Get Reel:

The Brooklyn Boy and Other Stories of Faith in the City

by Bill Reel

Newsday

ANDREWS AND MCMEEL
A Universal Press Syndicate Company
Kansas City

To my wife, Suellen,
who means everything to me.

Additional copies of this book may be ordered by calling (800) 642-6480.

Library of Congress Cataloging-in-Publication Data

Reel, Bill, 1939–
    Get Reel : the Brooklyn boy and other stories of faith in the city / by Bill Reel.
      p. cm.
    ISBN 0-8362-0809-9 (pbk.)
     1. Brooklyn (New York, N.Y.)—Social life and customs.   2. New York (N.Y.)—Social life and customs.   I. Title.
F129.B7R44   1995
974.7'23—dc20   95-23741
                                                  CIP

Book design: Diane Marshall

Contents

Chapter Three SIMPLE FAITH

Chapter Four HARD HABITS

Acknowledgments

I've been blessed by my colleagues at *Newsday*. Deep gratitude is due superb editors Ken Emerson, Kate McCormick, Janet Ungless (whom I love even though she made me rewrite several columns), Mary Suh, Walter Middlebrook, Steve Gunn, Mark Toor, Paul Moses, Debbie Henley and Mort Perksy. And boundless thanks to Bob Heisler, who conceived and put together this collection.

Introduction

∙∙

Should this book become a best-seller and make me rich, fine. Very fine. Excellent, in fact. But I'll be satisfied if it adds to the ranks of Reel people.

How might that happen? Well, let's say you're perusing a piece herein and you say to yourself, "Hey, I identify with this friend of Reel's who says the migraine headaches he had when he was in prison disappeared the day he got out. Brings me back to the great day I got paroled."

Maybe we'll have coffee and I'll use your story or your insights, or both. I won't reveal your identity. In fact, if your observations are especially brilliant, I'll certainly write them in a way that suggests they were original with me. You can be assured of total anonymity, and, in addition to that, no credit or recognition whatsoever for your contribution to my column. Thus would you achieve Reel personhood.

"I ought to give you half my salary," I often tell the Brooklyn boy, the source of many of the columns in this collection. By the way, he has a name like everybody else, but I call him the Brooklyn boy because that jaunty handle evokes the heart and humor of his home borough. Also, he's publicity shy, like a lot of Gowanus guys loath to awaken sleeping dogs at places like Household Finance.

Half my salary? Ha! Other than a few lunches at Italian restaurants in Bay Ridge, the Brooklyn boy has gotten nothing from me. And since Newsday paid for the lunches, I got not only a column but also cannelloni on the company, not to mention cream sauce on my suit jacket. So for the privilege of telling me numerous stories I turned into columns, the Brooklyn boy received only the satisfaction of knowing that without his input the paper would have come out with a big empty space under my picture.

How did we meet? The Brooklyn boy called one day and started talking. He figured I'd want to hear what he had to say, and he was right. He was a reader who sensed a kindred spirit and became a vital (to me) source. I've been blessed by many such angels—Reel people, I call them. One day a reader in Flatbush phoned to report that he'd saved a woman from drowning at Coney Island. "I gave her mouth-to-mouth restitution," he said. Beautiful, I thought. While we chatted he let drop enough malaprops to fill the next day's column. That was a decade ago. I only wish the Malaprop King of Kings County, as I dubbed him, would call again.

It's hard to know where to get stories, so I prefer to let them come to me. Oh, I suppose I could interview politicians, but an interesting politician is practically a contradiction in terms. The same is true of ballplayers, show biz people, celebrities. Their big egos make them boring. That's my experience, anyway.

For 20 years of column-writing I've lived off readers like the Brooklyn boy and the Flatbush fellow. Where would I be without them? Down at the unemployment office. So if you've got a timely human-interest yarn or something funny or thought-provoking to relate, know that I love to answer my phone and read my mail. Words can't express my gratitude to Reel people. May their tribe increase.

Chapter One:
The Brooklyn Boy

THE GAMBLER COMES A LONG WAY

One afternoon the Brooklyn boy came home from work and headed straight for the phone to call a bookmaker who, he prayed, would be rash enough to extend credit. The Brooklyn boy hoped to reverse a long run of bad luck by placing a big bet on the upcoming college basketball championship game. He was sure he had the winner. The smart-money wager would get him even, finally.

One problem, though: The wall was bare where the phone had been.

"What happened to the phone?" he asked his wife.

"Couldn't you at least say hello?" she came back.

"Hello. What happened to the phone?"

"A man from the phone company came and took it."

"What?"

"A man from the phone company came and took it."

"Why?"

"Because we haven't paid the bill for six months."

The Brooklyn boy frowned. "We have three little kids. What if one of them gets sick and we gotta call the doctor?"

She sighed. "Did you hear what I said? We haven't paid the bill for six months."

The Brooklyn boy snorted angrily. "Lowlifes! I'm down on my luck through no fault of my own, and right away the phone company cuts off service. They got no compassion."

His wife shook her head and went into the bedroom and slammed the door.

So it went for the Brooklyn boy. He contacted the bookmaker by pay phone only to be told credit was out of the question. Indeed, financing for his gambling habit seemed to have dried up entirely. He owed all his relatives, he owed guys at work, he owed loan sharks.

"Maybe God will give me a sign. I'll go to church and pray," he thought. He'd done this many times. His fervent prayer went as follows: "Let me sleep a number, Lord." The hope behind this petition was that the Almighty would arrange for a tipster to appear in a dream and advise the Brooklyn boy: "Do yourself a favor, kid. Play 211 tomorrow." The number would hit and he would gain breathing room. This celestial scenario had never materialized, but the Brooklyn boy was certain it was worth another shot. Hope keeps gamblers going, and false hope is better than none.

The thought of not gambling never occurred to the Brooklyn boy. In his neighborhood, if you got in trouble gambling, you got out of trouble gambling.

So the Brooklyn boy walked over to Fourth Avenue and Ninth Street to his parish church, St. Thomas Aquinas. Hadn't been a regular there for years, but his wife took the kids every Sunday. If God was going to bless him, this was where the deal would go down. He dipped his fingers in holy water and made the sign of the cross. He walked down the center aisle all the way to the altar rail. No mere pew would do. He would get as close to the tabernacle as possible to impress God with his deep piety and desperate need of divine intervention.

The Brooklyn boy kneeled down, blessed himself once more and said, "God, please help me stop gambling."

He blinked. Why had he said that? The prayer seemed to spring from his subconscious. He felt vaguely confused, uneasy, distracted. He remained on his knees for a while, then got up and walked out of the church. He noticed an old woman saying rosary beads in a back pew. He thought glumly: This is what I've come to at age 34—I'm visiting churches with little old ladies.

The next morning he was shaving. He kept his radio in the bathroom to get sports scores. A public service spot came on: "Did you gamble last night? Are you in trouble with gambling? Does gambling make your life unmanageable?" The announcement included a number to call for help. His wife, passing by, overheard and wrote down the number.

That night at dinner the Brooklyn boy said, "What do you think? Should I call that number?" Trying to sound supportive but not too eager lest he rebel, she replied, "Why not? What have you got to lose?" He said he might call. When he left for work she looked up and implored, "Please, God, let him call!"

This was what she had prayed for daily for years.

He came home after work and went right out again. He walked to Fifth Avenue and 12th Street. He used the pay phone outside OTB. A guy named Billy took his call. They talked about gambling. Billy asked for his phone number. "I don't have a phone." Billy asked if he had a car. "No." Billy asked if he could take the F train to McDonald Avenue the next night, a Thursday. "Sure." Billy told him a guy named Teddy would pick him up at McDonald Avenue and take him to Resurrection Church in Gerritsen Beach for a meeting of Gamblers Anonymous.

That was in March 1977. On his 17th anniversary in GA at Resurrection the other night, the Brooklyn boy read from the Old Testament:

"I will praise you, O Lord, for you drew me clear and did not let my enemies rejoice over me. O Lord my God, I cried out to you and you healed me. O Lord, you brought me up from the lower world, you preserved me from among those going down into the pit. Sing praise to the Lord, you his faithful ones, and give thanks to his holy name. For his anger lasts but a moment, his good will is for a lifetime."

The Brooklyn boy had come a long way from bad days of begging God to let him sleep a number.

April 3, 1994

How Two Gun Lucky Got Both Those Guns

The last time the Brooklyn boy saw him, Two Gun Lucky was waiting for a bus on Coney Island Avenue. The Brooklyn boy pulled over in his car. "Two Gun Lucky!" he hollered.

Two Gun Lucky looked great, like an aging Errol Flynn, just the way the Brooklyn boy remembered. They gabbed there for a while, with Two Gun Lucky sticking his head in the window on the passenger side. When the bus came along, the last thing Two Gun Lucky said was, "Kid, do yiz need any twenties?"

The Brooklyn boy laughed and drove off.

In the old days at the club on Third Avenue in South Brooklyn, Two Gun Lucky was always around pushing counterfeit $20 bills. Two Gun Lucky's $20s were notoriously amateurish—President Andrew Jackson was rendered with a very severe harelip, with his head tilted to the side like a rap singer's.

"You gotta pass this stuff at night to cab drivers," Two Gun Lucky always warned the young guys at the club willing to take the risk of passing his funny money. A batch of twenties he got made up in a hurry when his regular printer was on vacation had the Leaning Tower of Pisa instead of the White House on the back.

Besides counterfeiting, Two Gun Lucky was involved in various scams, hustles and con games in several Brooklyn neighborhoods. He was an agile thinker who talked his way out of situations that could have been fatal. Thus was he dubbed Lucky.

The Brooklyn boy remembers how Lucky became Two Gun Lucky.

It was a Sunday morning. The Brooklyn boy got up, had coffee and told his mother he was going to Mass. Then he went straight to the club to meet the guys. He figured only a handful of early risers

3

like himself would be there. But when he walked into the club, it was packed. There must have been 25 guys ringing the room. All eyes were on the pool table, where Lucky and Blue Beetle were playing. The Brooklyn boy let the door close very quietly. He stood there.

Lucky was a pool hustler, and Blue Beetle knew it, but he thought he could beat him anyway. Lucky made a tough shot to win a game, and Blue Beetle cursed and handed him $50, and as the balls were being racked for the next game, the Brooklyn boy eased over to where his friend Fatty was standing. "Hey, Fat, what's happening?" he whispered. Pool protocol demanded hushed voices.

"They been playing since 3 A.M. Lucky is hustling the hell outta Blue Beetle, saying how lucky he is to beat a great pool shooter like Blue. Lucky's up $600. Blue keeps losing and cursing and paying," Fatty told him.

Great action. This was South Brooklyn at its best, the Brooklyn boy thought, with wiseguys and con artists and hustlers and knock-around guys and kids like him hanging around the club watching a big pool game while the rest of the neighborhood was in church. Beautiful.

Just as Lucky leaned over the table and brought back his cue to break the rack, the door to the club flew open and in walked a great big young guy. A stranger. Must have been from another neighborhood. Everybody froze when the young guy reached into the waistband of his pants and came out with a .38-caliber revolver.

"Lucky, I want my *&¢%™%! money!" the young guy bellowed. He held the gun with two hands and pointed it at Lucky's chest. Lucky and Blue Beetle stood next to each other, pool cues at their sides. In an odd way, they evoked the Grant Wood painting "American Gothic." Blue Beetle discreetly took three steps away in case the young guy began throwing off shots.

Lucky's mouth motored at 100 mph even when he wasn't under pressure. Now he did triple time, the words running together. "I told you when I called you the other night I didn't have your money but I told you when I got it I'd call you and meet you and you'd get your money . . ."

The young guy was single-minded. He shook his head. He aimed the gun. "Lucky, I want my *&¢%$•! money!" he hollered. Geez, Lucky must have really scammed this poor kid to make him so mad, the guys in the club were thinking.

Lucky, cool under pressure, decided to try a different approach. "You think you're tough 'cause you got a gun?"

The young guy looked puzzled. "Huh?" he said. He lowered the gun a little.

Lucky had read him right: The young guy lacked the killer instinct.

"Let me go home and get my gun, and I'll come back and we'll see how tough you are," Lucky said.

The young guy exhaled. He slumped slightly. He put his gun back in his waistband. He began to weep. Tears ran down his cheeks. "Lucky, I want my *&¢%™%! money." By now it was a cry for help, a plea, not a demand.

Lucky walked over and put his arm on the young guy's shoulder and patted it. "There, there. I told you when I get the money you'll get your money. Now go along home."

The young guy turned and walked out of the club.

Lucky went back to the pool table as though nothing unusual had transpired, and calmly broke the rack. The balls spread out so that Blue Beetle had no shot. "Geez, I was lucky again," Lucky told Blue, conning him like crazy. Blue cursed, and the guys in the room resumed watching intently.

Two Gun Lucky. The gun the young guy had, and the gun Lucky was going to go home and get, added up to two guns. That's how the colorful handle came about.

The Brooklyn boy wonders whatever became of Two Gun Lucky. He wishes he'd get in touch for old times' sake.

August 2, 1992

RECALLING THE DAYS OF GAMBLING WAYS

The Brooklyn boy yawned. It was midnight. He sat in his favorite chair and scanned the channels one last time before turning in.

A pro-football game was winding up. The home team had the lead and the ball on the other team's three-yard line with 30 seconds to play. The quarterback took the snap from the center and dropped to one knee. The clock ran down.

The crowd booed the decision to forgo more points. The announcer was puzzled by the crowd reaction. Why run up the score? "The outcome of the game isn't in doubt," the announcer said.

His comment struck a chord in the Brooklyn boy. He flicked off the TV.

His mind flashed back to a Saturday afternoon in the old apartment on Fifth Avenue in Park Slope. His wife and kids were at her mother's. He stared at the TV. He was a young husband and father in

Brooklyn, and the biggest thing in his life was a college football game in Texas.

That morning he'd walked to the candy store up the block to call his bookmaker, Cockeye Tony. He owed Cockeye Tony $200 for bets lost the previous weekend.

"You calling to bet?" Cockeye Tony asked.

"Yeah. I like Texas A&M this afternoon," the Brooklyn boy said.

"I hope we ain't gonna have a problem if you lose. You already owe me."

"I made a big hit at the track yesterday. I can run by and pay you now if you like," the Brooklyn boy said, bluffing.

He was flat broke. He had to steal a dime from his wife's purse to make the call. Ma Bell disconnected his apartment phone, something about nonpayment.

Not wanting to insult a regular customer and steady loser, Cockeye Tony said, "No, don't bother coming by today. We'll settle up Monday."

The Brooklyn boy went back to the apartment and turned on the TV. He didn't move for three hours. The bet he put in with Cockeye Tony was what gamblers call "one hundred times." A one-time wager risks $5.50 to win $5; one hundred times, $550 to win $500. The Brooklyn boy gave 6 1/2 points. If Texas A&M won by seven or more, the $500 he would collect would get Cockeye Tony and a couple of loan sharks off his back. He could give his wife a few dollars for groceries. Maybe he could pay the phone bill.

The teams fought a hard defensive battle. He sat in a T-shirt, glued to the set, his face a foot from the screen. Perspiration drenched him. His stomach was in knots. He breathed heavily. His heart sounded loud and demanding.

Texas A&M scored a touchdown. His heart leaped for joy. He exhaled heavily. Relief flooded the Brooklyn boy from scalp to toes. The kicker put the extra point through the uprights. Whew! Seven points were on the board. Enough to win if the score held.

The game progressed with no more scoring into the fourth quarter. Confidence built in the Brooklyn boy. He liked his chances. He sat forward on the couch, anticipating $500.

He heard a yell from the street. It was his friend Harry, who knew better than to ring the buzzer. The Brooklyn boy had disconnected the buzzer so that bookmakers and loan sharks and others who might be looking for him would get no answer when they came calling.

The Brooklyn boy ran downstairs and let Harry in. They ran back up. "I bet a lung on Texas A&M," the Brooklyn boy told Harry excitedly. Just then a Texas A&M player ran around end and scored. The

Brooklyn boy let out a whoop. The extra point made it 14–0. The game clock showed 30 seconds to play. "I'm out," the Brooklyn boy said, greatly relieved.

When a gambler says he's out, he means he's out of debt, out of misery, the pressure's off—until tomorrow, of course.

Texas A&M kicked off. Jerry Levias of Southern Methodist took the ball on the fly and ran it back the length of the field for a touchdown. The score was 14–6.

"It don't matter," Harry said. "You still got eight points. You only need seven."

The Brooklyn boy noticed there was no kicker on the field. Panic surged up in him like a geyser. "They're going for two points!" he screeched, terror in his voice.

The Southern Methodist quarterback floated up a pass. In the corner of the end zone Levias leaped for it with three Texas A&M defenders draped all over him. Somehow Levias caught the ball. The foursome came down in a heap. "Out of bounds!" the Brooklyn boy screamed desperately.

He and Harry sat frozen on the edge of the couch. The officials in their striped shirts conferred for what seemed to the Brooklyn boy like hours, though it was less than a minute. The announcer observed that their ruling wouldn't mean much. "The outcome of the game isn't in doubt," he said.

The Brooklyn boy thought grimly, "That's easy for you to say. I've got a lung going."

The referee threw up his hands, signaling the conversion was good. Final score: Texas A&M 14—Southern Methodist 8.

Harry said nothing. He walked downstairs and out the door. The Brooklyn boy sat in shock, devastated, utterly destroyed, the world's unluckiest man. He wondered frantically: Could the Giants get him out Sunday?

That was then.

The other night the episode came back with utter clarity to the Brooklyn boy, now a happily recovered ex-gambler. He got up out of his favorite chair and went to bed and slept like a baby.

November 8, 1992

How to Find a Hero in the Nick of Time

New friend and mentor Paddy O'Botz called to invite me to Red Hook for a sandwich. Red Hook is his old neighborhood.

"Red Hook? Really? You can get a good sandwich there?" I said.

"What are you kiddin' me or what?" Paddy O'Botz replied. Paddy utilizes a special Gowanus dialect—the typical sentence is interrogatory, includes no commas and begins and ends with the word "what."

I was in my office in Manhattan. "I'd love to go to Red Hook for a sandwich. Could you pick me up?"

"What do you think I'm gonna make you walk to Red Hook or what?" Paddy retorted.

Paddy, who resides on 11th Street in Park Slope, came and got me. Through the tunnel we went. We took a right and a few rights and lefts and parked on Luquer Street off Columbia. We went into the place on the corner, Defonte's.

Paddy O'Botz introduced me to the owners, Nick and Nick Defonte, father and son. The younger Nick Defonte told me, "This is our 70th anniversary. My late grandfather—his name was Nick Defonte, too—opened this place in 1922."

Nick, Nick and Nick Defonte—three generations running the same sandwich shop in Red Hook. Remarkable.

"In an Italian family it's a tradition that the father names his son after him," young Nick said. Paddy O'Botz nodded. "Forget about it," he said.

"What?" I said.

"What what?" Paddy said.

"Forget about what?" I said.

"Like Nick told you, in an Italian family the father names the son after him. Forget about it. What are you kiddin' me or what?" Paddy explained.

Moving right along, I asked Nick, "How's business?"

Paddy answered for Nick. "What are you kiddin' me or what? Look at the line at the counter. It's three deep."

Sure enough, customers surged to place orders. Defonte's is strictly a takeout lunch place. No tables. Paddy and I stood in the kitchen while the two Nicks and several countermen worked feverishly to serve the hungry horde. When the crowd eased a bit, the younger Nick brought us hero sandwiches.

I took a big bite out of mine. I kid you not, of all the sandwiches I've eaten in my life, this Defonte's hero was the best. All sorts of spicy tastes exploded in my mouth.

"This is sensational!" I enthused. Paddy swallowed a mouthful and said, "What do you think I'd lie to you or what?"

"What's in this sandwich?" I asked.

"What what?" Paddy said.

"I'm talking to Nick," I told Paddy. Nick shrugged. "Salami, provolone, cooked peppers, fried eggplant."

"This sandwich is known as the Paddy O'Botz Special. What are you kiddin' me or what?" Paddy said, swallowing.

The elder Nick Defonte said business was off from the old days. "The neighborhood changed. Companies closed. Piers shut down. People moved away." But faithful customers remain, he said. "On Saturday morning we'll have people come in on their way to New Jersey or Connecticut and they'll have us make lunch for them and their relatives."

We finished eating. Paddy said he had another place to take me. Nick and Nick refused to let us pay for lunch. As we left I told Paddy, "Geez, I could lose my job for eating on the arm. Newsday is tougher than the police department about taking a freebie."

Forget about it, Paddy said; Nick and Nick were treating Paddy O'Botz and guest, and that was that. For emphasis he added, "What are you kiddin' me or what?"

We got in his car and Paddy drove under the expressway and out of Red Hook. We went along Smith Street into downtown Brooklyn. Paddy parked on Smith by Pacific. We got out and walked into a place called Nicky Specials. Paddy introduced me to owner Nicky Defonte.

"This is my day to meet guys with that name," I said.

Nicky Defonte turned out to be a cousin of the younger Nick Defonte at the Red Hook store. Sensing a clamor for superb sandwiches downtown, he opened Nicky Specials a few months back.

"Look at my menu," Nicky said proudly. "You know those fancy joints in Manhattan that name a dish for an important celebrity? I name my sandwiches for regular Brooklyn people."

Great idea. Some excerpts from the menu:

"The Animale" is named for the entire Long Island University baseball team. Ingredients: Marinated mushrooms, hot stuffed cherry peppers, capicola, provolone, lettuce, tomatoes, salami, fried eggplant, prosciuttini, oil and vinegar.

"The Ohio" recognizes Brooklyn Law School student Tom Leckrone, who hails from the Buckeye State: hot turkey, fried eggplant, lettuce, tomato, mozzarella, hot cherry peppers, mushrooms.

"The Vinny Pintus" honors the owner of an Exxon station on Stillwell Avenue: Hot roast beef, hot salad, chopped hot stuffed cherry peppers, fried eggplant.

"The Lee Silverman" celebrates stockbroker Silverman: Virginia ham, mozzarella, potatoes, eggs.

Needless to say, the Paddy O'Botz Special is prominent on the menu.

"I opened in December with 17 specials. People came in and demanded that I name a sandwich for them," Nicky said, "so I had to have a new menu with 32 specials printed in February."

Only in Brooklyn.

Paddy O'Botz drove me home. He wondered if I was going to write about all this. I told him, "What are you kiddin' me or what?"

March 8, 1992

HIS SECRET IS STILL BURIED

Moneywise, Made Man might have been the richest guy in Brooklyn. He thought nothing of taking a dozen guys to Atlantic City or Las Vegas and grabbing the hotel tab. He was an outrageous spender who literally had more money than he knew what to do with.

Made Man was in on the ground floor of the illegal drug trade. Back in the early '70s, when his career in organized crime began to blossom, he used to keep $250,000 in cash in a safety deposit box in a bank on Fifth Avenue in Park Slope. The account was in the name of his brother-in-law, Jackie, a blue-collar guy who worked hard for a living at a legitimate job.

Every now and then one of Made Man's bodyguards would show up at Jackie's house and announce, "He needs $75,000. I'll come by tomorrow at 9 A.M. and pick you up and we'll go to the bank and get it."

And that's what they would do. The money was bundled in thick stacks of hundred-dollar bills in the safety deposit box. Jackie counted out the money, handed it to the bodyguard and went straight to work at manual labor.

Jackie was never comfortable with responsibility for Made Man's ill-gotten gains. But he felt it would have been disrespectful to his wife to refuse to help her brother; Made Man was family, therefore Jackie obliged him. He was relieved when, for whatever reasons, Made Man eventually had him withdraw all the cash from the safety deposit box, turn it over to him and close the bank account.

About 2 A.M. one morning Jackie was awakened by banging on his front door. He ran in his underwear to see who was there. "Jackie, open up, it's me," he heard.

Jackie let Made Man in. "Jackie, I need a favor, you gotta help me out. Take a ride to Jersey with me."

Jackie's face fell. "If you got a body to bury, please, do me a favor, don't get me involved."

Made Man laughed. "Come on. I wouldn't jam you up."

Jackie sighed and went along. The bodyguard drove. Made Man sat in the front passenger seat. Jackie got on his stomach in the back of the car and jammed his face into the seat.

"What's with you?" Made Man asked him.

"I don't want to know where we're going," Jackie replied.

After an hour or so they arrived in a wooded area of New Jersey. They got out of the car. Made Man opened the trunk. A large metal container was inside. Jackie relaxed slightly; the container was not quite coffin-sized. Made Man unlocked it and lifted the top. Inside were stacks and stacks of big bills. Jackie thought it might add up to millions of dollars.

Made Man locked the box. "We gotta bury this," he told Jackie. The bodyguard took shovels out of the trunk and the three of them began digging. It took a couple of hours of hard work for them to dig a hole sufficient to bury the metal box full of cash.

They got in the car for the drive back to Brooklyn. Jackie resumed his face-down position in the back seat. "Look at me," he said. "See, I can't see nothing. Tell me when we hit the bridge to Staten Island. Then I'll sit up. I don't want to know the way here. I want you to know I don't know. If you come back for that money and it's dug up, don't look at me."

Made Man laughed. "You kiddin' me? If I didn't trust you I wouldn't have brought you. With you I got nothing to worry about."

Jackie got home and took a shower and went to work. Made Man offered many times to set him up in business, but Jackie always refused. He was happy coming home at night with dirt under his fingernails and no worries about cops following or rival gangsters pegging shots at him.

Only once did Jackie ever ask Made Man for a favor. He was reluctant to do it, but his wife insisted. They had a tenant upstairs. When their son got engaged and soon would need an apartment, they politely asked the tenant to move out. The tenant refused. "Have me evicted," he told Jackie. The tenant was a wannabe wiseguy who hung out in a pizzeria in Borough Park. He had no idea that his low-key landlord was the brother-in-law of somebody big.

Jackie took the problem to Made Man. "Please, no violence," Jackie implored him. "I don't want the guy hurt, I just want him out."

Made Man assured him that no violence would be necessary. "The guy is gone. Tell your son to order furniture. He can move in tomorrow." He sent a bodyguard to the pizzeria on New Utrecht Avenue to deliver a message to Jackie's tenant. The message was that the tenant was to be out of Jackie's house by midnight, and that he was to leave very, very quietly. The tenant nearly fainted when the bodyguard informed him that his landlord was related to Made Man.

Jackie and his wife were having coffee at their kitchen table that night when a moving van pulled up outside. The tenant and several moving men got out and walked into the house and up the stairs on tip-toes. They emptied the apartment without making a sound. "Them guys move like ballerinas," Jackie marveled.

It was only the fourth of the month, but the tenant left behind a full month's rent and a note that said: "Why didn't you tell me you was with good people?"

All the money and power he acquired are no good to Made Man now; he was shot to death on a Brooklyn street a couple of years ago. Most of the guys in his crew are either dead or doing time.

Meanwhile, Jackie gets up every morning and goes to work for a living. Once in a while he remembers burying millions in Jersey. It's a load off his mind that he doesn't know where.

November 28, 1993

FAITH WON OUT OVER NAGGING SUSPICION

The Brooklyn boy no longer plays horses. Didn't even bet the Belmont Stakes yesterday. But his recall of masochism at the track is keen.

The Brooklyn boy and his partner, Mario, got tips on horses from Nick in the liquor store on Third Avenue and Ninth Street. Nick was a neighborhood guy and a gentleman, and he was close with a trainer named Sid. Nick's tips didn't always pan out, but no true horseplayer doubted that his inside information provided an edge.

One spring day the Brooklyn boy and Mario were in the liquor store when Nick leaned over the counter and confided: "Boys, Sid's got a horse." The Brooklyn boy and Mario listened up. "The horse is kickin' down the barn!" Nick related.

News of a horse raring to run greatly excited the Brooklyn boy and Mario. Here was the chance for this pair of hapless losers to get even.

"The horse goes tomorrow. Her name is Mary Meacham," said Nick.

The Brooklyn boy and Mario shared the hot tip with no one. Why blab it all over South Brooklyn? Mary Meacham might pay only

$4 or $5 if too many bettors got down. They would keep this sure winner to themselves to protect the price.

They called in sick at their jobs the following morning and drove out to Aqueduct. Their chests heaved with hope as Mary Meacham went off at 12 to 1. They had $100 to win on her. The South Brooklyn worthies could practically taste their long overdue reward for years of devotion to the Sport of Kings.

The Brooklyn boy and Mario were disappointed when Mary Meacham ran dead last, but they had enough resignation to realize that something might have happened. Some horses kick down the barn in the morning but don't run well in the afternoon. Morning glories, they're called.

Two weeks later, Mary Meacham ran again. Nick said nothing, but the Brooklyn boy and Mario bet her anyway because they felt she owed them money. She finished way up the track.

Mary Meacham ran at least a dozen times that year and the Brooklyn boy and Mario bet her every time. They just couldn't let her go. Never once did she finish in the money.

Their lousy run of luck became legendary in their South Brooklyn social club, Nonchalants. "Are youse morons still feeding that nag?" guys asked them.

But the truth was that all the Nonchalants were playing Mary Meacham by now. The horse had earned a kind of losers' following in South Brooklyn. Guys would run up to the bookmaker on Fifth Avenue to bet her whenever she ran, no matter how long the odds.

The season ended and everybody forgot about Mary Meacham. In those days Aqueduct was dark from the end of November until around St. Patrick's Day. Spring came and, with it, hope eternal. In the liquor store, Nick leaned over the counter and told the Brooklyn boy and Mario:

"Mary Meacham had a great workout. We had a vet check her over the winter. Found a minor problem. She had surgery. Now she's kickin' down the barn again."

Half of South Brooklyn traveled to Aqueduct to back Mary Meacham in her initial outing of the new season on a glorious April day. Guys told each other with certainty, "We got a winner in this horse. All she needed was a little surgery." Mary Meacham ran seventh in a nine-horse field.

Three weeks later Nick said confidentially to the Brooklyn boy and Mario, "What are youse doin' tomorrow?" Nick explained that Mary Meacham would be running at Garden State in New Jersey. She was dropping down in company and should do better against lesser competition. Moreover, a top jockey, Braulio Baeza, would ride her.

"I think she's worth a bet," said Nick.

The Brooklyn boy and Mario raised $200 from loan sharks and set out the next morning for Garden State. They hit some early races and were looking forward to putting all they had, $400, on Mary Meacham in the seventh race. On the way to the ticket window, they encountered Nick. He looked deeply distressed.

Nick glumly reported a problem with jockey Baeza. Seems he'd asked off Mary Meacham, preferring to save himself for a mount in the eighth, a $100,000 stakes race on which he stood to make a lot of money. When trainer Sid refused to release him from his commitment, Baeza was overheard telling his agent peevishly, "If Sid wants me to ride, I'll ride." The implication was that he wouldn't ride too hard.

Their hearts sank as the Brooklyn boy and Mario absorbed this profoundly depressing news. They didn't know what to do. They were afraid to bet Mary Meacham and afraid not to. Finally, just before post time, they put a token $40 to win on her. A big wager would be reckless if the jockey was merely going through the motions.

Mary Meacham went off at 18 to 1. Turning for home, running sixth, Baeza brought her expertly between horses, swung to the outside and rode like his life depended on it. In a three-horse photo finish, Mary Meacham prevailed by a nose.

The Brooklyn boy and Mario were sure they were going to be sick. They collected close to $800. All they could think was that it should have been $8,000.

All the guys back in South Brooklyn played Mary Meacham with the bookmaker on Fifth Avenue, and they threw a party at Nonchalants to celebrate that night. They applauded when the Brooklyn boy and Mario walked in. The Brooklyn boy and Mario forced smiles. "Youse don't look as happy as you should," they were told. They shrugged. It would be too hard to explain that sometimes a horseplayer can have too much inside information. In fact, not until now did the whole story come out about the Brooklyn boy, Mario and Mary Meacham.

June 6, 1993

BROOKLYN BOY, VINNIE SPIN YARNS, YOU BET

Big Vinnie from Greenpoint was telling me about a friend of his who lost 56 bets in a row on college basketball. It was an unbelievably bad run of luck, the worst losing streak anyone in Big Vinnie's set could remember.

"The guy was game for more," Big Vinnie said. "He called his bookmaker on Sunday afternoon to get the betting line for that night. 'It's Sunday. No college baskets,' the bookmaker told him.

"So he asked the bookmaker what was available for betting, and the bookmaker said the only thing going was hockey. The guy thought this over for a few seconds, then he let out a sad sigh. 'Never mind,' he said, 'I don't know nothing about hockey.' "

If there were more stories like that to report, life would be a lot more fun.

Right after gabbing with Big Vinnie from Greenpoint, it was my pleasure to bunk into the Brooklyn boy from Bay Ridge. (In Brooklyn we say "bunk into" instead of "bump into." It's a tradition, like saying "Last night I stood home," instead of the prosaic and colorless "Last night I stayed home.")

I related Big Vinnie's yarn to the Brooklyn boy. The great thing about a funny story is that you get to laugh again every time you tell it.

"I know a guy," the Brooklyn boy said, "who had a dream about the number five. He woke up the next day and went straight to the track. He put $5 on the five horse in the fifth race." The Brooklyn boy paused for effect. "It ran fifth," he said.

As we gabbed, the Brooklyn boy was reminded of an old friend named Iggy who was a degenerate gambler. "Iggy was a clerk in a brokerage house in Wall Street. A guy in the office booked bets. The guy had no mob connection; he was a freelancer. Iggy looked to bust him out. One morning Iggy sneaked into his office when the bookmaker was getting coffee. He set his clock back five minutes.

"Iggy had a contact in Delaware. The contact had an open phone to somebody at the track in New York. Iggy called Delaware and by 1:33 he had the winner of the first race, which went off at 1:30.

"He ambled into the bookmaker's office and said casually 'Let me get this double in.' The bookmaker glanced at the clock. 'You're just in time,' he said. Iggy handed him a slip with the winner of the first race wheeled with everything in the second. Plus he made other bets, including $20 to win on the horse he knew won."

The Brooklyn boy paused to sip his coffee. "So what happened?" I asked. I could hardly wait for the windup. What a yarn!

"Iggy beat the book for $1,500. Later in the day he sneaked back into the office and put the clock ahead to the right time. The bookmaker never suspected a thing.

"Iggy had a good thing going. He didn't want to overdo it. He sat tight for a while. Then one day he took the bookmaker for a long lunch. They drank at the bar, which was crowded. He asked the bookmaker 'You want me to give you my bets now?' He knew the bookmaker, a nervous type, would say no. 'Later. You can gimme them in the men's room where it's private,' the bookmaker whispered.

"Iggy had an accomplice, his partner from the neighborhood, on the restaurant pay phone calling Delaware. Soon as the race was over his partner had the result and went in the men's room, wrote a slip and left it on top of the towel dispenser, as prearranged with Iggy.

"Iggy excused himself to visit the men's room. 'Give me a minute to go, then follow me in. I'll give you my action,' Iggy told the bookmaker. 'Fine,' the bookmaker said. He had no reason to be suspicious; Iggy hadn't been out of his sight.

The Brooklyn boy took another sip of java. "Iggy banged out the bookmaker for $2,800," he said.

You have to admit this stuff tops my usual Sunday sermon lamenting dirty streets and graffiti. Readership is bound to increase.

"Iggy very nearly pushed his luck too far," the Brooklyn boy said.

"Tell me about it." One more entertaining gambling episode should fill this space.

"Iggy beat a mob bookmaker in Staten Island for a bundle," the Brooklyn boy said. "He set the bookmaker up, betting for a couple of weeks, winning and losing like a regular player. He called in bets from his job.

"Then one day Iggy called right at post time. His partner was sitting beside him, talking to Delaware. His partner put up four fingers. Iggy told the bookmaker 'And, uh, $40 to win on number four.'

"Iggy won big. The bookmaker called him and said 'If yiz want to collect, come to my house.' Iggy was petrified. He almost didn't go. But not to collect his winnings would be an admission that he past-posted the bookmaker. He was afraid to go and afraid not to go. Finally he went.

"The bookmaker paid, but he looked Iggy in the eye and told him 'In the future, call 15 minutes before post time, no later.'"

"What became of Iggy?" I wondered.

The Brooklyn boy finished his coffee. "He's on the lam. He got jammed up. Seems he was involved with a mob guy's daughter. He wronged her. Had to leave Brooklyn in a hurry.

"I wouldn't be surprised," the Brooklyn boy said, "if Iggy was pulling a scam right this minute on a bookmaker in some place like Bismarck, North Dakota."

February 2, 1992

How Pinochle Almost Got a Kid Killed

The Brooklyn boy told me a story that gave us both chills. What prompted his recollection was last Sunday's savage execution of a clerk in a Brooklyn deli allegedly owned by wiseguys.

A gunman from a rival crew walked into Wanna Bagel in Bay Ridge and fired six bullets into counterman Matteo Speranza, 18. The kid was an innocent victim of the ongoing mob war within the Colombo family. He was buried yesterday.

A similar fate nearly befell the Brooklyn boy at 18. Anybody who ever had a close shave during a misspent youth will identify with this.

He hung out in a club on Third Avenue in South Brooklyn. A guy named Sallie ran the club. Sallie worked for Joey, who ran the neighborhood.

The club had a pool table, three card tables and a bar with a formica top. Sallie booked bets, took numbers and loan sharked money. Two Gun Lucky pushed counterfeit bills. There was always swag off hijacked trucks for sale.

Dishonesty was the policy of all club regulars, who included many neighborhood kids like the Brooklyn boy. The young guys would buy five phony $20 bills from Two Gun Lucky for $15, then take taxi rides to pass the funny money to cabbies.

At 3 A.M. one Sunday the Brooklyn boy was playing pinochle in the club with Sallie and an old-timer, Roger One Eye, who had one eye and went through life hearing guys say, "Roger, do me a favor—keep an eye out for me." Everyone else had left for the night. The club was very quiet.

Sallie got up to stretch. He ambled to the window, painted black except for a space at the top. He peered out and uttered a curse. He dashed across the room and into the little kitchen. He picked up a case of beer and threw it through the back window. The crash resounded like an explosion.

Sallie jumped out the window.

The Brooklyn boy and Roger One Eye sat utterly still. They could only assume that Sallie's hasty departure was because he had seen something extremely threatening that might still be out there.

"Roger, you wanna go?" the Brooklyn boy asked after 20 minutes. Roger nodded. The Brooklyn boy led the way. "After you," Roger insisted.

There was no one outside. Roger went home. Walking by 10th Street, the Brooklyn boy spotted Sallie across Third Avenue. Sallie called him over. He was packing a gun he kept stashed in the yard behind the club.

"Who was outside?" the Brooklyn boy asked. Sallie replied, "Junior and Mac."

Junior and his bodyguard, Mac, were mob rivals of Sallie's boss, Joey. They were known to kill people. "Well, they're gone now," said the Brooklyn boy with a shrug. He didn't think too much about it at the time. But this week, reading about the kid executed in the bagel shop, the Brooklyn boy shivered when he remembered that night in the club.

What if Sallie hadn't looked out the window? What if he hadn't lammed loudly, sending Junior and Mac on their way? If they had come in and rubbed out Sallie, surely they would have killed any unfortunate eyewitnesses.

The Brooklyn boy would have been dead at 18 for being in the wrong place at the wrong time, like young Matteo Speranza.

Today, Junior is in prison for life. Mac, behind bars for years, might make parole eventually. They're paying for lifetimes of crime. Sallie moved to California, where he died of natural causes.

The Brooklyn boy outgrew youthful folly. A good wife and a merciful God were on his side. He lives simply, happily, strictly legit.

And with gratitude for a narrow escape.

December 13, 1991

In South Brooklyn, a Death in the Family

The Brooklyn boy seemed sort of subdued. Not his usual jovial self. I wondered what had him down. "Funzi died," he explained.

Funzi was a prince among men in their neighborhood, the Brooklyn boy said. His personality and demeanor commanded respect.

Women appreciated Funzi because he was gallant, kids loved him because he was cheerful, and men admired him because he was a man's man. "Look up 'man's man' in the dictionary," the Brooklyn boy said, "and Funzi's picture will be there."

Seems Funzi grew up in a big family with plenty of brothers and sisters. Never married. Lived in South Brooklyn all his life. Made his living loading barrels onto flatbed trucks. Was as hard as Rocky Marciano in his prime, yet it was the gentle, soft-spoken side of Funzi that endeared people to him.

"Funzi was a role model before anybody ever heard of the term," the Brooklyn boy said. "A lot of guys in the neighborhood needed a man to look up to. Maybe their fathers drank or gambled or didn't set a very good example in other ways, and they needed to know what a real man was. Funzi showed them.

"Funzi treated everyone he met with respect. He would never slight or show up anybody. He hated to see anyone humiliated. He'd go out of his way to say something nice about you—although not so nice that you'd be embarrassed. He was sensitive to feelings.

"If he knew you were broke, he'd take you aside and slip you $100. 'Don't worry about it. Pay me when you can. I know you're good for it,' he'd say—and he'd say that even if he wasn't so sure you were good for it. The only way anybody would ever find out Funzi loaned you money was if you mentioned it, because Funzi would never tell a soul.

"Funzi was a big believer in family, and everybody in the neighborhood was part of the family as far as he was concerned. He was very quick to go into his pocket, and people took advantage of him the way they take advantage of family. We were saying at his wake that we'd like to have the money we lost at the track over the years, but even better would be to have the money Funzi loaned guys that they never paid back."

The Brooklyn boy was quiet, contemplating his dear friend Funzi, and then he smiled. "I just thought of something Funzi did that showed the kind of guy he was," he said.

"This goes back, oh, a couple of decades ago. I was about 30 at the time, and Funzi was in his early 40s. He and I were hanging around outside our club, the Nonchalants, on Third Avenue and 10th Street one night. There was a bar nearby, McGrath's. Mrs. McGrath came out looking upset. She walked over to Funzi and me and said a couple of guys she never saw before were in the place acting suspicious.

"We were all set to go in and give her moral support when suddenly the two guys ran out. They'd robbed the place while she was talking to us. One of them had a gun. He was waving it and running up 10th Street. Mrs. McGrath began running in the opposite direction. I was about to follow her when I saw Funzi chasing the two guys up 10th Street toward Fourth Avenue.

"There was nothing I could do but follow Funzi. If I let him chase them alone, I'd never be able to show my face in the neighborhood again. So I started after him. It was dark. Every few yards, I'd see a flash when the one with the gun turned and threw a shot at us. I stopped and ducked—but of course if the guy's aim was good it was too late to duck by the time you saw the flash.

"He fired a few times. Missed, thank God. Funzi didn't stop to duck because it would slow him up. He was gaining on them. Funzi was unarmed but he was determined to get his hands on this gunman who was blasting away at him.

"They ran into the subway at Ninth and Fourth. We ran in after them. A transit cop showed up. Funzi told the cop that two guys robbed a bar and they jumped down on the tracks toward Prospect Avenue. The cop calmly spoke into his radio. I suppose he was calling for cops to go to the Prospect Avenue station. Funzi said to him, 'Aren't you gonna run after them?' Funzi thought the cop should jump down on the tracks and chase them through the subway tunnel. 'Give me your gun and I'll go after them,' Funzi told the cop.

"And he would have, too. Eventually the cops picked up the two guys at Prospect Avenue and arrested them for the stickup. They were lucky the cops caught them and not Funzi. He would have made them pay for upsetting Mrs. McGrath."

"People would say Funzi was foolhardy for risking his life, but you have to admire his righteous indignation," I said. "Neighborhoods would be a lot safer with more guys like Funzi inhabiting them."

The Brooklyn boy nodded. "Funzi was the kind of guy who instinctively did what was right. Damn the consequences."

I always like to know what motivates people. "Was Funzi a religious man?" I wondered.

"He went to the early mass Sunday mornings at St. Thomas Aquinas, but he wasn't the kind of guy who talked about his faith," the Brooklyn boy replied. "Funzi died from a bleeding ulcer, and at his funeral mass the priest told us that when he got the last rites he didn't want to die. He said Funzi hated to leave his family, his sisters Mary and Susie, his friends and neighbors. 'Funzi always wanted to be there for people,' the priest said.

"I nodded at that. 'There for people'—that was Funzi, God rest his soul," said the Brooklyn boy, and now I understood why Funzi's death affected him so deeply. I felt like I'd lost a good friend, too.

August 15, 1993

REMINISCING WITH THE NIGHT RAIDERS

Sometimes the Brooklyn boy wonders how he survived childhood stunts like playing Tarzan above the Gowanus Canal. They were 8 or 9 years old when he and his friends unhooked a long piece of cable from a boom on a construction site by the canal after the workers had left. Using the cable as a rope, they competed to see who could swing out the farthest over the murky waters.

"Don't worry if you fall in," they told each other. "We'll send the

raft out for you." The battered old pallet workers used to move ma-
terials would float to the rescue of a drowning playmate, they were
sure.

Living dangerously got them in trouble with the law. Looking
back, the Brooklyn boy realizes they didn't appreciate how serious it
could have been. They were lucky the cops caught them early. They
weren't bad kids; they were just untamed.

One night he and his pals, fifth-graders at St. Thomas Aquinas on
Fourth Avenue, pushed in the big wooden doors of the First Machine
Corp. on 10th Street and slipped inside. They found a leather-bound
checkbook with 1,000 checks and a stamp machine that imprinted
the company logo. They swiped the impressive-looking stuff and
stashed it in a deep crack in the wall of a building behind the park
on 10th Street.

But, the caper that made them notorious in the neighborhood
took place on a Sunday afternoon. The Brooklyn boy recalls that he
and Lorraine and Eileen and Paddy and Wayne and Claudia and
Bobby and the rest of their urchin crew were still in church clothes
after Mass when they pulled a score that got a few paragraphs in the
old *Journal-American*. The paper assumed the heist happened after
dark and called the little perpetrators the Night Raiders.

They were fooling around by the toy factory on Third Avenue
when one of them managed to crawl under a door. The rest followed.
Inside they beheld a wonderland of kid stuff—cowboy outfits, board
games, dolls, sewing kits.

The Brooklyn boy filled two paper bags with dice from Mo-
nopoly games piled in stacks. "The older guys will love this," he
thought. Crap games were big in their South Brooklyn neighborhood. His little sister's birthday was coming up, he remembered, so
he grabbed a sewing kit.

Boys with cowboy outfits over church clothes and girls carrying
dolls were seen running up Sixth Street late that Sunday afternoon.

The next day, the Brooklyn boy was home from school for
lunch with his father, who worked nights in a shipyard, when detectives came by. Seems neighbors gave up the Brooklyn boy to cops
asking questions after the toy factory reported a burglary.

The Brooklyn boy's hard-working, law-abiding father was
stunned. His son in trouble with the law? Impossible! But he gave the
cops permission to interview the lad.

They got their confession, plus evidence. The Brooklyn boy produced the sewing kit he'd stashed under his socks in a drawer. The dice
were gone, appropriated by older kids to whom he showed the haul.

A stand-up little guy, he refused to rat out his accomplices. His closed mouth posed no great problem for the cops, who had the names of all the suspects from neighbors.

The Night Raiders story came out in the *Journal-American*. The Brooklyn boy's mother and father, and the parents of all 14 kids involved, were mortified and humiliated.

"If this ever happens again, you're on your own. We won't have gangsters in our family!" the Brooklyn boy's father told him.

At school, fifth-grade teacher Sister Maria Regina called him aside.

"I hear you're in trouble," she said. She was sympathetic.

He nodded glumly. "I might have to do five years upstate, sister. I'll be 14 when I get out."

An incident during the investigation greatly embarrassed his mother. She and several other moms were present when a detective asked the Brooklyn boy if he'd burglarized any place besides the toy factory. The cops were looking to clean up old cases. Had he ever stolen anything besides the dice and the sewing kit?

"Sure," he told them, pleased to be able to oblige the authorities.

"What?"

"A big checkbook and a stamp machine from the First Machine Corporation."

His mother wanted to die.

"Where's the stolen property?" the detectives demanded.

"It's in the crack in the wall behind the park," the Brooklyn boy told them. He felt pretty important leading the sleuths down 10th Street and climbing up the wall to recover the loot.

The Brooklyn boy wore his communion suit to Family Court. "Look at John Dillinger!" the older kids hollered, laughing, as he went downtown with his parents.

There were 14 little kids lined up before the judge, fathers and mothers standing behind them, hands on their shoulders. The judge gave the kids a tongue-lashing and probation. The cops would be keeping an eye on them, he warned. He admonished them sternly to stay out of trouble.

By and large, they did. Those Brooklyn kids of '52 grew up to be quite solid citizens, thanks to family and church and school and neighborhood and a society that generally supported right and condemned wrong.

May 17, 1992

Phantoms Haunt a Haze of Memory

The Brooklyn boy always sat with Ronnie Murphy in the cafeteria at Chelsea Vocational. Ronnie lived on Marcy Avenue in Williamsburg. His was one of the few white families in the projects there. Ronnie was a wiry little guy, tough as nails, and the Brooklyn boy admired his heart.

Ronnie walked with a swagger and wore a Sherlock Holmes hat adorned with a button that proclaimed "Phantom Lords," his street gang.

"We went up on the Chaplains last night," Ronnie told the Brooklyn boy as they ate their sandwiches. The Chaplains were one of the city's biggest and most feared gangs, with branches in several neighborhoods, including Williamsburg.

A girlfriend of a Phantom Lord had been insulted by a Chaplain, Ronnie explained. The Phantom Lords had to avenge the disrespect. A street battle ensued. The two gangs rumbled on Marcy Avenue until the cops intervened.

Ronnie was pleased to relate news of violence and was delighted to have been a participant. The Brooklyn boy felt uneasy for him, however. The Brooklyn boy belonged to a street gang, too: the South Brooklyn Boys, Irish and Italian guys who lived around Carroll Street and Third Avenue. He wondered how Ronnie survived as a white guy in a black gang that fought other black gangs.

Toward the end of lunch a big black kid named Gadson made his way over to the table where the Brooklyn boy and Ronnie sat. The Brooklyn boy knew Gadson. They rode the same subway. Gadson lived in the Red Hook projects. His stop was Smith and Ninth. The Brooklyn boy's stop was Fourth and Ninth. On the train to and from Chelsea Vocational, the Brooklyn boy hung with the whites and Gadson hung with the blacks. The two groups kept their distance but acknowledged and respected each other.

Gadson stood over Ronnie and announced, "I'm with the Chaplains."

The Chaplains were active in the Red Hook projects, the Brooklyn boy knew.

Ronnie cocked his head and eyeballed Gadson and said, "Yeah? So what?" His own affiliation was no mystery. He'd advertised it defiantly. The button on his hat shouted: "Phantom Lords."

"I'll bust you up," Gadson said evenly.

"Get a ticket and stand in line," Ronnie replied.

"I'll be outside at 3 o'clock," Gadson said.

"See you there," Ronnie said.

The Brooklyn boy thought: Where are we gonna send Ronnie's remains? Gadson will annihilate him.

Ronnie turned to the Brooklyn boy and Bobby O'Connor and the half dozen other whites who ate together. "You guys are gonna watch my back, right?"

Of course they would watch his back, even if it meant taking a beating. A beating was no disgrace. A disgrace was running away. A disgrace was deserting a friend in trouble. No matter what the odds, a guy stood with his friends. That was the code of the neighborhoods, passed down from generation to generation.

Three o'clock came, and the Brooklyn boy and Ronnie and their small crew walked out of Chelsea Vocational. News of a fight between Ronnie and Gadson had swept through the school, and the little park out front on Sixth Avenue overflowed with onlookers anticipating the scrap. No one doubted that Gadson would prevail. The question was would Ronnie show.

Gadson stood in the middle of a horseshoe formed by dozens of his friends and supporters, many of them fellow Chaplains, all of them black. His books were on the ground beside him as he awaited Ronnie.

Ronnie's pace quickened. He threw off his jacket as he approached Gadson. They raised their fists, circled for a moment and then waded into each other. Punches flew furiously. The Brooklyn boy noticed that the horseshoe had closed into a circle. He was surrounded.

The fight was a terrible mismatch. Gadson overpowered Ronnie. They went down in a scuffling heap with Ronnie underneath. Gadson pummeled him. Ronnie flailed futilely.

Gadson jumped up. Ronnie dragged himself to his feet. The Brooklyn boy thought glumly: Poor Ronnie looks like somebody just cleaned a pipe with him.

Ronnie raised his fists. Gadson dropped his. "That's enough," Gadson said.

Gadson was declaring the fight over. Everyone understood that he won. There was no need to press the point. Ronnie certainly realized that Gadson gave him a beating.

"That's enough," Gadson repeated. Ronnie dropped his hands. They looked at each other. All eyes were on them in the center of the circle. Gadson said, "You got a lot of heart, Murphy."

Ronnie replied, "You got a lot of heart, too, Gadson . . . for a Chaplain."

The Brooklyn boy got a sinking feeling. Would Gadson punish Ronnie with punches for that insolent remark? Would a riot break out?

But Gadson knew he had nothing more to prove. He slipped on his jacket, picked up his books and walked off. The crowd melted away.

Three decades later, the Brooklyn boy recalls that incident and wonders what became of Ronnie Murphy and Gadson. Ronnie was so arrogant that he probably caught a lot of lumps in life, the Brooklyn boy guesses. Gadson might have gone on to become a cop, or maybe a minister. He had character and self-esteem. He didn't need to humiliate an adversary. He was big enough to acknowledge the dignity of a valiant foe. That's how to earn respect and to show it, the Brooklyn boy likes to think, and that goes in every generation.

February 27, 1994

EVERYBODY'S SOMEBODY'S PRODIGAL SON

"I want to hear the sequel," the Brooklyn boy said. He was walking out of church Sunday in Bay Ridge. The gospel reading had been the story of the prodigal son.

"What do you mean, you want to hear the sequel?" I asked. "There's no sequel. The prodigal son returns to his father. That's it. It's a happy ending. It's the best story in the Bible."

"You say that because you like to think you're the prodigal son," the Brooklyn boy said. "Hey, Reel quit drinking—bring the best robe and put it on him, kill the fatted calf and let's celebrate with a feast! You like playing the lead role in a Bible story."

"What about you?" I came back, maybe a little defensively. "Aren't you the prodigal son, too?" Last Friday the Brooklyn boy celebrated 18 years without making a bet. Blessed abstinence after two decades of compulsive gambling during which he was more the Brooklyn bum than the Brooklyn boy.

"Sure I am, and I love the story as much as you do, but I wonder what happened after the happy reunion," he said. "St. Luke should have stuck in a sequel to let us know."

We stood on sunny Fourth Avenue outside Our Lady of Angels. "How might it go?" I wondered. It was typical of a couple of big egos like ours to try to improve on the New Testament.

"Let's review the story," the Brooklyn boy said. "The prodigal son asks his father for his share of the family property. The old man reluctantly obliges. The son squanders the proceeds on loose living. I can see you bellied up to the bar at P.J. Clarke's. A class joint, for openers. Before the night was done, you'd be walking on your knees in the Blarney Stone."

25

That sounded about right. But enough about me. "What about you?" I demanded.

"I'd start out with a girl on each arm in Atlantic City. After a few days you'd find me solo at Aqueduct, tearing up losing tickets."

"And after too many years of that," I said, "eventually we went home, like the prodigal son after he blew all his money and had nowhere else to go."

The Brooklyn boy nodded. "His father welcomed him with open arms. Even killed the fatted calf and threw a big racket for him."

"Showed him a lot of love, just like we got from our families—although our wives sure didn't host any celebrations right away," I said.

The Brooklyn boy paused. "But what must have happened after that?" he said. "We know the older brother resented the great reception the kid got from the father: 'I've been with you all these years. I never ran off and threw money away on hookers. How come you never threw me a party?' The old man calmed him down, but you have to figure the resentment simmered and surfaced again after the kid rejoined the family business. The older brother could forgive, but he couldn't forget."

That made sense. "And what about the prodigal son when he got the wrinkles out of his belly?" I wondered. "If he was bored before in the family business, how were they going to keep him down on the farm after he'd seen Paree? A few months or years of plodding along righteously, and he had to be tempted in the worst way to break out."

"I was tempted a couple of times," the Brooklyn boy admitted.

"Me, too," I put in.

"But God lavished so much love on us through our families and friends that we couldn't reject them," the Brooklyn boy said. "Despite ourselves we said no to another spree."

"Love conquers the urge to backslide. No one knows more love than prodigal sons."

"A Bible story hits home," the Brooklyn boy said smiling, "when you get to live the sequel every day."

March 29, 1995

BROOKLYNITES HAVE A WAY WITH WORDS

"What did yiz do last weekend?" a Brooklynite asked a friend sitting across the table in a diner on Fourth Avenue. And the reply came back, "I stood home."

I stood home. Overhearing this, I thought: What a great way to put it. Neighborhood dialect is colorful and expressive if not always precise. Seems to me that "stood" conveys the idea of a quiet weekend at home better than the prosaic "stayed," and so communicates the point effectively even though the sentence surely would get a failing grade in English class.

Manhattan talk can be as pretentious and stilted as an Academy Awards acceptance speech, and therefore annoying to listen to. But utterances overheard in the neighborhoods of Brooklyn and Queens cause the ear to perk up.

There is even a distinctively neighborhood way of describing the act of listening in on a conversation. "I was on the earie," a Brooklyn or Queens guy will say, meaning that he was eavesdropping when he picked up a particular piece of information. A splendid variation of this is, "I was on the Erie Lackawanna."

The first time I heard "on the Erie Lackawanna," it came out of the side of the mouth of a friend named John who is fluent in jailhouse argot, the result of having run afoul of the authorities during a misspent youth. John was one of the first guests in the Brooklyn House of Detention when it opened in the 1950s.

John has a neighborhood-style way with words refined by years of jailhouse conversations in the '50s and '60s, when the slammers were populated by Runyonesque characters.

"I pulled his coat," John will say, meaning that he took the initiative to speak to someone who needed to be made aware of some matter. "I told him to cop a mope," he'll say, getting across that he told someone who had overstayed his welcome to move along.

"Go see where you gotta go!" That's a South Brooklyn expression, I think. It means the same thing as "cop a mope." When a Gowanus guy directs someone to "Go see where you gotta go!" he's advising the individual in no uncertain terms to make himself scarce, pronto. This might be followed by a brusquely stated, "Don't let the door hit you in the rear end on the way out."

South Brooklyn also incubated the splendid rhetorical question, "Hey what are you kiddin' me or what?" That construction might appear to require a comma or two, but all the words run together seamlessly when the line is properly delivered by a typical burly South Brooklynite with plenty of hair on his chest if not much on his head. The proper position of the hands when inquiring if someone is kidding you or what is palms upraised.

I rarely eavesdrop on women's conversations because to do so would not be gallant, but no one who goes around Brooklyn and

Queens could have failed to overhear at one time or another the classic put-down of one female by another that goes as follows:

"She thinks who she is." This must be delivered in a tone of voice dripping with contempt. What a devastatingly scornful rebuff of a self-important female. The phrase really demolishes snobbery.

Neighborhood folks fracture the language in wonderful ways that recall the Bowery Boys. Remember Leo Gorcey telling Huntz Hall, "Don't be a'scared, it's only a fragment of your imagination." The Bowery Boys were Brooklyn boys at heart.

A couple of guys in a neighborhood bar were discussing a friend's son who had left home to join a religious order and study for the priesthood. "The kid went off to the monkastery," was the way one of them put it. His friend was appalled by the mispronunciation. "It ain't a monkastery," he corrected, "it's a monkstery."

Monkastery, monkstery, monastery . . . what's the difference? Neighborhood guys know what they mean even if they don't always say it just so. The guy doing the talking knows, and so does the one on the listening end.

My friend Artie from Canarsie ran into an old Bensonhurst buddy for the first time in a while the other day, and the conversation went like this:

"What's new?" Artie inquired.

"I just was at the VA hospital."

"Oh? Nothing serious, I hope."

"I went in for a CAT scam. While I was there they did a KGB. Good thing I got Medicare, or I'd be looking at an exuberant bill."

Artie related this wonderful dialogue to me. He added that when this same Bensonhurst buddy returned from a visit to the restored Colonial village in Williamsburg, Va., a few years ago, he told everyone, "Williamsburg is a very interesting hysterical area."

I shared these winning malaprops with my friend the Brooklyn boy, an avid collector of mangled phrases, and he was reminded of an acquaintance from Red Hook who picked up a check for retroactive pay earned during the previous fiscal year and remarked to friends, "I finally got my radioactive money from the last physical year."

"Not for nothing," neighborhood guys say. The phrase is used as a preface to take any possible offense out of the remark that follows. Example: "Not for nothing, but yiz have bad breath."

Last word goes to Mike the Rug of Bay Ridge, who assures me that the way to tell the college guys from the high school dropouts in the neighborhood is that the former say "not for anything" instead of "not for nothing."

May 2, 1993

THE PICTURE(S) OF PRIDE IN BROOKLYN

A happy, heartening scene in progress out in Mill Basin, Brooklyn: Three women artists are painting murals on the walls of the Ryder Post Office. Passersby pause to look, smile and comment favorably—a welcome contrast to motorists beeping horns and cursing one another on nearby Flatbush Avenue.

"I hope this is the answer to graffiti," Oscar Muller, a neighborhood old-timer, remarked as he watched artist Cathy Marshall render a portrait of Duke Snider on the brick wall.

Cathy was working from a photograph of the great Duke of Flatbush taken in the mid-'50s when he patrolled centerfield for the Dodgers before they lammed to Los Angeles. Her depiction of Duke is one of a series of portraits of ballplayers and other worthies executed by Cathy, a Park Slope resident, and fellow artist Cynthia Lechan of Cobble Hill. "You caught Jackie Robinson and Gil Hodges very well," I told them. Cathy, 23, smiled shyly. She admitted she'd never heard of Duke before this job. I felt old when she said that.

Cathy and Cynthia labored on the East 45th Street side of the post office just off Flatbush Avenue. Around the corner on the Quentin Road side, their boss, the artist in charge of the project, Bonnie Siracusa, was up on a ladder painting a sweeping mural of the Brooklyn Bridge illuminated by fireworks with Manhattan skyscrapers in the background. Somewhere in there she plans to put a soaring eagle, the postal insignia.

A post office customer, Eco Martorello, admired the mural. He broke out in a big smile. "This is like a museum piece out in the open," he told Bonnie. She smiled and said thanks, and continued painting.

Taped to the wall was a hand-lettered sign Bonnie composed: "We'd love to talk to you, but since we are extremely busy trying to concentrate in the extreme heat and traffic noise, we CANNOT BE DISTURBED WHILE WE ARE WORKING."

Another sign advises: "The mural paint contains an anti-graffiti agent that makes graffiti wash off. However, graffitists are artists in their own right and respect other artists' work."

Tom Roma believes street art can wipe out ugliness and transform the look of New York. Tom, manager of the Ryder Post Office, had a few thousand bucks in the budget to improve the facility. A Brooklyn chauvinist, he got the brainstorm of commissioning artists to beautify the building and build Brooklyn pride at the same time. After soliciting bids, he selected Bonnie to plan and execute the project. "I love what I see so far," Tom said cheerfully.

Now, you may say of this bit of uplift, so what? Decay mars so many neighborhoods that one isolated point of light way out in Mill Basin hardly calls for a whole story. Shouldn't I devote this valuable space to denouncing something or condemning someone rather than accentuating the positive, Pollyanna-like?

No. To hell with hand-wringing, at least for today. Let's be positive. If Brooklyn boy Tom Roma can bust out of the government-bureaucrat mold and provide an aesthetic experience for folks who walk by his post office, why can't everybody else light a candle rather than curse the darkness?

We aren't all artists, but surely every man, woman and child can do a little something to improve the appearance of the city. Pick up a piece of litter and deposit it in a trash receptacle. Be vigilant about keeping your block neat and clean.

Or, if you happen to own a building, commission an artist to put a happy face on it. Help New York become an outdoor art gallery. Call that the Mill Basin mission, and make it Gotham's motto.

September 11, 1992

RECALLING THE DAYS WHEN RELIGION WAS IMPORTANT

Brooklyn Bea noted the irony that in the innocent 1940s and '50s when we rarely did anything wrong, we went to confession regularly, but now that folks are doing wrong stuff day and night, confession hardly gets a play.

"Seems like it ought to be the other way around, now that you mention it," I said.

"When I was a girl, I used to go to Mass every day during Lent," said Bea, who grew up in St. Francis of Assisi parish on Nostrand Avenue in Flatbush. "And to confession every Saturday—even if I didn't have anything to confess."

I laughed. "Were you one of those girls who made up sins so you wouldn't disappoint the priest?"

Bea nodded. "Disobeying my mother or father was my old standby when I couldn't think of a sin I'd actually committed."

"In other words, Bea," I said, "you lied to the priest! That was a worse sin than the sins you didn't commit that you were confessing. You were a serious sinner and you didn't even know it."

We laughed. "I'd tell the priest I disobeyed my mother, and he'd ask, 'How many times,' and I'd say, 'Three times, Father.'"

"I'll bet you tried to sound real penitent when you said it."

"Like I was very sincerely sorry."

"You disobeyed your mother three times? How did you arrive at that number?"

Bea thought back. "Two times didn't seem like enough, and four or five times seemed like too many. I didn't want the priest to think I was too good or too bad. Three was a nice happy medium."

Bea, who lives out in Mill Basin, is good company. She and I are about the same age, and we like to indulge in nostalgia when we gab.

A repeated youthful indiscretion that caused special shame whenever she revealed it in confession, Bea recalled, was chewing gum in church.

I nodded. "That was a serious offense. Chewing gum in church came under the heading of blasphemy, if my theology is correct."

"Another big sin was swearing. If you said 'damn,' you had to confess it.

"A venial sin, for sure."

"And 'hell,' too."

"When you hear kids cursing today, you know foul language has come a far way," I said.

"Once in a while I'd be sick on Sunday and have to stay home," Bea said. "I was glad because I'd have a good sin to tell—missing Mass on Sunday."

"What about eating meat on Friday?" I put in. Friday meant no meat for Catholics not only during Lent but year-round when Bea and I were kids.

"We were very scrupulous about that," Bea said. "I remember one time a friend was eating an apple on the way home from school and she saw a worm in it. 'Oh my God, it's Friday!' she said."

We laughed. "What do you think, Bea—was all that emphasis on right and wrong, and the guilt that went with it, good or bad?"

We chewed that over and came to the conclusion that while too much guilt is bad, too little is even worse. We were better off than kids today who might never have had the fear of God drummed into them.

Maybe organized religion was too harsh in the old days, with its emphasis more on justice than mercy, but now the pendulum has swung too far the other way.

"What did you used to give up for Lent?" I asked Bea.

"Potato chips," she said. "Lent ended at noon Holy Saturday, and I'd run right to Henry's Deli on Nostrand Avenue and buy a five-cent bag of potato chips."

"With Lent over, you could stuff yourself with a clear conscience. A great feeling."

"On Holy Thursday, it was a tradition to visit three churches. We'd walk to St. Blaise on Kingston Avenue, Holy Cross on Church

Avenue and St. Jerome's on Newkirk Avenue, and go in each one and say a prayer."

Bea was going back 40 years and more. Religious devotions were important to folks. They obviously made a deep impression on Bea for her to recall them so vividly.

"On Good Friday, our mothers wouldn't let us listen to the radio, and we weren't supposed to talk from noon until 3 p.m., so we thought we might as well go to church. Good Friday was always a cloudy, dreary day, as I remember. I'd get scared. It was the day God died."

Bea and I were thoughtful for a moment. "There has to be a Good Friday before there can be an Easter Sunday," I said.

Bea smiled. "On Easter Sunday I couldn't wait to get to the nine o'clock mass to show off my Easter outfit—dress, hat, gloves, patent leather shoes. A couple of weeks before Easter my mother would take me downtown to May's for a new dress. Easter was such a happy day. The boys looked so nice in their new suits."

Kids nowadays are deprived of an appreciation of Lent and Easter, Bea and I agreed. The culture of faith has been diluted.

"When my son was in Catholic high school in the '70s," Bea said, "he was told he didn't have to go to mass on Sundays; it was up to the individual. What could parents say?"

Too bad we can't restore the best of the good old days. Bea and I will keep talking and trying, though.

April 11, 1993

CRIMES, MISDEMEANORS, SINS

The Brooklyn boy grew up believing he had no rights. In the late '50s and early '60s, when he was coming of age in Brooklyn, the police had the right to do whatever they wanted to young guys like him—run them off the corner, kick them in the rear end, drag them to the station house for questioning, lock them up on suspicion of having done something.

What reminded him of this was the O.J. Simpson case. Watching it unfold in court on TV, the Brooklyn boy listened to endless argumentation about probable cause and admissible evidence and motions to suppress. The police seemed to be on the defensive. They had to explain themselves and justify their actions. The rights of the defendant, Simpson, received the utmost consideration.

This was fine with the Brooklyn boy, who'd hate to see anyone wrongly convicted. And Simpson was no punk kid, but a high-profile fellow whom the system must treat with respect.

Still, the Brooklyn boy was struck by the emphasis on the rights of a suspect nowadays compared to their almost nonexistent status a generation ago. Punks testing the law today must have a field day demanding their rights, he thought.

The Brooklyn boy's mind went back to 1958, when he was 15 and longed to be a hard guy. His adolescent ambition was to hang out all day in Mitchell's, a pool room on Fifth Avenue and Seventh Street in Park Slope. Age of admission to pool rooms was 16. This was the law, apparently. Cops marched into Mitchell's regularly and demanded to see the birth certificate of anyone who looked underage.

Always quick with a scheme, the Brooklyn boy hit on the idea of altering his birth certificate. But his parents kept the precious document locked in a box at home. He knew better than to ask them for it. His father would smack him. Parents were like cops—they knew a kid was always up to no good, guilty until proven innocent.

The next best thing to a birth certificate was a baptismal certificate. The Brooklyn boy went down to Court Street to the parish in which he was born, Our Lady Star of the Sea, and paid a dollar to have the lady in the church office look up the record of his baptism, which included his date of birth, and copy it on paper stamped with a raised seal.

He took the certificate home to the family's tenement apartment on Third Avenue in South Brooklyn. By dipping it partially in Clorox, he managed to remove the number 3 from the date of his birth, January 8, 1943. He allowed the paper to dry overnight. The following day he took pen in hand and, using ink exactly the same shade as that used by the lady in the church office, wrote a 2 where the 3 had been. When the ink dried he scuffed and crumpled the certificate to give it a worn look. Then he put it in his pocket and set off for Mitchell's.

I'd better not get caught, the Brooklyn boy thought grimly as he walked along Fifth Avenue. Altering a baptismal certificate, he was sure, was a serious crime. The mere suspicion of forgery certainly would warrant a cuffing from the cops. He dreaded the possibility of interrogation in the 72nd Precinct on Fifth Avenue. He'd walked by many times and glanced furtively in the windows. The detectives were always eating cake from Larsen's bakery around the corner. They were all Irish and weighed 270 pounds. It was well known that when the bulls of the 72nd Precinct hauled in a suspect for questioning, they took him up a flight of stairs to a notorious room where they beat him over the head with the Brooklyn telephone directory. This brutal torture left no telltale blood or bruises. For altering his baptismal certificate, the Brooklyn boy was sure, the detectives would box his ears severely with the big directory. Then they'd throw him in jail. A judge would sentence him to prison. Tampering with a church document was undoubtedly a mortal sin as well as a felony, so if he died in prison he'd go to hell. The Brooklyn boy, stepping into smoky Mitchell's, swallowed hard and prayed his forgery went undetected.

Sure enough, the cops came that afternoon. The Brooklyn boy was shooting pool and strutting around the table and smoking a Lucky like a man when he heard, "The bulls are here!" His heart stopped. A plainclothes officer stood at the door to make sure nobody ran out, and his partner headed right for the table where the Brooklyn boy, trembling, tried to be cool and chalk his cue casually.

The cop got in his face and demanded, "What year was you born?"

So that was how they trapped a baptismal certificate forger. They didn't ask his age, but what year he was born, hoping the suspect would slip and tell the truth.

"1942," he said, thinking fast.

"You got proof?"

He produced the phony baptismal certificate. The cop eyed it skeptically. A slight smile played around his mouth. This probably wasn't the first doctored document he'd ever seen. "You sure this is '42 and not '43?" he said. "I swear to God I'm 16!" the Brooklyn boy, sick with panic, lied unconvincingly.

The cop gestured toward the door. "Get outta here!" he hollered. The Brooklyn boy fled, relieved to be free. He didn't ask for his baptismal certificate. He didn't want it even if he had a right to it.

Recalling this incident from his misspent youth the other day, the Brooklyn boy decided that growing up with no rights wasn't bad if the cops had a heart.

July 17, 1994

BROWNSTONE VETS GIVE BROOKLYN CHEER

There's a tendency to bad-mouth the block, the neighborhood, the borough, the city, so it's always refreshing to run into a New Yorker who loves living here.

"Fort Greene has definitely improved over the years. We've

never considered moving elsewhere. I can't imagine we would," Dave Wilson said with a smile.

Dave and his wife, Elise, settled on South Elliott Place in 1970. Their 130-year-old Victorian brownstone is worth, oh, a dozen times what they paid for it back then. But good neighbors and good living in Fort Greene, not improved property values, make the Wilsons high on the neighborhood.

I first met Dave and Elise and their kids, Josh and Sarah, on their block in 1976. Josh and Sarah were tiny at the time. Now they're in college. After all these years, Dave and I renewed our acquaintance recently.

"I don't know if you remember," Dave told me, "but when we met years ago the big problem in the neighborhood was a string of bars on Lafayette Avenue where prostitutes hung out. Well, the bars and the prostitutes are long gone. There was a seedy bodega on the corner of South Elliott and Lafayette then. Now there's a nice coffee shop there that caters to Brooklyn Tech students and teachers. Fulton Street has seen a lot of commercial development. A couple of jazz places and several good ethnic restaurants have opened in the neighborhood."

When we met in '76, Dave was teaching at a private high school in Manhattan, and Elise was a housewife. Today, he toils as an administrator in the dean's office at Baruch College in Manhattan, and she's a social worker for HeartShare (formerly the Catholic Guardian Society) in Red Hook. They both enjoy a healthy and inexpensive commute by bicycling to work.

"I have a rebuilt five-speed Peugeot the kids gave me for my birthday," Dave said. "I love commuting by bike. Only bad weather gets me on the subway. Last year I took the train a total of 20 times— I kept count. I can bike from my house to Baruch, on Park Avenue and 26th Street, in 35 minutes, the same time it takes on the subway.

"How do I go? Along Fulton Street through the mall, right on Adams Street and over the Brooklyn Bridge and uptown. The ride over the bridge is one of the great views in New York. I look forward to it every morning. Elise enjoys biking to work, too. She had a couple of bikes stolen, though. Now she's using one of Sarah's old ones."

Dave had a brush with crime while biking over the bridge one morning a couple of months ago. Ahead of him were half a dozen teenagers on foot. One of them kicked his bike as he rode by. The front wheel collapsed. Dave, no docile victim, came off the bike and went for the kids. They ran. "I'd have run after them but I had to look after the bike," he told me. "Cost me $40 to get it repaired."

As crime stories go, that's a minor one. Dave told me that, fortunately, his family has never been seriously victimized by crime during their almost quarter of a century in Brooklyn. "I admit, though, that the violence we read about and see on TV all the time demoralizes me," he said.

"But I disagree with those who think violence is an urban problem that they can escape by fleeing the city. There have been horrible incidents of violence in suburban and rural places lately. Running from the city is no guarantee of security. To get away from crime you might have to leave the country."

Many of the Wilsons' original neighbors in Fort Greene are still there, he said. Most of those who moved did so when their kids reached school age. Josh and Sarah attended a private grammar school, Packer. Sarah went to high school a short walk from home at Brooklyn Tech, which Dave praised highly. "A superb school. Sarah really blossomed there." Josh graduated from Friends School, where he learned an appreciation of Quaker spirituality that he transmitted to his parents.

"I grew up an Episcopalian, and Elise a Congregationalist, but we never joined a church in Brooklyn," Dave said. "That may be about to change. We've been going regularly to the Sunday morning meeting at the Society of Friends on Schermerhorn Street. We're very comfortable there. The service is a kind of meditation. Worshipers stand up at intervals to express a thought or offer a prayer. This has added an important spiritual dimension to our lives."

What prompted me to reestablish communication with Dave was seeing his picture in a nifty quarterly publication, *The Hill*, devoted to neighborhood life in Fort Greene and Clinton Hill. There stood Dave on his impressive stoop, and the caption read: "Dave Wilson in front of his bed-and-breakfast brownstone."

I asked Dave about that. "Elise and I had always rented out an apartment in the house. We got tired of being landlords. When a tenant left several years ago we decided to go the bed-and-breakfast route and rent the apartment to guests for short stays. It's worked out well. Quite a few of our guests have been foreigners. Fort Greene is a perfect place to stay for anyone who wants to really see brownstone Brooklyn."

It was good to get together with Dave again. His upbeat assessment of Fort Greene was heartening to hear. Brooklyn needs boosters. Families like the Wilsons sure help.

January 23, 1994

Here's to Those Who Stood Home

I propose an annual "Brooklynites Who Stood Home" celebration honoring a native son or daughter who has lived his or her entire life in the borough. Why should ex-Brooklynites get all the attention? Recognize those who stood home, I say.

A week from today the annual "Welcome Back to Brooklyn" festival is celebrated with a parade and entertainment at Grand Army Plaza. Singer Neil Sedaka will host the festivities. He and actress Marisa Tomei, actor Jack Scalia and basketball great Connie Hawkins will be welcomed to the Brooklyn Botanic Garden's Celebrity Path. These worthies all grew up in Brooklyn and left to achieve fame and fortune.

What about Brooklynites who never left and are unknown and broke? Don't loyal lifers deserve some kudos? There are tens of thousands of them, and borough president Howard Golden ought to select and cite one or more annually. A fitting tribute might be a party in Prospect Park or on the boardwalk at Coney Island. The honoree might receive a gift certificate for a sandwich and sundae at Hinsch's ice cream parlor on Fifth Avenue in Bay Ridge. Proprietor Johnny Logue would gladly donate the lunch to garner some publicity for his place.

Come to think of it, though, Johnny already got publicity in the last paragraph and it didn't even cost him lunch. Shows you how sharp Johnny is. I've been plugging his sweet shop for years. He gladly springs for coffee when I come by. "Reel is a cheap date," he once told Jimmy Laffey.

Johnny Logue himself could serve as a "Brooklynites Who Stood Home" role model. He grew up in Sunset Park and lives in Bay Ridge. He tends to stick pretty close to the old home borough except to visit a son in Florida. (Also, Johnny occasionally goes on safari to Staten Island). He came from a poor family and, to prove he was no snob, stayed broke for many years in adulthood. His bookmaker prospered, purchasing a new Lincoln annually, thanks largely to Johnny's loyal patronage.

So Johnny has some strong pluses for "Brooklynite Who Stood Home" honors. On the minus side, he's quite well known and gets many a big hello from friends and acquaintances when strolling along Fifth Avenue. This could work against Johnny because the honoree really should be a nobody, an anti-celebrity, an anonymous someone who just stood home.

Purists are probably wondering, "Why does columnist Reel, who certainly should know basic grammar, write 'stood home' when the proper construction is 'stayed home?'" The answer is that over the years I've noticed that if you ask a typical Brooklyn guy how he spent the previous evening, he'll likely reply: "I stood home."

Brooklynites speak colorfully. At a recent wake at Clavin's in Bay Ridge I ran into Pasquale from Park Slope, a fancier of fine Italian food. Pasquale loves to tell me about wonderful Brooklyn restaurants that never get reviewed. Food critics stay away because they fear that anything less than an unqualified rave notice—a mildly negative comment on the tortellini, say—might result in an unfortunate reprisal.

"Have I got a place for you! Marrone! The food is so good you'll fall down on the floor," Pasquale enthused. He vowed to take me to the place for dinner but was vague about when. To protect myself against the possibility that a concrete invitation might never be forthcoming, I said to Pasquale, "Can you tell me the name of the place in case I want to go by myself?" He gave me a look of reproof, put his finger to his lips and said, "I never devour a secret."

I accepted that. I just hope Pasquale from Park Slope and I can divulge a good meal together one day soon. He'd be a good "Brooklynite Who Stayed Home" except that Pasquale from Park Slope is much too well known. He's downright notorious, in fact.

My modest proposal is to cite annually an unknown Brooklynite of modest means—again, there's no shortage of them—who hasn't a single noteworthy accomplishment to his or her name but who has remained true to the borough of homes and churches, disdaining the exodus to Manhattan and Hollywood, not to mention Long Island and New Jersey.

At the party at Prospect Park or Nathan's or Hinsch's or wherever, the Brooklynite Who Stood Home would be expected to make a brief acceptance speech, and it might go something like this:

"Our family never missed 'The Honeymooners' on TV when I was a kid. My hero was Ralph Kramden. I wanted to be just like him. I guess I made it. I joined the Transit Authority after high school. I've spent 30 years driving a bus.

"Me and the wife live in an apartment. It was just right when we were married. Then the kids came along and it was too small. We used to talk about moving out of Brooklyn for more space, but we never had the down payment for a house. Now the kids are grown and living on their own, so our little place is just right again. I'm sure glad we stayed put!

"Everything we could want, or at least everything we could afford, is right here, so why go though the aggravation of moving? The wife likes the ocean in the summer. We're minutes from a beautiful beach, Coney Island. Some people think Coney Island isn't safe, but that's not so. We've never had a problem.

"I like the Mets. Takes me an hour to get to the ballpark. We like to eat. There's every kind of food within walking distance of the apartment. The doctor, the dentist, the church, the funeral parlor, the supermarket, the diner—everything is a walk away.

"So thanks for the free lunch. I promise not to go anywhere."

Those words would resonate with Brooklynites and uplift local spirits more than memories of the rich and famous who fled. "Brooklynites Who Stood Home." A breed not apart.

May 29, 1994

Chapter Two:

Saints and Sinners
••••••••••••••••••••••••••••••••••••

IS TRUMP A "SOFT AND TENDER LITTLE BOY"?

I was surprised that Donald Trump and Marla Maples could find a respectable clergyman to marry them. Any righteous man of God would beg off the assignment, I'd have thought. After all, Trump carried on an affair with Maples for all to see, humiliating his first wife, Ivana, before he divorced her.

We all sin, but Trump has always seemed immensely proud of his transgressions. Sinners should have the decency to show remorse. If we don't, shouldn't God's representatives rebuke us?

Monday I said to the Rev. Arthur Caliandro, who later that day married Trump and Maples, "This guy flouted God's commandment against adultery. He mortified his first wife and their kids. Now comes this tawdry extravaganza of a wedding. Doesn't the church look bad sanctioning it?"

This was stated with respect. I have a high regard for Caliandro, senior pastor of Marble Collegiate Church. The Dutch Reformed minister is the protégé of the Rev. Norman Vincent Peale, whose good words have given help and hope to millions.

"I'm a pastor," Caliandro answered evenly. "Trump is a public figure. I relate to many people who are not public figures whose lives are not straight and direct and proper in terms of religious understanding of morality. I don't judge them. I try to look for what in a person is redeemable.

"My contacts with Donald have shown me that within this man who is a very able and shrewd businessman is a soft and tender little boy always trying to express himself. A couple of years ago I had dinner with him and John Denver and a group of people, and the entire conversation was on faith and spirituality and morality. I watched Donald. He didn't say much, he was listening intently, didn't try to divert the conversation, didn't get cynical. I look for that in Donald Trump and in other people, and see God's presence and a desire to be loved."

I asked the minister if he got any sense that Trump was sorry for the pain he caused his first wife, Ivana, and their three kids. Could he tell if Trump felt shame or remorse?

"I think it's painful for him," Caliandro replied. "I think he has a strong awareness of what's right and wrong, and struggles with that all the time. That's the part of him that's very endearing. I see in him that kind, gentle little boy.

"Whatever sin was involved there, he's facing that and dealing with it. He's been very kind to Ivana. They're in touch. She told me the other day, 'Donnie's been good to me.'"

Caliandro knows Trump and I don't, so his opinion of him carries more credibility than mine. I've always considered Trump a blackguard. Almost nothing is worse than cheating on your wife in public. It's bad enough in private. Preening Trump paraded his infidelity—and his out-of-wedlock daughter, Tiffany.

"At the very least," I asked Caliandro, "after the scandal they've caused and the spectacle they've made of themselves for years, shouldn't Trump and Maples have kept the wedding simple rather than having a tacky spectacular at the Plaza?"

"Originally they wanted a small private ceremony. The Trump family has worshipped at Marble Collegiate for years. I wish they'd done it that way. I've emphasized to them that this is a worship service—it's God's time. My focus is on the sacredness of the service, and their commitment and pledge to strive to love."

Fair enough. Let charity prevail. No point in feeling contempt for Trump even if he warrants it. And let the Rev. Caliandro have the last word: "The older I get the more I acknowledge the fact that all of us are broken and very incomplete. None of us is in a position to judge. Jesus said, 'You who are without sin cast the first stone.' The more I see of life and of my own darkness, I have to honor that."

December 22, 1993

HE ALWAYS NAMES THAT TUNE

Fred Perri of Midwood has been in the record business for almost half a century. When he isn't selling music he's listening to it. As a result, Fred tends to think and talk in song titles.

The other day we were out for some air. "Where do you want to walk?" I asked him.

"On the Sunny Side of the Street," he replied.

That's Fred, to whom all of life is an old standard.

"I'm Beginning to See the Light," he said.

"Huh?" I said.

"I met my wonderful wife, Pat, the day she came into my store to buy a Harry James recording of 'I'm Beginning to See the Light,'" Fred related.

That store was on Whitehall Street in Manhattan. The year was

1951. Fred now owns WOW Music in Jersey City. Music is his life. His only greater love is Pat. They've been married 41 years.

"On our 10th anniversary, I told Pat how happy I was to be married to her. I told her, 'S'Wonderful!' " said Fred.

I smiled. "What did you tell her on your 20th anniversary?"

"Things Are Getting Better All the Time."

Fred was on a roll. Could he keep it going? I was curious. "How about on your 30th?"

"I Love You More Today Than Yesterday."

"And on your 40th anniversary, how did you express your undying love?" I wondered.

Without a pause Fred replied, "I got down on one knee, kissed her hand and said with feeling, 'Our Love Is Here to Stay.'"

"You sure do love your wife. You and Pat have a wonderful marriage."

Fred nodded and said, "Isn't It Romantic?"

"You don't mean to say you still romance her after all these years. Do you?"

"Night and Day," said Fred, grinning broadly.

"How has Pat treated you to make you such a devoted husband?" I wondered.

"Tenderly."

Fred is the only guy I know who speaks in songs. Brooklyn is just where you would expect to find such a unique character.

"Fred," I asked him, "when Pat walked into your store on Whitehall Street and you saw her for the first time that day in 1951, can you recall what went through your mind?"

"Ain't She Sweet?" he said.

"I'll bet you were quick to step out from behind the counter and ask the young lady if you could be of any assistance."

"Yes, Indeed."

"What were you thinking?"

"I'm in the Mood for Love."

"Do you remember anything about your first date with Pat? Did you get her home early or late?"

"In the Wee Small Hours of the Morning."

"After you walked her to the door, what did you say?"

"Give Me Five Minutes More, Only Five Minutes More!"

"Knowing you, Fred, I figure you probably tried to get fresh with Pat on your second date. How did she handle it? What did she tell you?"

"I'm Old-Fashioned."

"And what did you say to plead your case?"

"I've Got a Crush on You."

"By the third date you must have known you were serious. What did you tell her?"

"I'm Confessin' That I Love You."

"Can you remember your reaction when she said she felt the same way about you? What did you blurt out?"

"I Can't Believe That You're in Love With Me."

"What did Pat's father say when you respectfully requested his daughter's hand in marriage?"

"Take Good Care of My Baby."

"You're a pretty cool customer, Fred, so I imagine your marriage proposal was witty and whimsical. Can you recall what you said?"

"What Are You Doing the Rest of Your Life?"

"Did you consider the possibility that she might refuse your proposal?"

"It Never Entered My Mind," said Fred, smiling.

"I assume you were honest enough to level with Pat and tell her candidly that you were just a working stiff who never would make a million bucks. How did you put it?"

"I Can't Give You Anything But Love, Baby."

"I know Pat came from a family of modest means. When she told you there was no dowry, how did you respond?

"I Love You Just the Way You Are."

"At your wedding at St. Brendan's, how did Pat look?"

"Too Marvelous for Words."

"What were your first words to your new bride?"

"You Belong to Me."

"Not to be nosy, but how was the honeymoon?"

"Delightful, Delicious and Delovely."

"After four decades of marriage, do you still whisper sweet nothings in her ear?"

"Once in a While."

"And what do you whisper?"

"You're My Everything."

Unbelievable. "You're the Top," I told Fred. I guess song-title talk is contagious.

July 24, 1994

In Chelsea, They Were Neighbors to Live For

Maybe the lights on the Christmas tree sparked it. There may have been a gas leak. The cause was never clear, but when the blaze erupted it blew out the doors and windows of the tenement apartment where Tim and Irene Mahoney and their four young children lived in Chelsea.

At first it was thought no one was home. The Mahoneys had gone to a party that night at the Merrymakers Club on Eighth Avenue. But Tim left the party early and returned to their five rooms on the fourth floor at 315 W. 17th Street.

Firemen found Tim on the floor. When they carried him out, his mother, who lived next door at 313, fainted in the street. A rescue crew rushed him to St. Vincent's Hospital. He had severe burns over 35 percent of his body. A priest administered the last rites.

A worse Christmas was unimaginable.

Tim faded in and out of consciousness for six weeks. He has a hazy recollection of Dr. Jim Connell telling him, "I've gotta cut your throat." The doctor inserted a tube so he could breathe. And he can still hear the doctor saying, "I've gotta pull all that skin off your hands." The fire had charred his hands so badly that there was doubt he would ever use them again. He came down with pneumonia in the hospital, and Father Jim Gorman from St. Bernard's on West 14th Street gave him the last rites a second time.

Tim, a truck driver for a meat company in the West Side wholesale market, was 30 years old. "God, if You spare Tim, I promise we'll have another child," Irene prayed. Tim laughs about that today, because they had three more children.

Tim weighed 80 pounds and his hands were in plastic casts when he got home after four months in St. Vincent's. He was in and out of the hospital for another six months for skin grafts. One day during a treatment he told Dr. Connell, "Doc, my benefits have run out. I can't pay you." The doctor waved him off. Another of his patients at the time, as it happened, was a member of the Gimbel family, one of the city's wealthiest. "So don't worry about paying me, Tim. What I don't get off you, I'll get off the Gimbels."

Jack Haggerty, a longshoreman, met Irene in the street one day, clasped her hand and left $100 in it. That was typical of friends and neighbors in Chelsea. "What great people!" Tim says 35 years later, awe in his voice at the goodness of ordinary folks like Larry Sullivan and Johnny Lotito, to whom Christmas spirit meant loving their neighbors year-round.

The apartment was a shell after the fire, so the immediate need was for a place to live. Neighbors John and Mary Devers took in the oldest Mahoney child, Timmy, and in-laws John and Ellen Walsh took in the other three kids. Irene moved in with Tim's mother,

Mary. Irene had to make do on $40 a week from the truck drivers' union.

Charity had a personal touch, and raffles were a popular way to raise money for individuals and families hit by adversity in neighborhoods years ago. If an accident put a fellow out of work, the longshoremen on the West Side piers or the truck drivers in the meat market would run a raffle at the job. Each guy tossed in a buck or two. The winner of the raffle donated the proceeds on behalf of all the guys to the family in need.

Friends and neighbors did even better for the Mahoneys. They ran a big racket—that's what a benefit was called in those days: a racket—at the Sherry Club, a political clubhouse on Eighth and 18th. Money was collected at the door. When Tim's grandmother, Nellie, and her husband, Nick, arrived, Nick opened his wallet and took out $20. Nellie scowled and said, "Make it $50, you cheapskate!" Nick sheepishly peeled off three more sawbucks and handed them over.

The racket drew a crowd. Among those present was Joe Gorman, who owned a bar on Eighth between 18th and 19th. When Joe noticed the beer was running out, he sent a few fellows to his joint to fetch another barrel. Friends of the Mahoneys poured into the Sherry Club all afternoon and evening.

After it was over, a couple of the men who organized the racket, John Walsh and Walter Thole, visited Tim's mother's place. They brought two cigar boxes stuffed with money. They sat down in the living room and opened the boxes, and the green stuff sprung up and spilled out. Young Timmy, 8 years old at the time, was sitting with his mother. Wide-eyed, he asked, "Did you rob a bank?"

"I don't remember the exact amount," Tim says today, eyes glistening, "but I can tell you we wound up with a houseful of brand-new furniture, new clothes for everybody, all our bills paid and two grand in the bank."

His burns healed. He drove trucks for another 30 years. The Mahoneys left Chelsea in the mid-'70s. Tim and Irene are in Staten Island now. The kids are grown, with kids of their own, and living in New Jersey and Florida and Washington State. Tim and Irene go back to the old neighborhood occasionally for mass at St. Bernard's, and Tim drops into Flannery's on West 14th Street to gab with what's left of the old crew—Tom and Jim Mailley, Tom and Jimmy and Billy Hogan, Frank Lynch, Walter Thole. Every time he sees Walter he thinks of those cigar boxes stuffed with money for the Mahoneys.

Christmas of 1959 will always be seared in Tim's memory. He

nearly died. But it's not so much the pain and suffering that he remembers. "It's how great the people were," he says.

December 24, 1994

"YES" You Can

Clarence Nelson wants to pass on to kids what was passed on to him when he was a kid. Clarence was a shoe-shine boy in his native Bedford-Stuyvesant when a customer put the idea in his head that he could grow up to be an engineer.

Clarence did just that, and now, at 61, he's visiting high schools like Brooklyn Tech and Boys and Girls to persuade kids to excel in math and science—and perhaps eventually to enroll at Polytechnic University, where he is director of the Center for Youth in Engineering and Science outreach programs.

Clarence overcame the obstacles of poverty and a broken home. He studied at night for years to graduate from Polytechnic in 1967. Armed with a degree in civil engineering, he worked as an engineer for New York City and rose to become director of the Office of Parking in the Bureau of Traffic Operations. And later for the city of Norwalk, Connecticut. This year he went to work for his alma mater, Polytechnic.

Clarence is a self-effacing fellow who hates to talk about himself, but I dragged the shoe-shine story out of him in a conversation at Polytechnic on Jay Street the other day.

"I lived with my mother, brother and sister on Hancock Street," he said. "I shined shoes at a place on Lewis Avenue at the corner of Hancock—Wise Shoe Shop. The owner was James Wise. He was like a father to me.

"One of the regular customers was a fellow named John Surplus, the son of a state Supreme Court justice. The Surplus family lived on Putnam and Stuyvesant Avenues. John Surplus came in for a shoe shine whenever he was in Brooklyn. He was away a lot on his job in Alaska. He was an engineer, building an airport in Anchorage.

"He wore boots. He paid 25 cents for a shine and always tipped 15 cents, which was a lot of money to me. While I buffed his boots he would talk about his job. Alaska was the new frontier back then, and when he described his work there it filled me with the romance of the place.

"He was sowing seeds, although I didn't realize it at the time. He made me want to be an engineer."

It was good that Clarence was inspired by John Surplus, because he didn't get much encouragement at school. Or if he did, it was what you might called backhanded encouragement.

He remembers that a teacher at PS 129 on Lewis and Gates Avenues told him, "Clarence, you're a bright fellow, you have to train your hands."

That was the thinking in those days: A black youngster who showed aptitude and ability in school was steered into a trade where he could use his hands.

A good head was often wasted, because the white people who ran the school system assumed that blacks would not, or should not, aspire to become doctors, lawyers, engineers. The white-collar professions were for white people.

So at Westinghouse High, Clarence studied carpentry and cabinetmaking. But the thought of becoming an engineer stayed with him, and after graduation from Westinghouse he went on to what was then the Institute for Applied Arts and Sciences—now New York City Technical College.

Another bit of human interest I managed to drag out of a reluctant Clarence: He was broke when he started college, and about the only thing he owned that was worth anything was a clarinet he had played in high school. "I wasn't good at it but I liked to play. The clarinet came in handy. I hocked it to buy my books," he said.

After graduation from the two-year institute, Clarence went to work as a surveyor. He was married. He and his wife had four children. And he began the long process of taking courses at night at Polytechnic University.

As an engineer, Clarence was always conscious that minorities were underrepresented in his profession. He saw engineering as a golden opportunity for poor kids to pursue that would carry them up into the middle class. This was always true, of course, but truer now than ever because a shortage of as many as half a million engineers in the United States is anticipated by the end of the century.

Since 1975, Clarence has been visiting high schools as a volunteer under the auspices of the Institute of Transportation Engineers and also the Alliance for Community Education (a group he and other Brooklyn professionals founded) to involve kids in science and engineering projects and stimulate their interest in those careers.

Of his role with YES at Polytechnic, Clarence said with a smile, "I'm getting paid for doing something that I did for a long time for free."

Clarence made it clear when we talked that I should write about the YES programs and not about him, and I promised I would, so maybe I better get started. High school and junior high school kids with an interest in science who want to explore it here in Brooklyn, please listen. This might be an opportunity that will change your lives.

Clarence Nelson made his dream come true. Now he's passing it on.

April 28, 1991

A BANQUET FOR THE BODY AND THE SOUL

Harry Gorman, a big-hearted carpenter from rural Vermont, wanted to do something for Covenant House, a Manhattan-based charity that rescues street kids. He was too broke to write a check, but, like a lot of Vermonters, Harry raised his own poultry, and he could spare a few turkeys at Thanksgiving.

Harry's best friend, Gerry Dougherty, volunteered to transport the birds to Manhattan and cook them for the kids. Gerry's wife and partner in their catering business in Vermont, Eileen Bradley, was happy to join him. Friends and neighbors donated the trimmings to go with the turkeys. A contingent drove down with a U-Haul full of fresh food in tow and prepared and served a delicious dinner to 350 Covenant House kids, staffers and supporters at the charity's headquarters on West 17 Street.

That happened for the first time in 1988. Gorman has since moved to Ireland, but dinner via Vermont at Covenant House made such an impression that it's become an annual Thanksgiving tradition. Yesterday, Gerry, Eileen, their 6-year-old son, Sam, and a party of 15 adults, teenagers and preteens, all of whom made the six-hour trek from home to Manhattan in the rain Monday night and stayed over at Covenant House, got busy cooking a dozen 30-pound turkeys, a half-dozen Hubbard squashes and cases of carrots, cabbages and potatoes contributed by Vermont growers and gardeners. They'd brought 100 apple and pumpkin pies baked by students at St. Johnsbury Academy, and dozens of loaves of bread baked by well-wishers back home.

Gerry, a smiling guy with a red beard, surveyed the stacks of food his helpers were unpacking in the Covenant House kitchen yesterday. "All of it was donated. We have a network of 20 or 30 folks who get involved every year. It's pretty well organized. Vermonters love to grow their own food. They're proud of it and love to give it away. Some donate cash to pay for the U-Haul."

The turkeys were slaughtered Sunday. The 15 gallons of apple cider were pressed and poured at the orchard Monday morning. Nothing but the best for the Covenant House kids.

Gerry said that cooking for 350 was a labor of love for him and his wife and fellow Vermonters because they saw brotherhood in action all day. The kids from the country and their street-smart urban counterparts in Covenant House would make friends immediately, playing basketball in the gym and sharing food in the dining room, and differences of race and region would evaporate in the spirit of the holiday. This was his seventh Thanksgiving at Covenant House, Gerry said, and he's always heartened and reassured to see stereotypes shattered and barriers come down. "The kids learn that city folks and country folks are the same, they just grew up in different places."

"To me, this is the high point of the year," said Dave Gregorio, director of a Covenant House program called Rights of Passage, whose 114 young people get room and board and counseling at the agency while finishing school, learning a trade or starting work. Joining them for dinner last night in the big dining room were 35 women and their babies and toddlers who live in a Covenant House facility for unwed mothers on West 52nd Street, and scores of right-off-the-street kids from the charity's crisis center on West 41st Street.

Covenant House kids are poor, it goes without saying. The visiting Vermonters aren't rich, either. "Moonlight or starve—that's our motto," laughed Gerry, who works at his catering business by day and holds a second job at night.

But they all had plenty yesterday. And it happened because six years ago Harry Gorman was too broke to send money. Folks bearing food and goodwill came instead, and people came together for a Thanksgiving that blesses us all by its example.

November 23, 1994

"FLOYD" IS CONTENT WITH HIS STREET LIFE

A derelict lay under blankets on a mattress on the sidewalk as Anthony walked by on his way to work on West 14th Street. The cold bit into Anthony's face. He wondered how the derelict could survive in the street in such weather.

Anthony got about 15 steps past the poor guy and then turned and walked back. He thought: Everybody passes by these derelicts like they weren't human beings. How could I just walk by him? Anthony has a recurring daydream about someday opening a soup kitchen. Derelicts would come in for a meal and he would talk to them and they would change. He pictures them cleaned up and leading productive lives. He realizes it's a fairy tale. With a wife and three kids to support, he has to go to work every day.

His heart went out to the shivering derelict, who looked up from his grubby mattress.

"You wanna get out of the cold?"

"Yeah. Where?"

"Come on," Anthony said, and the derelict pulled himself to his feet and followed Anthony down the block. He was a big guy, maybe 6-foot-2, 200 pounds, with bushy gray hair and a beard. He wore a battered overcoat. His pants drooped. His feet must have been freezing because he wore no socks.

Anthony ushered him into a building and up the stairs one flight to his office. Anthony sat behind his desk. The derelict let himself down slowly on the couch. He smiled.

"Want a cigarette?" Anthony asked.

"Got my own," the derelict said. He took one out of his shirt pocket and lit up and asked, "Have you got an ashtray?" Anthony found one for him. A very mannerly and respectful derelict, he thought.

"I'm Anthony. What's your name?"

"Floyd."

They were silent for a moment. "Would you like to use the bathroom?" Anthony asked.

"No, that's okay."

Floyd reached into his overcoat pocket and came out with a pint bottle of vodka. He put it to his lips and drank.

"Want something to eat?" Anthony asked.

"No." Floyd shook his head.

Anthony smiled. "You're on one of those liquid diets?"

"Yeah." Floyd laughed.

"You and I are a lot alike," Anthony said.

"You know the deal?"

"I know right where you're at."

Floyd took another slug on his pint, and Anthony asked, "How could you stand it out there in the cold?"

"The cold don't bother me," Floyd said.

"You don't go to the shelters?"

Floyd shook his head.

"How long are you on the street?"

"I'm kind of embarrassed to tell."

"You could tell me."

"Oh, 20 years."

He was originally from North Carolina, Floyd said, and he played college football in Alabama. "I dropped a couple of passes. I had arthritis in my hand." After college he served in the Marines and then wrote songs and worked for a delivery service, he said.

Anthony didn't know what to believe. All of it or some of it or none of it might be true, he thought.

Floyd finished off his pint.

"Ever try to put that down?" Anthony asked.

"Yeah. I had some clean time once. About 20 months."

"What happened?"

"My girlfriend died."

"Ever try a detox? A rehab?"

"I tried everything," Floyd said. He shrugged. "This is just the way it is for me." He paused, then continued. "You want to know what's crazy? The very thing that got me in trouble was women—that's where all my money went—and right now I could really go for one!"

Anthony laughed. Floyd wouldn't be popular with feminists, he thought.

Anthony can't go a day without a shower, and Floyd looked like he hadn't bathed in weeks. "You want a shower? I got one here. You can use it if you want," Anthony said.

Floyd declined. He asked if he could fill his empty vodka bottle with water. Sure, Anthony said.

Anthony had an appointment for lunch. He got up to leave. "Lie on the couch if you like. Rest here as long as you want," he told Floyd.

Anthony ate well at the Old Homestead. He brought back a doggie bag with slices of steak, french fries and creamed spinach. He found Floyd under blankets on his mattress on the sidewalk.

"Thank you!" Floyd told him, accepting the food.

"You know where my office is. Come and visit any time you want," Anthony told him.

"God bless you," Floyd said.

Anthony walked to his office. Floyd seemed perfectly content to live in the street, he thought. The street was his home. The booze had taken everything from him. All he wanted to do was lie on his mattress and drink vodka. It was a shame that Floyd was a derelict, because he was a good guy.

Anthony took off his coat and sat at his desk and thought: We're all good guys, and there but for the grace of God go I.

December 18, 1994

How Helping Hands Warm the Heart

My friend Alan Luks, executive director of Big Brothers, Big Sisters of NYC, which matches kids from single-parent homes with adult mentors, was telling me that the conventional wisdom nowadays is that his work is a lost cause. When people he meets learn what he does for a living, Alan said, they give him a sad smile and say something like, "Oh, you work with inner-city youth? Too bad there's no hope for them."

Alan shook his head. "Even the die-hard do-gooders are giving up," he lamented.

It's a challenge to keep hope alive. Children from broken homes barely surviving in neighborhoods degraded by drugs and violence seem beyond whatever help the larger society can offer—especially when the larger society itself is beset by all kinds of moral and social evils. Prayer and fasting might drive out the inner city's demons, but no one in authority is proposing a spiritual solution.

The only antidote to despair, Alan Luks was saying, is constant rededication to the cause of kids in need. We have to believe we can do something for them—and, in the process, for ourselves, as the good we do comes back to bless us.

The statistics are numbing: 682,502 children living in single-parent homes in New York City—356,000 of them below the poverty line. All research shows that kids from broken homes are most at risk of becoming drug addicts and/or violent criminals.

Big Brothers, Big Sisters of NYC, founded in 1904, is devoted to rescuing these youngsters. Its trained adult volunteers and social workers serve about 1,000 kids. "All the mentoring programs in the city combined reach perhaps 40,000 youngsters—only a small percentage of those who need us," Alan said.

But we can't abandon kids in need. The rest of us will go down with them. Alan and I had lunch at Big Brothers on East 30th Street the other day with three successful young Manhattan men he's enlisted to raise money and recruit volunteers so the organization can reach out to more kids. Tackling the problem head-on is the only way to break through the feeling that it's hopeless. Stockbroker Andy Kramer, speechwriter Marty Galasso and marketing executive Jeff Rowland talked with Alan about a Big Brothers, Big Sisters fundraiser they put on recently in SoHo that attracted 150 young professional people. They discussed how that core group could involve their friends and get hundreds more young professionals to donate time and money to Big Brothers.

A kind of evangelism was going on in the room, I thought. It was heartening to see young fellows with good careers enthusiastic about doing something for poor kids and undaunted by the numbers who need help.

Volunteerism works because the giver derives personal satisfaction from helping the recipient, Alan Luks said. A large body of research supports the finding that helping others increases self-esteem. Therefore, Alan proposed, we should require kids to do volunteer work for their own good. "There are 47 million kids in U.S. schools from kindergarten through high school, and every one of them should do person-to-person community service on a regular basis," he said, noting that the state of Maryland has made 75 hours of community service mandatory to graduate from high school.

Alan would have kindergarteners draw pictures for old folks in nursing homes, and teenagers do grocery shopping for shut-ins, and the like. "A kid who has related to others by helping them and feeling appreciated is going to feel good about himself. That kid is less likely to commit violence," he asserted.

I must say, a radical reform like this seems warranted. We sure do have a radical problem.

July 14, 1993

Hard Drugs, Hard Time and a Helping Hand

John died of AIDS in the prime of his life. At the crowded wake last week, his father welled up when he told me, "A little black kid about 12 years old was here this afternoon. He shook my hand and said, 'Your son turned my life around.'"

I got a little teary myself at that touching tribute to John, who would have wanted nothing more than to have set a kid right.

John and I met over the phone. He used to call collect from an upstate prison. A critic by nature, he'd let me know when he disliked a column. He and fellow inmates agreed I was all wet for advocating stiffer prison sentences to deter crime. What society had to do, John argued, was figure out why so many young guys turned to drugs and violence, and then attack the root causes. Fine, I replied, but meanwhile society had to punish lawbreakers severely to send the message that crime was intolerable. That approach was doomed to failure, John insisted. "You don't know the guys in here. Believe me, they ain't afraid of nothing, including prison." Drugs were as available in prison as on the streets, he added.

I asked what he was doing time for. Stealing a car, John said. A prison sentence for car theft seemed harsh, I remarked. "There was somebody in the car when I stole it," he explained.

One night about four years ago, two friends of mine, Walter and Batts, walked into a place where I was having coffee. With them was a wiry, handsome fellow. Walter introduced him. "This is John, the guy who called you from the can. He just got out." They had known him for years from the neighborhood. I was flabbergasted. I'd envisioned a wizened old jailhouse face.

John threw himself into a job with a drug-treatment program. I saw him occasionally. One night we were talking about crime and punishment. I said something to the effect that convicts got what they deserved, and John flared up. For a moment I felt afraid of him. Another time he cursed out a cop for giving him a parking ticket. Called the cop every obscenity and challenged him to a fist-fight in the street. The cop smiled and calmly continued along his beat. "I don't know why I do things like that. I guess I just hate authority," John, remorseful, told me later. The cop who walked away was a better man than he was, he admitted.

John confided to only a few close friends like Walter and Batts that he was HIV-positive. "Keep it quiet. I don't want nobody feeling sorry for me," he instructed them. I had no idea.

The fatal virus sits and waits, and years after he last shot drugs, John got sick. "I put him in my summer home at the shore," his brother Bill, who's done well in Wall Street, told me at the wake. "My wife and kids and I went down to have Thanksgiving dinner with him. His temperature hit 105 that day and stayed there for a week. He had chills around the clock. He just wasted away the last 10 weeks. AIDS is a terrible death.

"How did he handle it? You know John. He was angry. Very bitter. 'I'm trying to do the right thing and look what happens,' he'd say. He'd drag himself to Sunday mass and come home and complain that the sermon was awful. 'The priest rambled all over the •$%¢&! place!'"

Bill and I laughed. That was John—resentful right to the grave.

The mourners were family and friends and neighbors and co-workers who admired John for overcoming addiction and working tirelessly to help kids beat drug problems and avoid the perils that put him behind bars—and ultimately took his life. Hard guys smoking cigarettes on the sidewalk out front looked like they'd probably known John in the joint. The mix of upstanding folks and ex-cons paying respects would have appealed to the deceased. I left John's wake hoping St. Peter had a mansion for him, and wondering if the unforgiving AIDS plague would ever end.

February 23, 1994

GREAT SMILE, GREAT MAN

"Do me one favor, huh?" Bishop Francis Mugavero said. He wasn't smiling. That was unusual; smiling was his natural way. We stood in his office in the chancery at 75 Greene Ave. This was 20 years ago, and I had just finished interviewing the bishop of Brooklyn for a piece I would write.

"Uh, what's that, bishop?" I asked.

(I called him "bishop," not the formal "your excellency," because the first time we met he told me, "I'm not excellent.")

"Do me a favor and don't compare me to Cardinal Cooke," he said. He frowned. He had been compared in print favorably to Cardinal Cooke in the past, and it embarrassed him.

The press, always quick to oversimplify, liked to portray Cooke as a princely Manhattan churchman ("a social worker among the rich," one writer sneered) and, for contrast, dub Mugavero the pastoral friend of the humble poor across the river.

Bishop Mugavero hated to look good at the expense of a fellow churchman. "Those comparisons are awful," he told me, shaking his head. "It's bad for Church." He repeated the statement for emphasis: "Bad for Church."

That was how Bishop Mugavero, who passed away yesterday at 77, looked at life. He liked anything that was good for Church, for faith, for families, for people, and he disliked anything that was bad for them.

He had a great smile, perhaps the best smile in New York in our time. It was ear-to-ear and always accompanied by twinkling eyes. He beamed when greeting folks on receiving lines at parish functions. Bishop Mugavero really loved people—not just humanity, but people one at a time.

People reciprocated. His wake won't lack for mourners of all faiths. No Catholic Churchman ever had a better relationship with Jews and Protestants. All prayers rise to the same God, knew Mugavero, a natural ecumenist.

Born in the back of his father's barber shop in Bedford-Stuyvesant, he was a lifelong Brooklyn boy, a regular guy, down-to-earth as could be. "Hey, ya' wanna be a pastor?" he would ask a priest. That was the Mugavero way of making a promotion.

He was a Brooklyn chauvinist who resented media preoccupation with glitzy Gotham at the expense of homey Brooklyn and Queens. "Manhattanopia" was the telling word he coined to describe media elitism. Thus he exacted wider coverage for his Nehemiah housing program in Brownsville. "He's like a great Italian tailor who sews so smoothly you can't see the stitches," an admiring Mario Cuomo, then a Brooklyn lawyer, once said.

Ed Wilkinson of the diocesan newspaper, *The Tablet*, recalls that when the bishop-publisher made him editor, he issued three directives: "One, make sure the story says what the headline says. Two, if you can ever do anything to keep me out of trouble, I'd appreciate it. Three, you know where I am; if you ever need any help, give me a call."

May he intercede for us up there where it counts, now that a peaceful death has concluded the fruitful and happy life in the Lord of Bishop Francis Mugavero.

July 13, 1991

PRINCETON'S LOWER EAST SIDE PROMENADE

Bronx guys don't forget where they came from, God bless 'em. He's studying hard for a doctorate in history at Princeton these days, but former Kingsbridge boy Jerry Podair will be back in his old borough tomorrow morning on a hike from 263rd Street, the Yonkers line, all the way down Broadway to Battery Park.

"It's about 22 miles and should take us about seven hours," the strolling scholar said cheerfully.

His friend and fellow Princeton historian, John Wertheimer, will join Jerry on the colorful trek through Riverdale, Kingsbridge, Inwood, Washington Heights, Harlem, the Upper West Side, Times Square, Herald Square and Greenwich Village. The purpose of the exercise is to raise a few bucks for Nativity Mission School on the Lower East Side.

Two Jewish guys schlepping for the benefit of a Catholic school that serves disadvantaged but highly motivated Hispanic boys. New York at its best.

Their stroll is a repeat performance. Jerry and John did it a year ago and raised $300 in donations of $5 and $10 from Princeton graduate students and professors who wanted to support kids from mean streets who aspire to be the scholars of tomorrow.

Jerry is a Bronx Science, New York University and Columbia Law School graduate with a wife and daughter. He practiced law for a decade before deciding to pursue a doctorate in history. How did he get involved in helping Nativity?

"A group of kids from Nativity visited Princeton for a football game a year ago last fall. They were some of the most impressive kids I've ever seen," Jerry said. "John had worked at the school for a year and always told me how special they were. They were remarkably mature. They were interested in the football game, but they were just as interested in the campus bookstore. I remember one boy asking another if he could borrow some money because he wanted to buy a copy of *Ivanhoe*. I never would have done that at that age. I would have been looking at T-shirts.

"When we were saying good-bye, a number of the boys came up to me and shook my hand and thanked me for having them down for the day. These boys were from deprived circumstances—some of their parents work in sweatshops. Their presence and maturity for boys 11 and 12 years old were so impressive.

"John and I had been idly talking about how long it would take to walk from the top of the Bronx to the tip of Manhattan. It hit us that we could find out and raise money for Nativity at the same time. So we did it last year and will walk again Saturday.

"We're always hearing about educational failures. Nativity is an educational success. These boys are going to make it. They're going to contribute. I'd urge everyone who can to send a donation to Nativity Mission Center."

By putting one foot in front of the other down Broadway, Jerry and John promote giving and also provoke a thought: Most of us don't have a lot of money, but most of us could spare $5 or $10. If we did, the sum of our donations would ensure the education of the 46 boys who attend the middle school.

The flyer Jerry and John put out to publicize their walk and attract donors says: "Jerry and John Hit Broadway, Part Deux. Don't be a putz, fork over some money for us." The rhyme is shaky, but the thought is right on as they put their best feet forward.

June 4, 1993

TRUE LOVE TURNS A BLIND EYE TO ROUND BALL

There are so many hate stories in the news that, once in a while, if only to restore faith in people and hope for the future, a love story deserves a play. So I'm pleased to announce that Don Costello, 42, and Laura Lewis, 40, are getting married.

Sounding ecstatic—almost giddy—Don called on Valentine's Day with the good news. I was happy for him but also a little surprised, because, like a lot of longtime bachelors, Don has his ways and he's pretty well set in them, and such guys can be reluctant to commit to matrimony.

"Does she know you have season tickets for the Yankees, and season tickets for the Giants, and that you've attended every college basketball championship since 1981 and intend to keep the streak alive through 2031, God willing?" I wondered.

"She knows, she knows," Don assured me. "This spring the Final Four is in Charlotte, two weeks before our wedding in Queens, and Laura insists that I go."

Really? I called Laura for verification. "I know Don is going to come back to me," she told me. "The cheerleaders are too young for him!"

No, she said, she wasn't the least bit jealous that her hubby-to-be was going off with the guys for several days. "He loves sports. Why take away something he loves and looks forward to?" she said.

This woman sounds like every man's fantasy.

Don is a police sergeant. Working out of the Flushing station house, he solves robbery cases in Queens. He's a lifelong Queens Village resident and a neighborhood celebrity of sorts because of his good works. A dozen years ago Don investigated a Christmas Eve burglary at a humble home on a poor block in Brooklyn. He never forgot the sight of the children crying because the burglar had stolen the presents from under the tree. For the past 11 years Don and several friends have sponsored an annual Christmas party at his church that attracts hundreds of guests. Each brings a wrapped gift suitable for a child. Don rents a truck and delivers the load of presents to Catholic Charities, which distributes them to needy kids in Brooklyn and Queens. Despite a severe snowstorm last December 11, more than 300 partygoers, an astonishing turnout, showed up at Our Lady of Lourdes in Queens Village bearing gifts.

Don is loved for his generosity. Laura puts it this way: "He's a sweetheart. He's unique—so kind and gentle and sympathetic. He hasn't become hardened by his job. I can't understand why somebody didn't just snatch him up. He's the sweetest guy on earth. We haven't found anything to argue about yet. We just have fun together. We like to go dancing, although we have a little problem with height—I'm five-three and Don is six-four."

Laura lives in Naples, Florida. Her job with a company that markets antique dolls brings her to New York occasionally, and she and Don were introduced by bartender Danny at a popular Bayside restaurant, Monahan and Fitzgerald's. Don made a good impression on one of their first dates, a day at Jones Beach. No sooner were they seated on their blanket than a seagull flew over and did something uncouth on his head. An insecure guy might have gotten upset, but Don calmly laughed it off.

Don't be surprised to see Don coaching Little League in Queens in the next century. Seems he and Laura are looking forward to raising a family. They love kids. "How many? We'll start off with one and see how I get to work if the baby keeps me up all night," said Don. Laura added, "We'll keep having them as long as they keep coming. Maybe we'll make headlines." For now, they make a column.

February 18, 1994

No Debate over Teacher

Harry Walters, a Manhattan lawyer who lives with his wife, Marie, and their four children in Maspeth, was telling me about the greatest positive influence on him outside of his family—his debate coach at Monsignor McClancy High School, Mr. Brophy, otherwise known as Broph.

Harry, 34, described Broph as a Brooklyn boy all the way—St. John's Parish, St. John's Prep, St. John's University. He taught at the Prep when it was alive and thriving in the Borough of Churches, then he moved to McClancy and taught English, ran the library and coached the debate team for 24 years at the Queens school.

Harry said that his four years at Fordham, where he studied philosophy and journalism, and three at Columbia Law School, taught him a great deal, but the truths Broph imparted were of the timeless, eternal variety.

"A lot of lawyers still haven't learned the lessons in advocacy that I started learning from Broph when I was 14," Harry said. "His lessons on debating and on life seemed simple enough:

"Advance only arguments that make sense.

"Be relentlessly self-critical, but enjoy yourself.

"Don't blame others for your mistakes—and never get paralyzed by your mistakes.

"Read. Work. Pray. Do your best."

Simple but profound. Harry was blessed indeed to hear such wisdom at a young age. Not only debaters and future lawyers but all of us could profit spiritually from Broph's sage sayings.

"Most debate coaches didn't really coach," Harry said. "Instead, they did their debaters' work for them, buying canned research, organizing evidence and programming their young charges to hear an argument and respond with a carefully scripted, pre-fabricated rebuttal.

"Not Broph. He taught us to listen, to think and to make a response that made sense. We'd be slaving away in the library, doing research while Broph sat at the front desk reading a book. Another teacher would come in and Broph would pipe up, 'Guess what I'm doing? I'm coaching debate!' He'd roar with laughter. We'd glower, of course, because Broph was making us do our work instead of doing it for us.

"His teams were successful, although not as successful as the programmed teams. That didn't matter to Broph. He knew we were learning something invaluable—something that the programmed debaters would have to learn, if at all, later in life."

A cheerful manner and keen sense of humor endeared Broph to McClancy kids, yet he was a no-nonsense mentor who made demands.

"One day he told me I was exempt from debate practice that afternoon," Harry recalled. "'Your hair is too long. Go get a haircut,' he told me. My hair was all right by McClancy standards but not by Brophy standards, which were slightly stricter. I went home. My mother said my hair was fine. The next day at school Broph asked how come I didn't get a haircut. 'My mother said I didn't have to,' I told him. Broph rebuked me for using my mother as an excuse. If I had a problem with getting a haircut, he said, I should have argued with him man to man, and left my mother out of it."

Like any good coach, Broph knew how to praise a kid and how to humble him. "If you did well in a debate, Broph would always congratulate you. But if you got too high an opinion of yourself, he'd put you down," Harry remembered. "Broph stepped up criticism commensurate with your ability to take it. When I was a senior he videotaped a debate practice. I did about eight minutes. The first minute was awful, but then I got rolling and made my case well. When Broph played the tape, he replayed the first minute over and over. 'Harry Walters can't speak a simple English sentence,' Broph said. I could feel his baleful glare on the back of my neck. 'Harry is using words that aren't even in the dictionary.' I kept waiting for him to play the rest of it so I could look good, but Broph fast-forwarded right through the last seven minutes."

And as an English teacher he was a staunch foe of grade inflation. "Broph would assign a short story to be read at home over the weekend, and in class Monday morning he'd say, 'Take out a piece of paper and convince me that you read the story. If you write something that half convinces me, I'll give you a grade of 50 percent.' And he would. Broph believed that a good grade must be earned."

Harry and Broph keep in touch. Harry and Marie took him to dinner at Niederstein's on Metropolitan Avenue recently. They sat in the restaurant for four hours, gabbing about everything from theology to sports.

"On the way home," Harry related, "Marie remarked that she'd learned a lot in four hours. Imagine, I told her, how much I learned in four years. Broph has that special combination of erudition and simplicity. He knows something about philosophy and something about shortstops."

Broph left McClancy a few years ago and entered Immaculate Conception Seminary in Huntington. God willing, he'll be ordained a priest of the Diocese of Brooklyn by Bishop Thomas Daily at St. James Cathedral in Brooklyn next Saturday. Harry and Marie plan to attend his first mass at Sacred Heart in Bayside a week from today.

The teaching profession's loss could be the church's gain. Folks in the pews crave down-to-earth wisdom from the pulpit. Good homilies are informed by the preacher's personal experience.

And a late vocation is always hopeful and heartening. Ad multos annos, Broph.

Father Edward Brophy, that is.

May 16, 1993

WHAT IF MADONNA REPENTED?

What sort of nation would make a best-seller out of a book of lurid pictures and prose by Madonna? A nation in which sexual harassment is a problem, perhaps?

When lust is celebrated and modesty ridiculed in the media, no one should be surprised by low behavior in the workplace and elsewhere.

Madonna brings out the worst in men. We can be awful even under the best of circumstances, I admit, but Madonna is the worst of circumstances.

Coming uptown on the bus the other morning I sat behind two middle-aged women talking about Madonna. "She's ruined a lot of young girls," one of them said. The other nodded.

Were they right? Who knows? But one thing is for sure: Madonna sets a terrible example. She's a lousy role model.

By the way, how does she manage to command so much attention? (Why am I writing about her, come to think of it?) If she merely sang and danced, she might make a living as an entertainer, but she wouldn't be a multimillionaire cult figure whose dirty book retails for $50 and goes straight to the top of the best-seller lists.

Madonna became a media sensation by shocking squares like me and the two middle-aged ladies on the bus, and thereby appealing to iconoclastic children of all ages. Her talent is dressing and undressing with a vengeance. Infamy made her famous. She scandalized her way to the top.

Madonna is bad in a big way, which raises the question: Is it possible to be good in a big way? Sure. It's been done. For centuries the name Madonna brought to mind "Hail Mary, full of grace, the Lord is with thee. Blessed art though among women . . ." Millions worldwide recite the rosary regularly, so even today the original Madonna gets more attention than her tawdry namesake, if that's any consolation to respectable folks.

But could an entertainer or public figure of any kind achieve prominence nowadays by representing goodness? Is a truly good role model possible, or would he or she be shunned by the media because of poor ratings (and profits) and low public support?

Suppose, for example, that Madonna underwent a conversion and decided, after much prayer and reflection, to assume a new persona of virtue. Imagine how her agent and publisher and newest court photographer and all the rest of her well-paid retinue might react if she came to them and said, "I'm feeling considerable remorse for flaunting myself in a vulgar way for years and making idols of pride, greed, lust and the rest of the capital sins. I want to make amends to all the impressionable young people I may have corrupted. Do you have any thoughts for a project that might redeem me and my career?"

Her agent probably would suggest some form of public penance, such as being flogged in the nude by a bullwhip-wielding Ice T, also in the nude. Do it as a video.

If Madonna persisted and seemed sincere in her quest for redemption, would anyone take her seriously? Not for long. The appeal of a repentant sinner would soon fade. She could take herself to a nunnery, and that would make a big splash in the paper and get lots of TV coverage the day she entered the convent, but Madonna would never be heard from again—unless, of course, she tired of prayer and meditation and went over the wall to meet and run off with, say, Marky Mark. That would assure a triumphant return to page one, and massive public interest.

The bottom line is: We'll take a good role model if one comes along for free, but we won't pay for one.

October 30, 1992

Sins of the Fathers Grace Their Sons

Doug from Dyker Heights took his son, Mike, 7, to the Mount Manresa Retreat House in Staten Island the other Saturday afternoon. They visited a grotto on the grounds. Retreatants slip away to pray there in solitude. Set in a wooded area, the deep, still grotto with its religious symbols evokes a sense of sacred mystery and God's presence. Little Mike was awed.

"Dad, how did you find out about this place?" he wondered.

"A priest told me."

"Do a lot of people know it's here?"

"People who make retreats know. Every year I come here on a retreat with my friends," Doug explained.

Mike's reaction tickled Doug, who thought with a smile: My kid thinks I'm an important man with inside information.

Doug was grateful he could show his son a place set aside for prayer, and that it made such an impression on the boy. He hoped the impression would last forever. He thought it might, because what a father imparts to a son tends to take hold, for better or worse.

Doug recalled that when he was Mike's age, his father took him to a bar on Fourth Avenue in Bay Ridge on Saturday afternoons. He got a Coke and chips while his father drank whiskey. He remembers his father telling him, "Son, you're a lucky man if you have one friend in life. I have that friend. His name is Cutty." Then he'd signal the bartender, "Gimme another Cutty and water."

His father died at 44, when Doug was a teenager. The cause of death was alcoholism. Standing in the grotto with his son, it occurred to Doug that he was now about the age his father had been when the two of them first went to the bar on Fourth Avenue. Thank God, he thought, that he was able to take his son to a grotto at a retreat house and mention prayer without self-consciousness or embarrassment.

His father, God rest his soul, couldn't have spoken about prayer. It wasn't suitable for a conversation between fathers and sons. They could talk about drinking or gambling or fighting, but certainly not about prayer. The subject couldn't come up in a man's world. Prayer wasn't manly.

His father's attitude was typical of the times, Doug realized. Couldn't blame the old man for being a creature of his generation. A real man drank and gambled and got into brawls that spilled outside the bar where the combatants rolled on the sidewalk. You knew you were a man if you did virile, violent things and bragged and laughed about your behavior the next day at the bar. Church on Sunday and faith and prayer were all right for women, especially old women who made novenas. But a man's man scorned such stuff.

Doug grew up with those twisted beliefs. The values were immature and irresponsible, and he adopted them wholeheartedly. They were gospel in his crew of junior gingerellas who cut classes at New Utrecht High School in the mid-1970s. They drank in the park and hustled football slips for a dollar ("Pick four winners and win $10"). They thought they were pretty slick. None would be caught dead in church on Sunday, for sure. If they ever prayed it was only when cops were chasing them: "Get me out of this one, God, and I swear I'll be good." But didn't mean it, of course.

God blessed him, Doug thought, by letting him get jammed up so desperately that the ordeal turned his life around. His prayer changed; instead of "Get me out of this one, God," it became, "God help me; I can't help myself." When his humility was sincere and his dependence on God unconditional, then and only then did God show mercy. Doug fell in with a new set of friends with backgrounds like his, knock-around Brooklyn guys who used to gamble and drink and abuse drugs. His annual retreat at Mount Manresa is with them.

All this ran through Doug's mind in a minute. He considered how different his life was from his father's, by the grace of God, and how different Mike's childhood and adolescence would be from his, God willing.

Oh, Doug reminded himself, it was foolish to predict how your son would grow up, of course. But he would steer Mike in the right direction with spiritual pointers. By example he would show Mike how to pray, teach him to say: "God grant me the serenity to accept the things I cannot change, courage to change the things I can, and wisdom to know the difference. Thy will be done, God, not mine."

And he would tell Mike: "Never ask God for favors. What you want might not be good for you. Tell God you want whatever He wants. Pray for the strength to do His will."

Pray for other people, he would urge Mike, especially for people he might not like so much. If Mike fought with Butch, for instance, that night he should pray: "God, I forgive Butch. I hope you love Butch as much as you love me."

And Doug would teach Mike a favorite prayer of his to keep a big ego in check: "Lord, to bless, not to impress." When you aim to bless a person, he would explain to his son, love guides you. When you strive to impress someone, pride takes over and fear creeps into the relationship.

Doug looked down at Mike standing beside him in the grotto at

Mount Manresa. Gratitude flooded through him. God was with them, he was sure. God gave him the gift of faith and a new life, and he would pass it along to his son. He thought of his father, and his eyes filled. The old man did the best he could; may he rest in peace. "Come on, Mike, your mother and sister will be waiting for us at home," Doug said. They walked out of the grotto.

November 7, 1993

SIX-YEAR-OLD TEACHES HOW TO HANDLE LIFE

Plainclothes cop Don Costello, known in Brooklyn and Queens for the many good robbery arrests he's made, is hard-nosed but soft-hearted. He told me about a little girl in his neighborhood, Michele Mykolyn, who's an inspiration to him.

Don related that he was grabbing a snooze at home in Queens Village the other afternoon when 6-year-old Michele came in the house and walked into his room and woke him up. She shook him and said, "Uncle Donald! Uncle Donald!"

He opened his eyes. Michele stood there beaming at him. She was all bundled up because it was cold out, but nothing could hide her happy face.

"What's up, Michele?" Don said sleepily.

"Uncle Donald, I'm going to school! I start this week."

"Hey, that's great!" Don said.

She had another surprise for him. "Watch me walk," she said.

She turned and walked—a little unsteadily, but pretty darned well—into the living room. As she left his room she turned and smiled at Don. She and he knew that her short walk was a huge accomplishment.

"You're doing great walking!" Don enthused. He swallowed hard. He was so moved he wanted to cry.

Courageous Michele puts all of life in perspective, Don was telling me. That's because he knew the story behind those unsteady steps.

"You can't imagine the agony that kid has experienced," he said, shaking his head in awe of the brave little girl. "When she was 3 she was diagnosed with brain cancer. Operations. Chemotherapy. Hundreds of days in the hospital. More pain and suffering than we can imagine. I've known her for years because she plays with my sister's kids. They're neighbors on 222nd Street in Queens Village.

"I've never heard Michele complain or show any self-pity. She's full of life. The kid is just amazing. When you think about what

Michele has been through, your problems are nothing in comparison. The usual worries about money or complaints about work seem so petty. Michele makes you ashamed to feel sorry for yourself."

Don told a wonderful story about Michele's heart. Seems his mother, Mary Costello, was hospitalized last summer for treatment of emphysema. Afterward she visited her daughter, Pat Poslett, on 222nd Street. Michele was there playing with Pat's girls, and she overheard Mrs. Costello mention that she might have to return to the hospital for more treatment of the emphysema.

"Don't worry, Mrs. Costello, you're going to be okay," little Michele assured her. "It hurts a little bit at the hospital, but then you get better and you come home. Everything will be fine."

Don related that and added, "Here was a 6-year-old girl trying to comfort a 70-year-old woman. And it helped my mother. It took her mind off her illness. It was as though she got a shot of energy from Michele that did her more good than a whole canister of oxygen."

Michele is the daughter of Tom and Laura Mykolyn and the sister of Lauren, 9. Tom works for a Manhattan brokerage house. The Mykolyns have shown real heroism in all they've been through. Laura, a Brooklyn native who grew up in Bensonhurst, explained the ordeal.

"We thought it was the flu when Michele first got sick late in 1990," Laura said. "We all had the flu at the time. But she didn't get better. She was lethargic. We were back and forth to doctors. Finally I took her to Schneider Children's Hospital in New Hyde Park.

"They found a tumor on her spine. They removed it. The surgery took six hours. Six months later Michele blacked out at home. We rushed her back to Schneider. She was diagnosed with multiple brain tumors.

"She got three chemotherapy treatments followed by a bone marrow transplant. Since then she's had a brain biopsy and a leg biopsy. She's on medication to prevent seizures.

"One doctor told me that kids who have what she has almost never make it. But she's made great progress. Michele is a fighter. When we go to the doctor she always tells me, 'Mommy, I'm a big girl. You don't have to come in the room with me.'

"She was finally well enough to start school this month. She goes to PS 136 in St. Albans, a special school for kids with handicaps. She loves it. The teachers love her. The other day the bus didn't come for some reason. 'Call car service,' Michele begged me. She just had to go to school. I got a neighbor to drive us.

"Michele is very bright. Very verbal. Her memory is sharp. My brother, Michael, passed away at 27 some time ago. Recently a man on the block, Eddie, died of a heart attack. Eddie had been wonderful to us through this whole thing. All the neighbors have been wonderful. Michele asked me what happened to Eddie. I told her he went home to God. 'With uncle Michael,' she said.

"She's very friendly. She says hello to all the neighbors in the courtyard. They all know her."

Don Costello loves kids. He throws a big Christmas party at Our Lady of Lourdes every year. Don's many friends each bring a toy, and Don gives the toys to Catholic Charities to distribute to needy children. That's the kind of guy Don is, and Michele is a hero to him.

"Nobody ever had it tougher than that little kid, but she's just grateful to be able to walk and go to school. Most kids complain about going to school. Michele can't wait to get there," said Don. "The kid has a tremendous spirit."

Thanks, Michele Mykolyn, age 6, for showing us how to live.

February 21, 1993

SEARCH FOR A LAUGH IN A SERIOUS WORLD

I used to gab with a bartender who lived in Flatbush and toiled in a place in lower Manhattan. I'd visit his saloon in the morning and drink coffee while he polished glasses and sliced lemons. His name was Billy but I nicknamed him Hands because his hands were so swift and graceful as he served a drink, took the customer's money and polished the mahogany with the bar rag.

"You're poetry in motion, Hands," I used to tell him. He loved the compliment. He was a real Brooklyn guy. He had an easy laugh. We enjoyed each other.

Hands was a wonderful raconteur. One morning he related an incident that happened years before when he was tending bar in a joint in Flatbush. Seems a well-known judge who lived in the area was a regular customer. The judge came in shortly before closing time one night. He looked sour. "I just had a bad blowout with the old lady. Gimme a double shooter," he told Hands. He asked to run a tab because he'd left his wallet home. No problem, said Hands. The judge was good as gold, and a great tipper.

Hands poured a couple of generous belts of top-shelf booze into a water glass. The judge swallowed the blast in one gulp and called for another. Hands obliged. "Go sit in a booth and nurse this one, judge, and after I close we'll have breakfast at the diner."

At closing time the owner of the joint came in to lock up and count the night's receipts. Hands put on his coat and walked over to the booth where the judge was sitting. "Come on, judge, let's go for eggs," he said.

No answer. Geez, the judge must have nodded off, Hands thought. "Judge! Judge!" he said, shaking his shoulder.

Well, to make a long story short, the judge had more than nodded off. The judge had died. Expired right in the booth with glass in hand. The look on his face said he was still mad at his wife.

Hands was deep in contemplation of what to do next when the phone rang. Grateful for the distraction, he grabbed it. The caller was none other than the judge's wife. "Is the judge there?" she demanded to know.

Narrating the saga to me, Hands paused for effect at this juncture. He leaned over the bar and said, "A sticky situation such as this is where a bartender earns his salary. People think we have it easy, pouring booze and socializing with customers and maybe clipping the cash register for a double sawbuck when the owner isn't looking, but there's a lot of delicate human relations problems in bartending. If I tell the judge's wife, 'Yeah, he's here,' what am I gonna do if she insists on speaking to him? And if I say, 'The judge is here, all right, but he's dead,' the poor widow might go into shock. So I took the easy way out for both of us. 'No, he isn't here,' I told her. In a way that was true—the judge was in the hereafter. And the answer was tactful, which a good bartender always is."

I asked Hands, "How did the owner react when you broke the news to him that a customer had passed away on the premises?"

Hands replied, "The owner wanted to know if the judge died running a tab or paying cash. I said he was running a tab. He said, 'Just my lousy luck the judge croaked owing me money!'"

If you get the idea from this that it was fun to shoot the breeze over the bar with Hands, you're right. I enjoyed him immensely. I have no idea what became of him. Last time I saw Hands was a decade or so ago. He'd left the tavern in lower Manhattan and was working the day shift behind the bar in a big fish restaurant near Flatbush and Nostrand. I happened to stop there for lunch with a Brooklyn College dean and was pleasantly surprised to see Hands walking the duckboards. We only had a minute to chat. He told me he liked working near his home.

What I'm hoping is that Hands, if he's still in Brooklyn and happens to read this, will get in touch with me. I'd love to resume our conversation. If anybody recognizes Hands and knows where he is, I'd appreciate it if you'd pass this message to him. You see, I need Hands for column material.

Everything nowadays is so serious. Politics is serious. Sexual politics is especially serious. Social and spiritual ills afflicting the city are terminally serious. But I can't write about serious issues all the time. Too depressing. There's a surplus of deadly seriousness and I'll be damned if I'll contribute to it! I need regular communication with the likes of Hands in order to keep up my spirits and yours.

Maybe I'm just getting old, but it seems to me there was more humor in the papers years ago. I loved those columns of witty one-liners Bob Sylvester, may he rest in peace, wrote for the Daily News. Most columns nowadays, it seems, are either too intellectual or too gossipy. What became of old-fashioned fun in print?

A scribe needs his sources. Hands, my man, where are you when I really need you?

March 28, 1993

WE'RE ALL VICTIMS OF URBAN DREAD

A Haitian immigrant in East Flatbush makes his living delivering circulars for local stores. He walks around all day dropping the circulars off at houses and apartments. He works long hours. His mother and sister, who has several children, live in Haiti, and he sends them money.

He loves this country and wants to learn English, so he goes for tutoring in basic reading and conversational skills to St. Catherine of Genoa School two nights a week. The instructors are volunteers.

It so happens that one of them has expertise doing income taxes, and when the Haitian learned this, he asked the instructor to help him file a tax return.

"I make big money. I want to pay taxes," the proud newcomer to Brooklyn said in broken English.

The reading instructor agreed to assist him with the Internal Revenue Service forms. Turned out the Haitian immigrant's income from delivering circulars, the "big money" he spoke of with such pride, was $200 a week. Nothing was deducted by his employer last year, and he owed $1,000 in federal taxes.

He doesn't have the money, of course. But paying taxes to support the U.S. government is important to this immigrant who truly believes America is the land of opportunity, so he painstakingly wrote a letter to the IRS pledging to pay $100 a month.

Hannah Coughlin, the volunteer director of the reading program at St. Catherine's, related this to me. The Haitian immigrant determined to do the right thing for America typifies those she's met since starting the program two years ago, said Hannah, a lifelong Brooklynite who lives in Old Mill Basin.

Enrollment has grown to 120. Hannah and fellow volunteers tutor the Haitians two nights a week. The program utilizes five St. Catherine's classrooms.

Going into a tough neighborhood at night to teach immigrants to read isn't the most glamorous charity imaginable, but it sure is God's work. Hannah is assisted by fellow volunteers Lesley Nozier, 28, a hospital worker who lives in East Flatbush; Jay Morrel, a widower who lives in Canarsie; Bill Kemper, a retired New York Telephone manager who lives in Old Mill Basin; Catherine Higgins, a mother of 10 and grandmother of 17 who lives in Old Mill Basin, and Frank Richard, a New York Telephone retiree and East Flatbush resident.

"Our first class of 12 just graduated in June," Hannah reported the other day. "They were so happy they hugged us! We handed out diplomas, and we all celebrated with cake and soda. They were so grateful to us for working with them! But I'll tell you the truth, I always feel they give me more than I give them."

Hannah wasn't saying that to sound humble. She meant it. Folks who donate their time to one good cause or another usually see themselves as the truly blessed. Givers get more than takers. It's paradoxical but true.

Hannah told me she was considering inviting some of the Haitians to her home for tutoring while St. Catherine's is closed for renovations this summer, but decided against it because of their reluctance to visit a white neighborhood. She recalled one of them remarking that he and several friends were chased by a gang of whites on Flatlands Avenue one night. Others in the class nodded in sympathy because many of them also had encountered prejudice in white areas.

The Haitian immigrants she tutors complain bitterly about street crime in East Flatbush, Hannah said. There the violence is black on black. Seems they can't escape the threat of assault wherever they go. They fear white racists will attack them if they venture into white neighborhoods.

How disheartening. And America fancies itself the land of the free. Certainly there is no freedom from fear in urban America.

Still, life is a whole lot worse in Haiti, and the Haitians are grateful to be in Brooklyn.

As countries go, the U.S. is still a good one. But you won't hear me mouthing the old cliché, "This is a great country" because, frankly, I no longer believe it is. Let's be honest: In a great country, it would be safe to walk city streets.

We've slipped so badly as a nation in recent years that making a lot of noise to proclaim patriotism on the Fourth of July seems foolish. What's to celebrate when folks are afraid to go out in their neighborhoods, or to visit other neighborhoods, because of the threat of assault?

Haitian immigrants illustrate the point dramatically, but the rest of us are victims of urban dread, too, no matter what our skin color or nationality. Many of us are full of trepidation in a strange neighborhood. Violence and racial tensions mock the ideal of one nation under God.

Is it too late to recapture that?

People like Hannah and her fellow volunteers Lesley, Jay, Bill, Catherine and Frank, and the grateful immigrants they tutor, provide a glimmer of hope.

So much depends upon what we choose to look at. If a hate crime happens, we lose heart. "Geez, there's no place safe," we say, demoralized by violence.

But the reading program at St. Catherine's has been going on for a couple of years with good feelings all around. We can choose to focus on that as an example of how folks love their neighbors—even neighbors a few neighborhoods away.

"Their gratitude inspires me," said Hannah Coughlin, explaining why helping Haitian immigrants does more for her than for them.

When such charity prevails, then God will bless America.

July 4, 1993

LUCK AND LOVE ON ST. VALENTINE'S DAY

Candyman Johnny Logue was in a gloomy mood when I visited his sweet shop, Hinsch's on Fifth Avenue in Bay Ridge, exactly two years ago last week. Chocolate hearts, chocolate kewpie dolls and chocolate roses manufactured in his Third Avenue factory were lavishly displayed, and I would have expected Johnny to be jubilant in anticipation of guys buying sweets for their sweethearts for Valentine's Day, yet he sat in a booth and drank coffee and looked melancholy.

"Why so glum, John-o?" I wondered brightly.

Johnny sighed and replied, "Ash Wednesday falls the day before Valentine's Day. This is bad for business. I don't mind competing with Overeaters Anonymous, but I hate to go up against Lent."

That was in 1991, when Ash Wednesday arrived unusually early—on February 13. From personal experience of more than 40 years in the candy business, Johnny knew that Valentine's Day sales would suffer somewhat due to a certain percentage of old-fashioned Catholics forswearing sweets for Lent.

His good humor was fully restored when I spoke to Johnny the other day. Lent is a fortnight in the future, and Valentine's Day is upon us. "I should get some last-minute guys. When they wake up Sunday morning and remember they forgot, I'll be open for business," said candyman Johnny, a lovable guy who, now that I think of it, bears a slight physical resemblance to Cupid.

Candy isn't for everyone, of course. Some females favor flowers. Others might prefer just a card. Men appreciate being remembered, too. I have a friend in Bay Ridge whose daughter gives him two cards every Valentine's Day. One is lovey-dovey and mushy, the other needles him about losing his hair and getting a paunch. He loves both cards.

This fellow always makes a big deal out of Valentine's Day. He painstakingly pens a card to his wife to tell her in his own words how much he loves her. He doesn't care how gooey-gooey it sounds, and neither does she. She proudly puts his Valentine's Day card on the TV in the living room where the kids and visitors can read it. It's all right to get gushy when you love somebody, my friend and his wife believe, and I agree. What's wrong with telling loved ones that you love them? Repressed Irish Catholics like me usually aren't very good at it, but that's a shortcoming, not a virtue.

Speaking of love, got a letter from Elizabeth Cuttitta telling me that her grandparents, John and Elizabeth Ingrassia, have lived in the same house in Canarsie since their marriage on October 3, 1936. That's almost 57 years! "Six children, sixteen grandchildren and six great-grandchildren later, they're still together and an example to us all of love and commitment," Elizabeth Cuttitta wrote.

"An example to us all of love and commitment." That's as fine a tribute as could possibly be paid to a married couple. I called Elizabeth Ingrassia to ask the secret of her successful marriage of 57 years.

"John is very loving, he really is," she said of her husband. And she added, "Patience on both sides, patience with each other's thoughts and ideas, and loving each other—I think that's the whole thing."

Contemplate that paragraph, all you young couples out there, and meditate on the wisdom of the words. Cultivate patience and love, and you might celebrate a golden anniversary one day.

Then there's Randy Caleskie of Bensonhurst. "My grandparents, Ed and Mary Freeman, have been married 65 years, and they've lived the whole time in the same house in Bensonhurst. My grandfather's lived there since he was five. Now he's 95."

Wow.

I called Ed and Mary. Turns out Ed and I worked together briefly at the *Daily News* in the early '60s. He was a printer. We talked for a while, and then I asked to speak to Mary, a sprightly 92.

"We eloped," Mary revealed, laughing. "We met at Brooklyn Jewish Hospital. I was a nurse and Ed was a patient. We eloped, and later we had a regular ceremony to please the old folks—on November 13, 1927."

This Bensonhurst couple was married the year Babe Ruth hit 60 home runs.

How are they doing 65 years later? "We go out every day if the weather is nice. We'll walk to Bay Parkway, or to 86th Street. We're doing pretty well for a couple of old fogies. Right now I'm trying to decide what to cook for supper. Chicken, I think."

This sounded to me like a happy marriage. I asked Mary about it. I think she thought it was a dumb question. "Why do we have a happy marriage? Because we love each other. And, my husband is very good-natured."

That says volumes in a few words.

And may I conclude with a touching Valentine's Day couplet dedicated to the Polish-American princess who's been my better half since 1964:

I love my Mrs. Polonia
and that's no balonia.

When she reads that, I'm gonna get hit in the head with a rolling pin.

February 14, 1993

ANNIE SHAND'S GOOD-BYE

Annie Shand of Brooklyn called to say good-bye. I was flattered that she remembered me. Seems I mentioned her in a column some years ago. She came across the clipping while packing. That prompted her to pick up the telephone.

"You're leaving Brooklyn? Where are you going?" I asked Annie, 67, of East Flatbush.

"Back to my old hometown—Clayton, North Carolina," she

said. "I'm retired, my husband is deceased, my children are grown. God has been good to me. I still have my health and strength. I feel like I'm starting life all over again.

"I retired two years ago from the Department of Social Services. I started there in 1969 as a clerk. I worked my way up to office manager in the agency for child development. Before that I worked 13 years in a garment factory, sewing dresses, doing piecework. Before that I was a live-in maid. I came to New York as a live-in, making $100 a month, in 1950.

"My husband, Hubert, passed away in 1990. My children are all doing well. John is retired from the Air Force. He's a minister in North Carolina. Frances is a public school teacher in Brooklyn. Pearl works for Champion, the sportswear manufacturer, in North Carolina. She never liked New York. Benjamin is in Greece with his wife, Elaine, who's stationed there in the Air Force.

"Why am I going home to Clayton? For the same reason I came to New York in 1950—a better quality of living. Back then the economy was better here, and it was easier to make a living, and the living was better. I lived on Park Place in those days, and we would walk to Ebbets Field at night and home afterward. We would walk to a movie at night, too.

"Now, even though I have a car, I don't go out at night. Nothing has ever happened to me, but you still have that fear or apprehension that it's not as safe as you would like it. The people in New York are wonderful, but there are just so many of them crowded together. The South is more open. Most of the houses aren't attached. You don't have as many people so close together, so there isn't as much going on."

I asked Annie if she thought there was any hope for New York. Crime, corruption and racial tension are so demoralizing that you sometimes wonder if the city can hold together. You can easily lose heart.

"Yes, there's hope—in the church," Annie replied. "We have to love each other and be concerned about our neighbors and people in general. If we don't have the love of God in our hearts we can't do it. If we keep stepping on each other for the almighty dollar, there's no hope.

"My advice is to look at each other as equals. But we don't. I'm not condoning anything that black children do that's wrong—wrong is wrong—but don't just play up the bad and never say anything about the good. We have numerous good black kids who are striving, working, going to school, not getting into trouble. But it's got to be out of the ordinary for them to get any recognition. I would like to see all of us treated equal because we're all God's children."

Thanks for calling, Annie Shand. New York really can't afford to lose you, but may your life be long and blessed in North Carolina.

June 19, 1992

Chapter Three:
Simple Faith

The Faith That Dare Not Speak Its Name

Most of us middle-aged, middle-class white males have great difficulty in discussing intimate experiences, feelings, desires, needs, etc. Self-consciousness prevents us from sharing intimacies.

Am I talking about sex? Heavens, no! We came along before the sexual revolution, so our sex lives have always been mainly in our minds. And now our minds are slipping a little as years go by.

No, I'm talking about how we discuss what means most to many of us: faith.

The Brooklyn boy is convinced that he was saved from becoming a bum only by his Irish mother's prayers to St. Jude and the intervention of a merciful God.

The Brooklyn boy can't bring himself to come right out and say that in so many words, however. To talk of God by name would cause him to cringe with embarrassment. He'd almost rather admit he sneaks a look at *Penthouse* at the barber shop.

Instead, to describe his relationship with God he invokes a colorful euphemism worthy of a Brooklyn boy. After talking easily and with no shame about a misspent youth and young adulthood that featured numerous brushes with the law and the underworld, the Brooklyn boy puts down his coffee cup and sums up his salvation as follows:

"The Big Guy rescued me, with an assist from Mom." The Big Guy. God is fine for old ladies and little kids, but not for a knock-around Brooklyn guy to mention by name.

The Brooklyn boy typifies the reluctance of men our age and in our set to speak openly about what's ultimate. Another acquaintance, Big Mike, an old sandlot ballplayer who lives in Staten Island, refers to God as "The Skipper," as in, "Every morning when I wake up I thank The Skipper for another day."

Other guys in my set speak of the healing power of "The Man Upstairs." Anything but God. The Brooklyn boy was telling me about a young guy he met on a retreat in Long Island last weekend. "This kid used to be on the fringe of the mob," the Brooklyn boy related. "He spoke for a few minutes at the retreat, and at the end he said, 'I want to thank my Higher Power, the Man Upstairs, the real, true Boss of All Bosses.'"

The Boss of All Bosses. Not bad.

What brings all this to mind is an experience I had at the Billy Graham crusade at the Brendan Byrne Arena at the Meadowlands in New Jersey last week. In five nights of preaching, evangelist Graham drew 106,000 people. The crowds spilled over into the parking lot, where they watched the proceedings on a giant screen.

I was there to get a preview of the Graham rally on September 22 in Central Park, which more than 1,000 New York City churches are sponsoring. Some 25,000 evangelical pastors and their congregations nationwide have been asked to pray for its success and contribute to its $1.5 million budget, mainly for advertising.

Graham was workmanlike but not inspirational in the Meadowlands pulpit, I thought. On the way out of the arena I struck up a conversation with a Catholic priest in the ecumenical crowd. He looked at me and said, "Do you know the Lord?" It sounded like an accusation. "Uh, yeah, sure," I babbled, sounding defensive. I got the feeling he didn't believe me. I felt uncomfortable.

Oh well, I thought, I belong with my own kind—the Brooklyn boy and Big Mike and the like. We're not real buddy-buddy with the Big Guy, the Skipper, the Man Upstairs. It takes a lifetime, maybe an eternity, to get to know the real, true Boss of All Bosses. No need to rush to be on a first-name basis with Him.

September 11, 1991

IF YOU LOSE YOUR JOB, DON'T LOSE YOUR FAITH

In my set, we reassure one another that God has a plan for our lives and that our job is to cooperate with it. Do God's will, in other words. We know by faith that God cares for us and calls us to follow Him. Our life experience tells us this is true. We can look back and detect the presence of God even in the worst of times.

And what is God's will for us, and how do we know it? Prayer and spiritual fellowship reveal the answers. "Where two or three are gathered in my name, there am I in the midst of them," our Lord said. So we pray, and our conversations are prayerful (profane, too, sometimes, because we're human). We talk easily of God and His will for us. Faith is the center of our lives. Millions of people live this way.

I was sitting in the Church of Our Saviour on Park Avenue on Wednesday morning when a friend joined me. After Mass he said, "Have you got time for coffee? I'd like to talk." As we walked to the coffee shop he said, "Yesterday afternoon the boss called me in and fired me."

My heart sank. I love this guy like a brother. We talk just about every day. He has—or had, I should say—a high-powered job in the investment business. Profits are down drastically in the financial services industry, and layoffs are up. My friend has even more bills to pay than I do. I knew how I'd feel in his shoes: devastated by getting fired, terrified by the prospect of no income. I'd be beside myself.

We got our coffee and I said to him, "Well, this is easy for me to say and maybe hard for you to hear right now, but we both know it's true: God didn't bring you this far to abandon you. Losing your job is an opportunity. God has something better for you."

He believed this was true but wished he felt it more fervently, he said. He dreaded the search for new employment. We drank our coffee and talked about the need for faith, and more faith, and more still. "Lord, I believe, help my unbelief," as the father of a sick boy healed by Jesus said.

Later that morning I went to the press conference at which the winner of the annual Templeton Prize for Progress in Religion was announced. I wish I could say my faith got a boost, but it didn't. The winner was mathematical physicist Paul Davies of Australia, who defined God as "something which underpins this ordered universe." (I wondered: How should this deity be addressed? "Our Underpinner"?) Davies was born and brought up an Anglican but thought better of it and dropped out of organized religion, he said, explaining that his conception of the Almighty is "quite a long way removed from the personal God of popular religion." I was surprised and disappointed. Past winners of the prestigious award have included Mother Teresa and Billy Graham, the kind of believers who make religion relevant in the traditional sense.

But maybe the discovery of a Great Underpinner serves a theological purpose. We partisans of a personal God can't expect everybody to endorse our conviction. After all, sometimes God Himself seems to ignore us. Frequently we don't get what we pray for. One of the foremost religious thinkers and most eloquent believers of this century, C.S. Lewis, put the problem bluntly: "Every war, every famine or plague, almost every death bed, is the monument to a petition that was not granted." That's certainly true, and not neatly reconciled with the gloriously hopeful words of Jesus: "Ask and it will be given to you; seek and you will find; knock and the door will be opened to you."

Maybe the answer is not to pray for what we want but for God's will to be done, and for the grace to do it cheerfully, even if the task can be an awful drag, like looking for a job. Times like these call for a lot of faith, but no faith seems such a grim alternative.

March 10, 1995

HAND OF DEVOTION SPANS THE YEARS

John Byrne of Stuyvesant Town attended the annual fund-raising dinner for LaSalleAcademy. His son, Christopher, is a student at the 147-year-old Christian Brothers school on Second Street and Second Avenue. During the cocktail hour John saw a face across the room that jogged his memory back almost four decades to his sophomore year at Bishop Loughlin High School in Brooklyn.

Rheumatic fever caused John to miss most of the second semester in 1956. He was bedridden when his social studies teacher, Brother Edmund, visited him one Sunday afternoon. Brother Edmund had taken the subway from Brooklyn to the Byrne home in Queens.

"John, I want you to try to keep up with your studies as best you can," he told him, "so I spoke with your other teachers and we've put together some assignments for you to do while you're recuperating. If you're well enough to take final exams and you pass them, you can be promoted." He wished John a speedy recovery and left a load of homework for him.

John's mother and father thanked Brother Edmund profusely for caring enough about their son to travel all the way to their home on a Sunday. He certainly had gone out of his way for a student. "Oh, don't mention it, I'm glad to do it," Brother Edmund said, and he bid the Byrne family good afternoon.

John himself wasn't so sure he was thrilled by Brother Edmund's dedication. He hadn't been doing well in his classes even before he got sick, and he was kind of looking forward to flunking out of Loughlin. The brothers were strict. They punished antisocial behavior like fighting. They expected students to pay attention in class and study at home two or three hours a night. John, at 15, wasn't keen on devoting his teenage years to such a demanding regimen. He thought he might rather go to public high school in Queens and maybe cut classes and hang out with a crew of local guys who liked to stand on the corner, smoke cigarettes, drink beer and pursue girls. Loughlin was all-male in those days, which John thought was too bad.

There wasn't much else to do while sick at home, so John studied the assignments Brother Edmund had delivered. By late spring he was well enough to go back to Loughlin. He took his finals and managed to get passing grades. He didn't believe he had done well enough to earn them. He suspected that Brother Edmund must have influenced his teachers to give him a break. He guessed he was grateful. In any event, John was promoted to the junior class.

He grew up over the summer. His attitude was more positive when he returned to Loughlin in the fall. He began to grudgingly appreciate the wisdom of a no-nonsense approach at education. He turned into a decent student. He graduated on schedule. He became a police officer. He spent his career working Midtown. He went to John Jay College and earned a degree. Now he's retired from the NYPD.

At the LaSalle dinner in a restaurant in Little Italy, John made his way across the room. He introduced himself and said, "You're Brother Edmund, aren't you?" He got a nod and a smile. John said, "Brother, I can never thank you enough for what you did for me. You really changed my life."

What struck John about their reunion that night was that Brother Edmund had no particular recollection of him. John was surprised that his old social studies teacher didn't remember going to such great lengths to help a sick student.

John related all this to LaSalle's development director, Pat Cunningham, who agreed it was odd that Brother Edmund failed to distinctly recall the boy with rheumatic fever 40 years ago.

Pat told several LaSalle faculty members the story. They assured him it was no surprise that Brother Edmund had forgotten a mission of mercy to John Byrne in the 1950s, because he had traveled many extra miles for many students over the decades. Pat mentioned this to Brother Edmund. "If a student is sick or out of school for any reason I'll try to do whatever I can for him," Brother Edmund said. He considered it simple Christian charity to take the subway to a sick kid's house to bring him homework.

John Byrne was saying the other day how privileged he felt to have a son at a school with Brother Edmund on the faculty. "He'll be Christopher's guidance counselor when he's a senior next year," John said. "To think that Brother Edmund did so much for me and that after all these years he can influence my son means an awful lot. I really appreciate the Christian Brothers."

Thanks to teachers like Brother Edmund, a little school like LaSalle, tucked away in a corner of the city where it gets little notice, makes a big contribution. The principal, Brother Michael, spent 20 years in Africa before his current assignment. He was principal of a school in a town where water was pumped by hand and the basic mode of transportation was the donkey. The natives ate two meals a day—bread and tea for breakfast, and a mush of ground grain for dinner. Brother Michael helped deliver tons of grain provided by Catholic Relief Services when a crop failure caused famine.

Brother Michael and Brother Edmund and their colleagues on the faculty provide the 535 LaSalle students with a special perspective on life, learning and faith. Classes at LaSalle begin with a prayer: "Let us remember that we are in the holy presence of God." The Christian Brothers live the prayer as well as say it.

February 12, 1995

IF IT'S AUTUMN, THIS MUST BE ASSISI

Brisk fall mornings rejuvenate me and I love them, but I feel a loss this year. No, not baseball. I notice the absence of baseball, of course. The sports section of the paper struggles without it. But I feel no loss. Baseball lost me a couple of decades ago. When the World Series moved from beautiful Indian summer afternoons to frigid fall nights in pursuit of TV lucre—the greed was insatiable, alas—I turned it off in favor of a good night's sleep.

No, I miss a man I saw every morning for the past half-dozen years greeting the faithful on the church steps as they visited for mass or a prayer before work. Courtly, quiet-spoken Monsignor Tom McCormack was a devoted New Yorker as well as beloved pastor since the late 1980s of Our Lady of the Rosary on State Street at the foot of Manhattan.

Msgr. McCormack told me a memorable only-in-New-York story a dozen years ago, when he was principal of Cardinal Hayes High School in the Bronx. As a young priest in the 1950s he taught history at Hayes, and eventually was appointed principal by his friend Cardinal Terence Cooke.

Seems that one night after another long, hard day in three decades of trying to pound sense into adolescent heads, he finished working late and trudged wearily to his living quarters by the Grand Concourse in the Bronx. He flopped on the couch and flipped on the TV. He always liked to catch a few minutes of Johnny Carson. But on this night the host was off and comedian George Carlin was subbing. Carlin gabbed with a guest, author Vincent Patrick, whose novel *The Pope of Greenwich Village* had been made into a popular movie.

"You know, you and I have something in common," Carlin said to Patrick.

"Really? What's that?" Patrick replied.

"We both got thrown out of Cardinal Hayes High School in the Bronx," Carlin said.

Msgr. McCormack almost fell off the couch. A dim recollection of Carlin in history class came back to him. "It was quite a remarkable feeling, I have to admit, to hear these guys telling millions on TV that they got thrown out of Hayes—and to still be there myself!" he told me, laughing at the irony of it as he related the story.

Msgr. McCormack died in August. He was 70. I still look for him on the church steps every morning when I'm walking from the ferry to the bus. I miss him.

Life goes on, especially the life of faith at this invigorating time of year. Seems like it picks up. The Jewish high holy days give the Christian churches a lift, I like to believe. All prayers rise to the same God, and the spiritual benefits redound to us all. Churches were busier yesterday than on the usual weekday—it was the feast of St. Francis of Assisi, who died in 1226 yet is remembered reverently by millions worldwide.

Gratitude is called the aristocrat of attitudes because when you're feeling grateful you can't simultaneously entertain self-pity, envy, anger or other negative thoughts or emotions. Though he embraced poverty and thus had nothing in a worldly way to be grateful for, St. Francis is probably the patron saint of gratitude. He was always praising God and God's creatures.

"He understood down to its very depths the theory of thanks; and its depths are a bottomless abyss. He knew that the praise of God stands on its strongest ground when it stands on nothing. He knew that we can best measure the towering miracle of the mere fact of existence if we realize that but for some strange mercy we should not even exist."

So wrote G.K. Chesterton in his biography *St. Francis of Assisi*. Despite strife and suffering and sadness that make life grim at times, and the passing of a man like Msgr. McCormack that makes his friends feel a loss, the gratitude personified by St. Francis still fills churches. In this bittersweet season I can't imagine a better consolation.

October 5, 1994

ANONYMOUS MIRACLES OF COINCIDENCE

"Coincidence is often a little miracle in which God has decided to remain anonymous," observes Fulton Oursler Jr., editor of *Guideposts*, a Manhattan-based monthly magazine devoted to human interest and spiritual living. Listen to him and see if you don't agree that coincidences can be providential.

It seems there was no God in his home when he was a boy. His father, Fulton Oursler, was a founding member of the Freethinkers Society of America and the author of articles that ridiculed the Bible. His father often said he hoped to write a book to debunk Christianity—as a teenager he had made a living as a magician, and he suspected Jesus of using magic tricks to hoodwink credulous followers.

Young Fulton was sent to boarding school in Riverdale in the Bronx. He hated it. The only legitimate way to get off the grounds, he learned, was to take religious instruction at one of the local churches. "I started with the Lutherans," recalls Fulton, a big man with an easy laugh. "I went to the church class, was marked present and then asked to go to the little boys' room. I ducked out the door and ran six blocks to the drugstore, where I could get a chocolate milkshake and buy comic books. I got away with this for two weeks and then announced that I did not want to be a Lutheran."

Next stop was the local Episcopal church. He soon wore out his welcome there. On to the Presbyterians. Following a parting of those ways, he tried a Catholic parish in Riverdale. Slipping out of catechism early one evening, he was apprehended by a believer with a missionary bent, PeggyJo Reilly. She sat him down and told him the story of Christ. "Faith seized me that night and has never let go," Fulton says.

He told PeggyJo he wanted to be baptized. Good, she said, but first he needed to learn about the faith. He confided that his parents wouldn't approve. She told him to pray for them, and to pray that they would accept his conversion. Meanwhile, there was no need to tell them he was taking instructions. They toured the great churches of Manhattan. Fulton was awed by St. Patrick's Cathedral, but fell in love with St. Francis of Assisi on West 31st Street. His favorite place was the grotto in the lower church devoted to St. Bernadette.

He visited his parents' New York apartment once a month. His father was a popular radio broadcaster. Father and son were together in a cab one Sunday. The boy noticed they were going in the direction of St. Francis of Assisi. He was flabbergasted when the cab stopped in front of it. "Follow me," his father said, and they got out and walked down the steps to the lower church. Young Fulton thought his heart would stop.

"I thought the game was up," he remembers, "so I was not surprised when we walked straight to the grotto—somehow my father must have discovered my secret trips to the city. But instead of turning to confront me, he sank to his knees! I watched in complete amazement as he bowed his head and prayed." Back in the cab, his father said he had become a convert at that grotto, and that he would make his conversion public the next day. He explained that this would cause controversy. Their lives would change. Some long-time friends would reject them. But their family would be stronger than ever. Was there anything his son wanted to say?

"Was there! I remember the stunned look on my father's face," Fulton says, "as I told him about PeggyJo and my instruction in faith. When I mentioned the trips to New York and the unbelievable coincidence that the grotto where he had found faith was the same one I had so often visited in secret, tears spilled from his eyes. He hugged me and said: 'Oh, what wonderful tricks the Great Magician plays on us!'"

His father went on to write a bestseller about the life of Christ, *The Greatest Story Ever Told*. The book has never been out of print. His mother, Grace, a writer, returned to her faith after an absence of many years. And when Norman Vincent Peale founded *Guideposts* in 1945, he put Grace in charge as executive editor.

Fulton Oursler Sr. died in 1952. Grace Oursler died in 1955, when young Fulton was 23 and just starting a job with *Reader's Digest*. He worked there until 1987 when he retired as deputy editor-in-chief to become a freelance writer.

One day in 1991 he got a call at home from an executive recruiter. Would Fulton be interested in the job of editor-in-chief of *Guideposts*? He was speechless. The headhunter wondered if he had ever heard of the magazine. Fulton replied that indeed he had—his mother had been the first editor! "The headhunter was astounded," Fulton says.

"As I was pondering whether or not to leave the freedom of freelancing and return to the world of deadlines," he remembers, "I received a letter, out of the blue, from a woman who had been the subject of a piece my mother had written many years before. The woman enclosed a letter my mother had sent a few weeks before her death. It was the first time I had seen my mother's signature in more than 35 years."

Fulton accepted the job. *Guideposts*, with millions of readers worldwide, is the most successful magazine in the history of spiritually oriented publications. Reflecting on his and his parents' path to faith, he offers a thought that seems timely:

"God has a plan for everyone, and it's become an article of faith for me to believe that sometimes we can catch glimpses of the Spirit at work on the grand design through the anonymous miracles of co-incidence."

November 27, 1994

CAN ONE BE CATHOLIC AND ACTIVELY GAY?

The Catholic Church teaches that homosexuals are called to chastity—no exceptions—and sponsors a 12-step program, Courage, to help them abstain from sex. I was once a guest at a Courage meeting in a room off the kitchen of a Catholic Church in Manhattan. About 10 men and a couple of women were present. The meeting proceeded according to the format followed in 12-step programs for alcoholics, drug addicts and gamblers. But here the participants talked about homosexual episodes and inclinations. They sought relief from temptation by sharing experience, strength and hope with one another.

Over the years I've run into one of the men who was at the meeting, and we've paused to chat. He was always very congenial, but I was uncomfortable. If he had been an ex-drunk or reformed gambler, conversation would have come easily. I might have pumped him for a story or two about the bad old days, and we'd have gotten a laugh recalling humiliating but hilarious (in retrospect) escapades in the bars or at the track. But with the fellow from Courage, I was reluctant to talk about homosexuality.

Why is homosexuality so vexing for some heterosexuals? Why does it make me profoundly uneasy? Did I keep this good man at arm's length emotionally because our religion condemns the sexuality God gave him and urges him to reject something so fundamentally human in himself?

What brings this to mind is a plea by Andrew Sullivan, editor of the *New Republic,* for the Catholic Church to eschew the Courage approach and rethink its demand that homosexuals embrace chastity. Sullivan describes himself as both a practicing Catholic and a practicing homosexual. A contradiction, perhaps: the Bible proscribes homosexual acts. Saint Paul explicitly condemns sodomy in several epistles. Sullivan has argued humbly and respectfully and with love for his church that it should welcome homosexuals without demanding they be celibate. Celibacy is too much to ask of a mere layman, he found from personal experience. Sullivan tried mightily for years to be chaste, but the austere religiosity required to fortify his will left him anxiety-ridden, depressed and spiritually bereft. "The command to love oneself as a person of human dignity yet hate the core longings that could make one emotionally whole demanded a sense of detachment or a sense of cynicism that seemed inimical to the Christian life."

Before reading Sullivan, I had always thought the analogy between addiction and homosexuality was valid. Catholicism regards both conditions as disorders that are blameless in themselves but sinful and self-destructive if acted upon. So, just as the alcoholic in recovery practices steps that emphasize humility and prayer to stay sober, why shouldn't the homosexual, buttressed by the sacraments, do likewise to keep chaste?

The alcoholism analogy fails, says Sullivan, because while the sober alcoholic is healed to enjoy the fullness of matrimonial love, the homosexual who renounces his sexual and emotional core is deprived of fulfillment and "liberated into sacrifice and pain," as he puts it.

Ask veterans of 12-step programs who have defeated alcohol or drugs or gambling and they are likely to say that the greatest benefit of recovery is the restoration of their family. "I have the love and respect of my wife and kids today," they'll declare gratefully. I once heard an ex-drunk say, "I missed my kids growing up, but I'm sober for my grandchildren, thank God." A happy home made recovery worthwhile. But the Catholic Church denies homosexuals the realization of human love in a faithful union. Some may thank God for calling them to heroic holiness, but others must wonder why He made them to be lonely.

February 22, 1995

An Elegant Prayer

No one in the well-to-do congregation will know that the woman and two adolescent children kneeling in a front pew are a welfare family from a shabby neighborhood a subway ride away.

The mother could take the kids to Easter Sunday mass at their home parish this morning, but she prefers the elegant Park Avenue church because it evokes life's possibilities. They'll pray for a better future and thank God for what little they have. They count survival among their blessings. They once lived for 18 months in a city shelter.

"I'm not ashamed, but don't use my name," the mother said when we spoke recently. She had just made her monthly visit to a food pantry on East 109th Street. She got powdered milk, bread, cereal, three cans of tuna fish and four teabags. "This isn't much, but it tides me over after food stamps," she said.

She grew up in a stable neighborhood in the days when Manhattan was full of them. Her father worked for a utility company. She went to Catholic schools. She held a promising job but gave it up after she got married. Her husband would work, they would have kids and she would stay home and raise them. That was the plan. But, a decade ago, he died suddenly.

The death of a spouse can have a debilitating effect. Probably she should have gone back to work right away. In retrospect, that would have been the thing to do. But she had been out of the job market for almost six years when he passed away. Her confidence was shaky. The kids were infants and one of them was sickly. She didn't trust anyone but herself to care for them. So she stayed home. The rent was $1,100 a month, and before long they lost their lovely apartment.

So they went from a comfortable middle-class existence to a shelter on Henry Street and the grim world of welfare. Her search for permanent housing seemed endless. Whenever the city sent her to look at an apartment, she always had the same disheartening thought: "If I took this place, the first thing I'd have to do is lead a rent strike."

But she found a livable place eventually, and she and the kids have been there for half a dozen years now. "It's not too bad. Occasionally there's gunfire, but not too often." Though she and many of her neighbors have little in common besides poverty, she's made many friends among them. She used to believe some stereotyped generalities about poor people, but since she joined their ranks, she sees them as individuals. She predicts their numbers will swell as businesses and government shed workers. "I have a friend who lost her job. Unemployment ran out. She's charging the rent on her credit card."

She often wonders how life would have gone if her husband had lived. His job was solid. There would have been Catholic schools for the kids, vacations at the Jersey shore, occasional dinners out. By now, maybe they'd be living in a nice house in suburbia. A while back, she ran into an old friend she hadn't seen in decades, someone who knew nothing of her hard times. The friend, married to an executive and residing in the suburbs, wondered what kept her in the city. "Oh, you know, the convenience of being near everything," she lied airily. She hoped she sounded convincing.

She won't succumb to envy or self-pity. Nobody has it easy, she knows. "I have a friend whose life looks comfortable on the surface, but her son died of AIDS," she said. What sustains her? Hope. An Easter attitude. "We're surviving. My kids are doing well in school."

She may be the only one in that stately church thanking God for a food pantry. A prayer like that should get a hearing.

April 16, 1995

EVANGELIST FOR GOOD LIVING

Mike Williams grabbed a cab after another busy work day at his personnel agency in Manhattan and headed home to Roosevelt Island. Going up Third Avenue he felt the seat getting warm. He smelled smoke. The cabbie jerked the hack to the curb on East 59th Street and said, "I think we're on fire."

Mike threw open the door and leaped out as the cab rolled to a stop. The driver bailed out, and they stood and watched as flames leaped from under the body of the cab. Smoke consumed the night air. A couple of cops on foot patrol moved toward the cab but wisely retreated at the sight of the blaze.

A taxi rounded the corner. Mike hailed it and climbed in and went over the bridge to Queens. No need to wait and see if the cab exploded. He was just grateful to be out of the inferno.

Mike was still shaken by his narrow escape when he told me about it a couple of mornings later in the coffee shop of the Lincoln Building across from his office on East 42nd Street. Mike, 36, looks successful, which he is. The personnel agency he founded four years ago has prospered. He recently opened a branch office in White Plains. No one would guess that this rising executive once lived in a grim single room in the Greenpoint Hotel—and that was when he had a few bucks. He slept nights on the L train when he was broke.

"Another minute or two in that cab," I told Mike as we sipped our coffee, "and you wouldn't be making the retreat this year. We'd bow our heads for a moment of silence in your memory." Mike and I belong to a retreat group that meets this month at St. Ignatius on Long Island, and in January at Mount Manresa in Staten Island.

Mike wondered aloud, "Why was I so fortunate? Getting out of that cab before it went up in flames makes me feel I have a greater responsibility to do something with my life."

Mike is alive for a purpose, he believes. Building a business that provides jobs for secretaries and messengers and data processors and programmers is one way to fulfill it. Education is another way— Mike graduated from John Jay College in June after years of taking classes at night. Spiritual growth is another—Mike is active in a spiritual fellowship and has made a weekend retreat annually since he got on his feet a dozen years ago. And reaching out to others is yet another way—several young men, homeless and hungry for hope, visit his office regularly. Mike encourages these poor guys who remind him of his old self to keep the faith.

"I don't know where I'd be without belief in God and faith and prayer," Mike was saying over coffee the other morning. I often say the same. Mike isn't ashamed to thank God for blessings received. God works through people, of course—in Mike's case, his godfather took an interest in him when he was a boy and left a lasting impression that motivated Mike to get up when he was down.

I always marvel at Mike's story. Hundreds of thousands of New Yorkers, through no fault of their own, live in poor and violent neighborhoods. Many probably feel hopeless. Welfare and gunfire seem to hold them hostage. They must be terribly deprived and discouraged and mad at the world. I would in their circumstances. But despair is useless. Mike is a powerful example of a man who prevailed despite awful disadvantages.

Mike was the sixth of 12 children. He grew up in the South Bronx. His father was murdered. His mother died when he was 12. He lived in a group home in Richmond Hill, Queens, until he was 17. From there he went out on his own. Failure dogged every step for the next seven years. He moved from one menial job to another, with stretches of unemployment in between, and from furnished rooms to subways. He favored the L train for a night's sleep because the cushion seats were comfortable.

His godfather, Montague Pendergast White, who had always visited Mike when he was a boy on birthdays and at Christmas and Easter, passed away, and he left a few thousand dollars to Mike in his will. Mike went through the money in a matter of days. Guilt and shame filled him with self-loathing. But he pulled himself together. His godfather, he knew, would urge him not to give up but to go forward in faith.

Mike worked as a security guard, taking all the overtime he could. After a few years, a job in the personnel field presented itself. Mike grabbed it. He found he was a natural-born salesman. But why settle for small commissions and leave the profits to the boss? Why not be the boss? Mike opened his own agency in March 1991. Though the economy was slumping, he worked hard and his agency succeeded despite the downturn.

Not that life has been a bed of roses. Mike got married along the way, fathered two daughters and, a few years ago, was divorced. The girls live with their mother in Park Slope. They visit their father on weekends. When he moved to Roosevelt Island recently, he took an apartment with an extra bedroom so the girls could feel at home there. Mike knows there is no success as important as being a good father.

I wish every young person who suffers from self-doubt and low expectations could meet Mike, an evangelist for good living. "Reject the lie that failure is inevitable. You're a creation of God. You're priceless. Make the most of it," Mike would tell them, and it wouldn't be just talk, because Mike Williams walked the walk.

September 11, 1994

GOD'S WILL, NOT HIS OWN, SAVED HIM

A fellow was leaving his Manhattan office to drive to a prison to speak to inmates involved in a drug-and-alcohol rehabilitation program. A friend ran into him just as he was departing. When the fellow mentioned his destination, the friend wondered how he felt about it.

"Funny you asked. Earlier today I wasn't looking forward to it at all. I was thinking, 'Geez, you gotta fight the rush-hour traffic all the way there. Then you gotta speak. You won't get home until midnight.' I was sorry I agreed to go.

"But then another thought came to me: 'You ingrate! Don't forget where you came from.' And suddenly I was filled with gratitude, and I wanted to share what's been given to me with the inmates.

"They're right where I used to be. This time of year is the worst in prison. I'd lie in my cell, heartsick and ashamed, remembering Christmases at home when I was a kid, seeing myself decorating the tree with my mother and sisters. We were poor but happy. I'd lie there wondering what a nice guy like me was doing in the slammer. Where did I go wrong? I had no answers, only sadness and remorse. I was miserable.

"Memories of holidays behind bars hit me hard. I felt so grateful for my life today that any regrets about tonight's commitment vanished. My whole attitude changed from self-pity to gratitude. Now I can't wait to get to the prison and talk to the inmates.

"They stole to support their habits, and they got locked up. That's my story, too. I never wanted to be a thief, but the craving for drugs and alcohol made a thief out of me. That craving is too powerful for mere willpower to resist.

"I've said it many times: There's no human explanation for my recovery. It was a gift from God. I believe God answered my mother's prayers. She was always making novenas for me. I can still hear her yelling at me when I'd come out of jail or off a drunk: 'Go over to Holy Name Church and throw yourself on the altar of God and beg Him to forgive you, you blackguard!'

"I have to laugh when I think of it. I like to believe she's laughing now in heaven. It was no joke at the time, though. I broke her heart. She used to tell me the only time she had any peace of mind was when I was in jail. She felt I was safe there. I couldn't die of an overdose or get killed in the street in jail. Imagine what it must be like for a mother to be happy when her son is locked up.

"All she could do was pray for me. I thought prayer was superstitious. I ridiculed her. 'Forget that pious hocus-pocus, Ma,' I used to tell her. I knew everything. Meanwhile, I worshipped heroin and blackberry brandy.

"I can't explain the power of prayer, but how else did I get sober? I couldn't stop drinking on willpower. My will was to drink, not to stop. Detoxes, rehabs, hospitals, prison, jails—nothing could stop me. I'd get released and go straight to a liquor store and buy a bottle of blackberry.

"A turning point came when I was behind bars. I'm sure I'll mention this tonight. Maybe it will give the inmates encouragement. It was a miracle. There's no other way to describe it.

"I was out of detox and sober for six weeks or so, making meetings every day, staying away from the people, places and things that got me in trouble for 20 years, when there was a knock on my door one night. 'It's the super,' a voice said. But it was two big detectives. They had warrants. A couple of old burglaries had come back to haunt me. Next thing I knew I was in Rikers Island.

"I didn't feel sorry for myself. That sounds impossible under the circumstances, but it was so. I had a prayer card in my pocket that someone gave me in a meeting. I read the prayer: 'God grant me the serenity to accept the things I cannot change, the courage to change the things I can, and the wisdom to know the difference.'

"I sat in my cell and thought about it: I couldn't change the fact that I was there. Apparently it was God's will. I didn't understand it, but I accepted it without bitterness.

"Within days my sisters bailed me out. I had disappointed them dozens of times over the years, but they said they saw something different in me this time. They were willing to take a chance on me.

"What they saw, although they didn't realize it at the time and I wasn't fully aware of it, either, was that I'd been touched by God's grace. A probation officer interviewed me and saw it, too. The probation officer gave the judge a glowing report.

"Still, I was sure I was going to prison. My sheet showed arrests that went back to when I was 15. There was no way I could walk out of court a free man. So I showed up for sentencing with a toothbrush and a carton of cigarettes.

"You could have knocked me over with a feather when the judge said: 'I sentence you to a year in the penitentiary, suspended on the condition that you continue to attend meetings of Alcoholics Anonymous.'

"That was over 18 years ago. I haven't had a drink or a drug since. If one inmate gets a spark of hope from hearing me tonight, it will be well worth driving in traffic and getting home late. I'm grateful for the opportunity to be used by God," the fellow said.

His friend was glad he asked. Hope the fellow's answer gives you a lift, too.

December 4, 1994

THE EARTHLY LIMBO OF ANNULMENT

It caused a stir in Catholic circles when Sen. Ted Kennedy received Holy Communion at his mother's funeral mass last week, because Kennedy was thought to be estranged from the church. He divorced Joan Kennedy after 22 years of marriage in 1982 and married Victoria Reggie in a civil ceremony, witnessed by a federal judge, in 1992. His archbishop, Cardinal Bernard Law of Boston, voiced disapproval at the time: "Senator Kennedy, in the eyes of the church, is married, and, as long as he is married, is not free to enter into another marriage."

Explaining his reception of the Eucharist the other day, Kennedy's press office said his marriage to Reggie "has been blessed by the church." There was no elaboration. The statement implies that his marriage to Joan was annulled—in other words, that it never happened.

Over the past 25 years, hundreds of thousands of divorced and remarried Catholics have gotten first marriages annulled to regain good standing in the faith. The Catholic Church considers divorce a grave offense against God's law, and a second union permanent adultery. An annulment is a declaration by the church that a marriage never existed—that it was invalid from the beginning because one or both partners was incapable of making a lifetime commitment. It paves the way for a second church ceremony and a lifetime of entitlement to the church's sacraments.

But doesn't annulment of Kennedy's first marriage consign those 22 years with Joan—and the three children they produced—to a kind of earthly limbo? And while the church doesn't declare the children of an annulled marriage illegitimate, what does it imply by saying their parents were never married?

Annulments used to be rare, but have been granted liberally in recent years as the Catholic divorce rate has risen to about the same level as that of other religions. Priests who heard marriage cases used to demand evidence of physical impotence or the refusal of a spouse to have children in order to invalidate a marriage, but now they accept a variety of reasons. A spouse's alcoholism, for example, can be the basis for an annulment. Joan Kennnedy is an admitted alcoholic. Ted is no teetotaler. Perhaps a church tribunal saw drinking as symptomatic of spiritual ills that invalidated their vows.

Some are skeptical when Kennedy's press office says his second wedding has been blessed by the church. Church officials, citing privacy considerations, won't confirm or deny the statement. It's possible Ted decided on his own to take communion at his mother's funeral. Many Catholics in so-called irregular marriages receive the Eucharist without ecclesiastical permission. Some refuse to apply for an annulment as a matter of principle. They're appalled by the suggestion that their first marriages didn't exist. "I was married, but the marriage died," they say. The typical grounds for an annulment nowadays, psychological immaturity, strikes them as pretty lame. Of course they were immature; isn't most everybody in their 20s, simply because they're young? Love didn't last, but they can't deny they were married.

And maybe they learned something about themselves in a failed first marriage that prepared them for a successful marriage later on. All experiences, good and bad, happy and painful, contribute to personal growth and made them what they are. They don't disagree with the church that divorce is wrong, but for them it was unavoidable. They don't want to seem defiant toward the church they love, but they meant their vows when they spoke them.

Happily, a pious past is no requirement for church membership—nor is a pious present, for that matter. To quote Father Ben Groeschel, the great Franciscan priest of the South Bronx: "We must reject the phony image of holiness. A saint is just a sinner who is more repentant than most of us."

February 1, 1995

DEAD SON SUSTAINS A DAD'S BELIEF

Marty Doherty hates to argue with Pope John Paul II, for whom he has the utmost respect and reverence. Marty takes his

Catholic faith and his Holy Father very seriously. But he can't accept the condemnation of capital punishment in the papal encyclical, "The Gospel of Life."

Marty's son was shot to death in East Flatbush by a man who served six years for the crime and came out of prison to take five more lives in Brooklyn. Had the shooter been executed for killing his son, Marty reasons, those five citizens would be alive and their families spared the awful anguish of losing a loved one.

"I believe the Pope is speaking for Catholics everywhere when he says the death penalty is wrong," Marty said. "But situations make a difference in some cases."

Marty certainly isn't the only practicing Catholic to cite so-called situational ethics to justify disagreement with church teaching. For instance, birth control and abortion are proscribed by the church, but some married couples—and some theologians, too—would argue that exceptions are allowable in certain hard cases, such as a wife who has been told by her doctor that another child would endanger her health.

Last week's encyclical rejected the death penalty in language stronger than had been heard before from Rome. So the many Catholics who favor capital punishment will have to defend themselves against the charge that they're disloyal to the church—just as Catholics who support legalized abortion have had to do for years. Our Catholic mayor, Rudy Giuliani, and governor, George Pataki, are publicly at odds with their church on both issues. Marty Doherty's experience may not justify dissent from church teaching, but it makes dissent understandable.

It was 15 years ago tomorrow night that Marty's oldest son, also named Marty, was shot near the Doherty home on Glenwood Road. He was 21, about to graduate from Kingsborough Community College, looking forward to a promising job he'd accepted on Wall Street. He was leaving the house after dinner to visit his girlfriend when two neighborhood kids told him they had been menaced. Young Marty caught up with the assailant, who shot him in the head. A neighbor hurried to the Doherty home and pounded on the door. "Your son's been shot," he said. Marty ran to the scene. The sight of his son lying in a pool of blood in the street has haunted him ever since and always will. Young Marty died hours later in Kings County Hospital. That was April 3, 1980—Holy Thursday, as it happened.

It took police three years to track down and arrest the killer, Eban Robbins of Snyder Avenue. Marty attended the trial daily. Robbins was convicted of manslaughter in 1983 and sentenced to five to eight years behind bars. Marty didn't think it was enough. If you take a life you should forfeit yours, he believed.

A couple of years ago, Marty, who is the athletic director at John Adams High School in Queens, heard on the news that a man had been arrested for a murder rampage that left five dead and three wounded in Crown Heights, Brownsville and East Flatbush. When he heard the name, Eban Robbins, he felt shock and pain. He thought how the victims' families would undergo the same suffering he and his wife, Catherine, and their four other children experienced when they lost Marty. Only faith got them through a soul-wrenching time that lingers still. And "The Gospel of Life" reminds Marty anew that faith is hard.

And this time, Eban Robbins is doing 199 years.

April 2, 1995

A HISTORY TO BE THANKFUL FOR

They were all involved in illegal gambling. Indictments were expected. Everybody could go to jail. Tony was on the fringes. He had a couple of arrests for disorderly conduct, but nothing serious yet. The district attorney couldn't be too interested in him. If he made a clean break he might save himself.

He fled Brooklyn and landed in a college town up north. He took a laborer's job and hung out at night with the college students. He was their age. He fit in. They never suspected he was a semi-wiseguy from Brooklyn.

College kids like to carouse, and Tony was happy to join them. One morning he woke up on the grass in front of the college administration building. He was cold. "This would never happen in Brooklyn," he thought. "Drinking buddies in Brooklyn make sure a guy gets home. Maybe they have to pour him into his house, but they don't leave him lay all night on a strange lawn."

He had lost his car, or maybe it had been stolen. He swallowed his pride and called his father. "Come and get me," he said. His father drove up and brought him home to Brooklyn.

That episode taught Tony something: You can't run away, because wherever you go, no matter how different the environment might be, you take yourself with you.

Conditions at home hadn't improved during his absence. A couple of very close associates had gotten locked up. They were going to do time. The heat was on. Everyone in the crew was very bitter, always cursing the cops and the district attorney. Tony had grown up in that negative atmosphere. As a kid he was disappointed by movies because the good guys always prevailed in the end. He rooted for the bad guys in movies and in real life, too.

But somehow Tony had the sense to know that this attitude was wrong. He was led to visit an uncle who had always impressed him because he had the courage to be different. The uncle was a churchgoing, hard-working family man. A legitimate guy. He drove a truck for a living. It wasn't glamorous, but he never had to worry about getting indicted. His son, Tony's cousin, was in law school.

"The hard way is the best way. Remember, anything that comes easy is no good," his uncle lectured Tony. For some reason Tony was disposed to pay attention. His uncle told him he ought to reform his life and should begin by going to church.

Tony had visited churches a couple of times when he was up north in the college town. He'd stop in when lonely and depressed to sit in a pew and try to pray. He didn't know what to say to God, or even whether God was listening. His faith was shaky. He'd graduated, barely, from the parish school at St. Bernadette's. As a kid he'd go to church, grab a bulletin and then hang out at the candy store on 13th Avenue. When he got home he'd show his mother and father the church bulletin and tell them he'd been to Mass. They probably didn't believe him, but they couldn't say much because they weren't churchgoers themselves.

"Church is boring. I hate sitting through Mass," Tony told his uncle. He had no patience, no attention span, no ability to listen. He was too self-absorbed to give God a whole hour a week. "Just go to church. God's grace will work on you, don't worry," his uncle assured him.

So Tony began showing up on Sunday mornings. He got down on his knees and poured out his heart to God. Before long he felt his life improve—not suddenly, but gradually. He avoided bars and social clubs where his crew congregated. He concentrated on getting a job.

Something his uncle told him made an impression:

"Go to work at an honest job. The hard way is always the right way. You're a sharp guy, but life is not about getting over on people. If something bad happens to you—you get shot, you go to jail—I'll mourn you and feel sorry for you, but when the alarm goes off in the morning I gotta get up and go to work. I got a family to take care of."

Looking back today, on Pentecost Sunday, birthday of the church, Tony understands it was the grace of God enlightening him that cop-hating and corner-cutting and racketeering were no way to live. He knows it was no coincidence that his life got better when he began obeying his uncle.

He went to church on Sundays. He looked for work. A no-show construction job was offered by a guy in the crew who had a connection in the union. Tony was tempted to grab it for the money but resisted. Instead he took a menial job at $3.35 an hour. That took humility, a virtue new to him.

It was a turning point in his life. He's since gone on to better-paying employment, but on that lowly job he met a wonderful girl. Within a year they were married. The wedding was another turning point. Minutes before the ceremony Father Saporito pulled him aside.

"Tony, did you go to confession?"

"Geez, father, I haven't been to confession in years."

"Marriage is a sacrament. You gotta go to confession."

"OK, father." Tony divulged a dozen years of sins, Father Saporito gave him absolution and the limousine arrived with the bride.

It was a wonderful day, and it helped Tony realize that his life began to turn around when he got back to church. He was a Brooklyn prodigal son. He vowed to worship every Sunday, pray every day, keep God in his life. And he's done that since he made that vow, a little over a decade ago, despite hard knocks that tested his faith at times.

A tested faith is only strengthened, he's learned gratefully. Tony will take his wife and kids to church this Pentecost Sunday and thank God for his uncle and all the other disciples going back 2,000 years.

May 22, 1994

A VISION OF HOPE IN SUNSET PARK

What was Christmas like in the old neighborhood? I put the question to my good friend Richie, who grew up on Fourth Avenue in Sunset Park. "Cold," Richie recalled. "I remember it was cold."

Anything else? Richie thought and said: "My job was to take the 52nd Street bus to 13th Avenue and go to the Jewish bakery and try to buy day-old bread. I didn't have much success because they didn't know me there. Everybody in our neighborhood bought day-old bread at the bakery on Third Avenue and 48th Street. I can still see the line out front. But it was closed on Christmas."

Something special came back to Richie. He smiled at the recollection. "I saw Santa Claus. I was maybe 4 or 5 at the time. I was standing at the window late on Christmas Eve, maybe it was early Christmas morning, looking out over the harbor. Everyone else was asleep. I'm not sure if I was up because I was excited about Christmas or because I was uncomfortable. I slept on two chairs in the kitchen.

"From our apartment on the third floor, you could see the Statue of Liberty and the ships coming and going. There was a big full moon, and, sure enough, I saw Santa go by the moon in his sleigh. Looking back today, 55 years later, I suppose it was a vision of hope. I wanted to believe. I knew better than to tell anybody I saw Santa. They'd laugh at me. I don't think I ever told a soul about it until now."

"Thanks for the scoop," I told Richie. We laughed.

I was interested in his family's living arrangements. What did he mean when he said he slept on two chairs?

"Space was at a premium—there were nine of us in a three-bedroom apartment, my mother and father and seven of us kids. We doubled up and tripled up, slept on the living-room couch, put two chairs together and made a bed out of it in the dining room. The youngest slept in the bed between my mother and father. I was second-youngest.

"I didn't think of it as a hardship. Everybody we knew lived the same way. The family on the second floor had seven kids, the family on the first floor had eight. Big families were the rule in the neighborhood. You moved around from one room to another to find a place to sleep. One night you might be in a bedroom, the next in the living room, the next in the dining room."

The '90s are supposed to be hard times in places like Sunset Park. Richie remembers the '30s and '40s as no bargain, either.

"I don't go back to the old neighborhood too often because it kicks up sad memories. I remember how cold and hard it was. The laughs were few and far between even though we had a good family. My father was a hard-working man. He was a driver for the city. He became a chauffeur for a city commissioner. He took pride in the job. He did well for a man with no education. He probably made $30 a week. He worked every day. One day I wanted him to take me to a ball game. The other fathers were taking their sons. I met him when he came up out of the subway that night and asked why he'd had to work. He said, 'Did you have to eat today?' After that I didn't ask him many questions.

"I usually got one toy for Christmas. Got a fire truck one year. That was great because I wanted to be a fireman. Another year I got a wallet. I was probably about 10. A wallet meant you were entering manhood. When you got to be 13 and were truly a grownup, you proved it by carrying a condom in your wallet.

"I don't have happy memories of those years. Was it a sad time to grow up? I don't know, but I was a sad person. All I could see ahead was gloom and doom—I'd never get out of the neighborhood, and it was always gonna be cold. Yet I realize now we were comparatively well off. Our building had a boiler. The people who lived in cold-water flats had it really rough. They had to make their own heat. I remember them walking down to First Avenue, where trains made deliveries to Bush Terminal, and they'd be hoping to pick up pieces of coal that fell off. We were the elite compared to them.

"What was the difference between the neighborhood then and now? Fathers and mothers put all their energies into making sure their kids got to the next level. With all the single-parenting today, it's much tougher. There's more hostility and anger now. People didn't used to be so afraid. I think they helped each other more. I recall a boiling hot July day when my father was standing at the window looking out at beer deliverymen unloading their truck. They were delivering kegs to Shreck's deli. My father called me over and told me to take a clean shirt of his down and give it to one of the deliverymen whose shirt was soaked through. 'My father said to give this to you,' I told the guy, and he said, 'Tell your father "thank you very much." ' "

Hard to imagine that happening in the '90s. Did religious values contribute to better relations back then? Perhaps, Richie thought.

"Everybody in the neighborhood went to church on Christmas. And every Sunday, too. Church was mandatory. We didn't want to go, but we just went. We quit going when we got to be teenagers. We'd tell our parents we were going, and halfway to St. Michael's, we'd peel off to the candy store. But we grew up in contact with religion.

"I remember getting the message as a kid in catechism that God made me to know, love and serve Him, and to be happy with Him forever in Heaven. That meant nothing to me at the time, but 50 years later I see the truth of it. If you love and serve God, you'll find happiness and freedom and be prepared for the next life.

"What would I tell kids growing up in Sunset Park today? I'd tell 'em to look for Santa Claus. Try to like yourself, I'd tell 'em, and know that God loves you."

December 26, 1993

"GOD NEEDS TRAGEDIES TO SHOW HIS LOVE"

The earthquake collapsed his building, but he got out alive. The shaken, disheveled survivor was interviewed on TV in Los Angeles.

"God spared me," he declared, sounding absolutely certain of it. Then he made the sign of the cross, raising his right hand and touching his forehead, chest and left and right shoulders.

I saw that Monday night on one of the networks, and was struck by the fellow thanking God for allowing him to live through a natural disaster that took at least 33 lives. His home was gone, but he wasn't angry or resentful. Quite the opposite. He was grateful. His world had been violently disturbed, yet his reaction was a statement of faith in God.

Why didn't he blame God for putting him in harm's way? That reaction would seem justified. A close shave might provoke anger at God, you'd think. Yet folks who narrowly escape sudden death rarely make the Almighty the heavy. Instead they tend to express gratitude. "God was good," they say. Or, "Thank God." Or, "God spared me."

Come to think of it, I've never heard a survivor tell a reporter, "Why did God have me anywhere near this disaster? God could have done me a favor and put me somewhere else when this happened. Why did God destroy my house? Now I'm homeless. I'm not lucky to be alive—I'm unlucky to have no place to live. Thank God? For what? I resent God. His earthquake killed a lot of people and terrorized me. Anyone who thanks God for not killing him in an earthquake is too easily pleased."

Adversity, and even tragedy, seem to strengthen faith in God rather than diminish it. I can't explain this, but I've seen it often, most recently on a religious retreat led by a Long Island Jesuit priest, Father Bernie Shannon, who thanks God for what he calls "the gift" of mental illness.

Your first reaction is: How could anybody be grateful to God for mental illness? Wouldn't such an affliction be among the worst fates that could be visited on a human being, probably harder to bear than a physical injury or handicap? How could a sufferer thank God for demons?

"God trained me more in mental hospitals than in the seminary," Shannon told 75 men gathered at Mount Manresa Retreat House in Staten Island last weekend.

He suffered a severe nervous breakdown in 1953 while studying to become a priest. Mental illness persisted for two decades. He was hospitalized several times. His Jesuit superiors allowed him to remain in the order to do menial work, but told him that ordination to the priesthood was out of the question. He found healing, however, in a mutual assistance program for the mentally ill, Recovery. He attended meetings regularly for three years. His sanity restored, he asked the Jesuits to reconsider. A special dispensation from Rome was required. It was forthcoming, and he was ordained a priest in 1980, 33 years after he began studies.

"I owe my priesthood to a Jewish psychiatrist, Dr. Abraham Low, the founder of Recovery, and to the Blessed Mother. I dedicate my work to her," Shannon, who lives at St. Ignatius Retreat House in Manhasset, likes to say.

And he's enjoyed a fruitful ministry, working primarily with people with emotional problems and addictions. He encourages them to help each other. "Wounded healers," he calls them.

"God needs your tragedies to show His love," he insisted. By the looks of them, no one in the room doubted him, and many had personal stories as harrowing as his own.

There has to be a Good Friday before there can be an Easter Sunday. The New Testament tells that the earth shook on Good Friday, too.

January 19, 1994

AND YOU THOUGHT WE DIDN'T HAVE A PRAYER

Had a sidewalk conversation in hushed tones with my friend Anthony from Bensonhurst, a meat salesman. We spoke barely above whispers because the topic was so sensitive we'd have been embarrassed if anyone overheard us.

"I pray the rosary when I'm driving to work in the morning," Anthony confided. He had to get it off his chest.

I was shocked. I figured Anthony, 36, a street guy, probably listened to a raunchy talk show while commuting to his office by Kings Plaza. "No Howard Stern?" I questioned him sharply.

Anthony looked a little sheepish. "I get the news on WINS, and then I turn off the radio and say my beads," he admitted. "Praying makes me peaceful even in rush-hour traffic with lunatics cutting me off."

I took a deep breath. "I'll tell you something I never thought I'd mention, not even to my wife," I said. "Monday morning I had to drive to see a sick relative. It was the first weekday morning in years I didn't take public transportation to work, and I looked forward to listening to the radio. But I was disappointed—Imus was making fun of Frank Sinatra fainting on stage the night before in Baltimore. That made me feel bad. I had to turn it off."

Anthony nodded. "Stuff like that ruins your day. Who needs it?" he said.

"Know what I did while I drove?" I said. I looked around. No one was within earshot. "I prayed."

We were like a couple of conspirators.

Sex has been topic A in public conversation for three decades now. Could it be time for prayer to get a play? Might Anthony and I be on the cutting edge? Hardly seems likely, but he said he saw a sign that we pray-ers might be coming out of the closet, so to speak.

"Go out and buy *Life* magazine. The one with the girl on the cover," he advised.

"There's a girl on the cover of every magazine," I said. "Even the sports magazines have girls on the covers."

"But the girl on the *Life* cover is praying," Anthony said.

Sure enough. It features a lovely girl in a prayerful pose, eyes lifted to heaven. "The Power of PRAYER. How Americans Talk to God," the headline announces.

A revealing story. A survey done for *Life* by the Gallup Organization discloses that nine out of 10 Americans pray, and three-quarters of us pray once or more every day. The majority devote a few minutes to prayer. (I fall into that category—a little time for my Maker, but not too much.) Fully 28 percent of us spend an hour or more praying.

The *Life* article quotes a cross-section of Americans—among others, a U.S. senator, a black woman pastor, a former pro-football coach, a prostitute, and a Jewish mother of seven who's twice survived cancer—describing how they open up to the Almighty.

"I pray with all my heart the homeless and hungry will make it. I don't know if that prayer helps them, but it prevents me from becoming blind to other people's suffering," says San Francisco record producer Jim Hicks, 43. "I pray that wars will end. If we all did that, they would have to stop."

True, people who pray for each other seldom fight. Since he's been praying while driving on the Belt Parkway, Anthony told me, he hasn't once shot the old Bensonhurst salute at a honking motorist. "I smile and wave," he said.

If prayer can work such a miracle, surely it's time to talk it up.

March 11, 1994

HOLY ORDERS? THE BIBLE'S RULES FOR COPS

Jimmy Devine assured 1,800 rookie cops that theirs was truly God's work because His messenger, John the Baptist, personally set the guidelines for the job. The recruits gave Jimmy a standing ovation. He recalls it as the highlight of his police career, even though he may have overstepped the line that separates church and state.

Maybe cops need bold spiritual affirmation and inspiration regularly to cope with the killing stress of their work—eight New York City police officers have committed suicide this year, and 52 since 1985. That startling toll of self-inflicted mortality testifies to the awful pressure of dealing on a daily basis with violence and depravity. No mere police commissioner, even the reportedly charismatic William Bratton, could possibly contrive and manage the reforms required to impart inner peace to embattled police officers. Surely there's a crying need for help from a Higher Authority.

"It was about 10 years ago. I was a lieutenant in the job and director of the department's counseling service," Jimmy Devine, 50, retired from the NYPD and now a clinical social worker in private practice, recalled at lunch the other day. "I got a last-minute call to go to Brooklyn College and address an auditorium full of newly appointed cops. I had no time to prepare. I said a fast prayer for guidance, grabbed a Bible out of my desk and made a hurried search for references to cops.

"I walked out on the stage and began talking. About 2,000 years ago, I told the rookies, a guy who looked and sounded like a raving EDP—emotionally disturbed person—came out of the desert and into the towns and cities around where he lived and demanded loudly that everybody get their act together beginning immediately. His name was John the Baptist and he claimed to speak for God, and many flocked to hear him.

"Two occupational groups approached John seeking direct consultation. One was tax collectors. They wanted to know what they should do, and he told them to collect only what they were entitled to and not a penny more. The other group was soldiers, who were the local peacekeepers—in other words, the cops."

Jimmy, relating this, sipped his coffee and told me, "I was composing the speech as I went along, and I noticed that the auditorium was absolutely still. Every one of the 1,800 cops in the audience was hanging on every word. I had their undivided attention. I sensed a real hunger for the spiritual message I was delivering. I was glad I hadn't had time to prepare a speech because probably it would have been full of the usual clichés instead of these words from the heart and the Bible.

"I told the rookies that when the cops asked John the Baptist what they should do, he didn't tell them they'd made a poor career choice and they should get out of the job or be condemned and lost.

He told them: Don't bully anyone, denounce no one falsely and be content with your pay.

"In other words, no use of unnecessary force, no phony collars or perjury, no bribes, shakedowns, gratuities or stealing. As an aside I noted that when John said to be content with your pay he didn't mean the PBA couldn't negotiate a raise. Got a laugh with that.

"With those reasonable boundaries he spelled out, I told the rookies, John the Baptist issued to us as police officers the highest blessing of the vocation we chose. Cops are a ministry of justice, on the front lines between good and evil, and as such we're God's instruments, His agents. Few professions have been so honored."

When he finished talking that day a decade ago, Jimmy recalled, the young cops stood as one and applauded loudly and at length. The spiritual message gave them hope.

Commissioners come and go. Cops are beleaguered today perhaps as never before. The message of divine approval bears repeating.

December 3, 1993

RELIGION DOESN'T COME FROM THE CHURCH

Went to a christening Sunday. A very heartening and happy affair. Little Angelina, daughter of Ernie and Grace, was baptized along with six other infants at stately St. Pancras Church in Glendale, Queens.

Angelina let out a pretty good yelp that resonated in the cavernous sanctuary when the priest poured water over her head. Ever notice how people laugh when a baby hollers? Good thing Angelina didn't know we were amused at her discomfort; probably would have made her madder still. I know how it infuriates me when people fail to take my complaints seriously, and I've had almost 54 years more than Angelina to grow up.

The ceremony was dignified despite the occasional racket made by the babies and their slightly older brothers and sisters in attendance. Gridlock seemed inevitable, what with seven sets of parents and godparents traipsing from pews to baptismal font and back, plus proud grandparents crowding in with cameras, but the priest, a smiling young man with a pleasant manner, expedited traffic smoothly and with aplomb.

He also said something interesting in a short homily. He observed that the World Trade Center bombing on Friday made frightfully clear just how dangerous a world these babies had been born into. He had no glib words to dispel families' fears for the future. Only strong faith would see us through the violence and brutality of the times. "And," he said, looking at the parents and sponsors, "religion does not come from the church." Yes, the family is the church in miniature. He let that sink in and added, "Religion comes from the home. We in the church are here to serve. But the faith comes from you." He urged the adults to live their religion and set a good example for the children, and said he was confident they would.

I paraphrase the padre slightly, but that was the gist of his remarks, which struck me as simple but profound—the sort of message that needs to be heard more often. I pass it along because, if you think about it, spiritual wisdom is rarely reported in the media. The lords spiritual are seldom quoted—unless, of course, they say something traditional-minded about sex, in which case newspapers ridicule them, or they excoriate a fellow clergyman.

But that's another column—for a day when I'm in a bad mood.

I'm in a good mood since the christening. After the ceremony at St. Pancras (pronounced, in authentic Glendalese, St. Pancreas), nearly 200 family and friends of Ernie, Grace and Angelina repaired to a nearby catering hall for a wonderful celebration. It was a gathering that made me glad to be a New Yorker. Ernie is a police captain, so there were many police officers and their wives and kids present, and there was also a table presided over grandly by Angelina's grandfather and occupied by old-neighborhood guys he ran with five decades ago down around Myrtle and Bedford in Williamsburg. Of this group, none was in law enforcement, although a few may have encountered the authorities at one time or another.

The dance floor cleared and burly Ernie, clutching tiny Angelina to his right shoulder, stepped out nimbly and twirled her around to the sentimental strains of "Daddy's Little Girl." I'm not ashamed to admit I shed a joyful tear. This was life at its best. There's a lot of good life in New York, and it will get better if we heed the young priest at St. Pancras.

March 3, 1993

THE WINNING HAND'S FOR CHARITY NOW

When I was a little boy, my grandfather, Billy Reel, taught me to play poker. He was a lovable man, and I wanted to grow up to be just like him. I didn't, but if I had, I'd be spending a couple of late nights a month looking for a poker game at the Knights of Columbus.

When my grandfather died in 1952, one of his brother Knights told my father at the wake, "Billy used to smoke one cigarette after another at meetings, waiting for the business to be over so the game could begin. How Billy loved to play poker!"

My father, Joe Reel, who died 10 years ago this week, never joined the Knights of Columbus. He once told me that when he was asked to join, the member who extended the invitation said, "If you don't belong to the K of C, you won't have any friends."

That hard-sell approach annoyed my father so much that he declined to become a member and always bad-mouthed the Knights around the house.

I grew up thinking of the K of C as a place to drink, sort of a Mory's for Catholics. Every council I ever visited had a big bar. Beer and pretzels—that was the popular image of the Knights of Columbus.

Was I wrong? Or has the K of C changed? A little of both, probably.

"What brings you all the way from Sacramento?" I asked Bishop Francis A. Quinn, who heads that Catholic diocese in California. We were at a reception at the Knights of Columbus international convention at the Marriott Marquis in Times Square exactly 500 years after Columbus set sail. Mother Teresa of Calcutta was due to receive an award from the Knights and thank them for supporting her work among the poor.

Bishop Quinn, who is regarded as a liberal in a conservative Catholic hierarchy, said he came to the convention to show his deep appreciation for the charitable work the Knights of Columbus do in his diocese and worldwide. The 1.5 million members contributed 42 million hours in volunteer service and donated $95 million to church, community and youth programs last year.

But there was something more, Bishop Quinn said: "The Knights never protest. I appreciate that. I'm a protester myself. I think the church needs a lot of protest. But bishops and priests love the Knights because they're one group we know we can always rely on to give us their full support. They only want to serve."

With dissenters always getting the biggest play in the Catholic Church—and everywhere else, for that matter—it's reassuring that a service-oriented outfit like the Knights of Columbus is around to devote itself to quiet good works. "What do we do? Well, in my K of C council in Hamden, Connecticut," Richard McMunn told me at the reception, "we just painted the parish rectory. That saves the pastor some money. And we ran fund-raisers to send handicapped kids to summer camp, and to support a religious education program for them. And at Christmas we had parties for inner-city children in New Haven and gave them presents."

Such low-profile stuff rarely makes the media, but multiply it by 10,000 councils in the U.S., Canada, Mexico and the Philippines, and the charity performed is formidable.

The K of C has gained 400,000 members and 3,000 councils in the last 15 years, defying the trend of a time during which organized religion in general suffered losses. Beer-drinking and poker-playing have been greatly de-emphasized, I'm told, in favor of programs of the kind that Mother Teresa would approve. Maybe the Knights deserve another look from some of us who scoffed.

August 5, 1992

ASHES TO ASHES ON THE FLOOR OF THE 5:33

"When I was on the floor of the train, and really accepted the fact that I was about to die, I could only think about how absurd it was for my life to end this way," related Frank Barker, who was hit by four bullets when a gunman opened fire on the Long Island Rail Road.

"My wife and I were to leave that week for Bermuda for our first trip south since our honeymoon 14 years before. I was about to start a new job in a few weeks. We had just moved into our new house four months earlier. Our seventh child was only six months old. I had a lot of living to do, so how could I die on the floor of the LIRR?

"I've always believed that life is a gift. It is a gift I've enjoyed with gratitude for 36 years. My wife and I have been blessed with terrific kids and I've been blessed with a good career. So it appeared to me that I had a job to do on earth, that I couldn't die.

"Once I survived the incident, my only emotion was gratitude. I can't and won't blame God for the actions of people who choose to commit violence. I can and do thank Him for my life, before and after this shooting.

"You know, as I do, that there are plenty of stories in the Scriptures regarding how we don't own our own life. This event has just reconfirmed my faith that we are working toward a fuller life after death—and that, in fact, I could die despite my own feelings that I could do so much more by being alive."

There's the Ash Wednesday message up close and personal. Many Christians get ashes placed on their foreheads as Lent begins today to remind them that life is fragile and finite. "Remember you are dust and to dust you will return," the priest or minister utters when applying the ashes.

Frank plans to take his wife, Mary Anne, and their seven kids for ashes at their parish church, St. Anne's in Garden City, after he gets home from work tonight. "This Lent is obviously a big time for our family. We're going to focus pretty heavily on trying to be grateful for what we have. I make a retreat every November at Bishop Molloy Retreat House in Queens to refocus my faith. We'll try to do that this Lent as a family."

Frank grew up in Whitestone and attended St. Mel's, Holy Cross High School and Queens College. Did graduate work in computers at Stevens Institute in New Jersey. He's the kind of regular fellow many men can identify with. While bullets flew and he covered his face with his hands ("Just don't take it in the head!" he told himself), the thought hit him that if it weren't for basketball he would have caught a later train and avoided this real-life nightmare. He and friends from Garden City and Stewart Manor play for a couple of hours in a local school gym Tuesday nights, then repair for refreshment to Sweeney's on New Hyde Park Road. So as not to feel too guilty about a night out with the boys, Frank hurries home early on Tuesdays to help wife Mary Anne feed the kids.

So there he was in the third car of the 5:33 out of Penn Station, where Colin Ferguson was emptying a 9-mm. semiautomatic, killing six and wounding 19. A bullet pierced Frank's left hand, penetrated his neck and came to rest in his mouth. ("My friends rib me about how my tongue stopped a bullet," Frank remarked.) He was hit twice in the right leg and once in the left buttock.

Pins protrude awkwardly from his still-healing hand, but otherwise life is back to normal for Frank and family. He finally begins his new job today as technology manager of a Wall Street securities firm. Tonight the family goes to church. Frank summed up his thinking: "I'm grateful to have survived this, and hopefully in time I'll be a better person because of it."

February 16, 1994

Chapter Four:
Hard Habits
•••••••••••••••••••••••••

IF I HAD MY WAY: A JACKPOT EVERY DAY

I'm waiting for a politician to stand up and proclaim: "Read my lips: No new benefits!" And then propose a strict freeze on all federal spending until the budget deficit has been eliminated.

Won't happen, of course. Voters demand their expensive entitlement programs, military bases, postal services, etc. We hate big government in principle but embrace it in practice. A pol who campaigned against benefits would get buried at the polls.

The new tax bill under concoction amid much confusion in Washington assures only that you and I will pay more for government. As a typically tax-gouged American I accept ever-rising taxes as inevitable. But couldn't President Clinton and Congress please give us a circus for our money?

I've got an idea for a fun new tax that would rake in record revenues and, at the same time, make politicians popular with the masses. President Clinton, Hillary, members of the House and Senate, listen up: I suggest a national game of chance. Let's dub it Reel Bonanza, since it's my modest proposal. All citizens would be taxed to support Reel Bonanza, and all registered voters would be eligible to win one of the 25 cash prizes of $1 million bestowed daily on lucky Americans.

Imagine a government that created 25 millionaires every day of the year. Cleaning ladies, bond traders, welfare mothers, big-league ballplayers, migrant workers, executives, ex-cons—daily winners inevitably would include the whole spectrum of society, from folks who really need the money to those who have plenty already but could always use another million in cash.

Why make being registered to vote a condition for eligibility? Because that would invest the lottery with civic virtue. Killjoys inclined to oppose a game of chance could be persuaded to endorse it as a good-government measure aimed at increasing participation in our great democracy. High purpose always goes down well with editorial writers and other skeptics.

How would Reel Bonanza work? The Senate Finance Committee, headed by Senator Pat Moynihan, would devise a formula to raise $100 million a day via a levy on family income. Call it the Reel

Tax. (I'll take the heat and let the pols off the hook.) Low-income families would contribute, say, 50 cents a day, middle-income families $1 or $2, and the affluent $5 or $10, to bring $100 million a day to Washington.

Every evening around 6:30 (timed for the convenience of TV news), in a gala ceremony at the White House or on Capitol Hill, prominent political personages would draw at random the Social Security numbers of 25 registered voters. Hillary could announce the winners one night, President Bill the next, Senator Moynihan the next, and so on. Sen. Al D'Amato would demand a turn, of course, and that would be fine, but he'd have to swear not to call out his brother's name. Reel Bonanza would be strictly kosher. I'd want Attorney General Janet Reno, looking stern, present at every drawing to ensure integrity.

No taxes would be levied on winnings. Lucky guys and gals would get a cool million—and not doled out over 10 or 20 years, either. Winners would receive within a couple of days a certified check from the U.S. Treasury without a cent deducted.

The populace would be wildly diverted and deeply grateful for a federal program that, for a change, showed tangible benefits—25 instant millionaires and $75 million for the federal treasury 365 days a year. Politicians could commit the $75 million to deficit reduction. Voters would not fail to re-elect the pols who enacted this largess. The program would soon be as sacrosanct as Social Security. I can hear voters in the year 2000 hollering: "Cut federal spending, but don't touch Reel Bonanza!"

June 23, 1993

FOR ONCE, HE'S A WINNER

The snow money was due. The job pays the snow money in the spring. He would get his check that afternoon for last winter's overtime. It would amount to almost $2,000.

He sipped his coffee and read the paper, and she looked across the kitchen table and said, "Just to remind you—I've got bills backed up. We're late with the rent. I owe the deli. The kids need some things."

Her voice trailed off. She hated to sound like she was afraid he would blow the snow money gambling. But she was. His gambling was ruining them. They were always broke. The tension was terrible. They argued all the time. She didn't want shouting and crying this morning. She tried to sound casual.

"So," she said, getting up and taking her empty cup to the sink, "just to remind you, soon as you get home with the snow money, I'll go right down and pay the landlord."

He looked up from the sports pages. "Didn't I tell you I'd be home at 3:30?" His tone suggested: How could you doubt me? Isn't my word my bond? Don't I always come straight home from work and hand you my check?

She stifled a sigh. She desperately wanted to believe him. "Fine," she said.

His intentions were noble. They were always noble. Never in his life did he say to himself: "Today I'm going to gamble and lose and make my wife and kids suffer." He was basically a good man who loved his family. He didn't mean to hurt them. It was just that he couldn't catch a break. He was down on his luck. A loser.

He finished his coffee and gave her a peck on the cheek and went to work. A man's world. All the guys were in high spirits, pumped up about the snow money.

"Dice game in the garage right after we get our checks," one of the guys, Butch, told him during coffee break. He nodded. He didn't commit himself. He didn't say he'd shoot dice after work and he didn't say he wouldn't. He'd keep his options open.

They got their checks and went to the bank and cashed them. He cleared $1,850. He felt flush. He usually took home $500 a week, never enough for a gambling man.

Guys were heading for the back of the garage. He had a decision to make. He'd told her he'd be right home after work. But why not take a shot with $50? Even if he lost, he'd have $1,800 for her and she'd be off his back.

Guys rolled the dice on the floor up against the wall. The action was fast and furious. Adrenaline ran so high it was almost audible. Cash was everywhere. One of the guys, Batman, lost all his money in half an hour and punched a wall so hard he made a hole in it and everybody laughed.

He reached into his pocket for $50. "When I lose it, that's it," he told himself.

A couple of rolls of the dice and it was gone.

He went right back into his pocket and came out with $20 and got in the game with a vengeance. He was transported. Time seemed to stop. That was definitely an illusion, though; next time he looked at his watch it said 5:30. He was due home two hours ago.

The 25 or so guys who began the game had dwindled to six. He had gone into his pocket so many times he was afraid to take out what was left and count it. "It's getting late. Know what we'll do?" a guy named Jimmy said. "We'll shoot once around." The others nodded. Each of them would roll the dice until he crapped out and then the game would be over.

He slipped into the men's room. He took a deep breath and reached into his pocket and pulled out what was left. He counted it: $90.

He walked out with a lump in his throat. Jimmy pushed the dice at him and said, "Go ahead. You're up."

He put down $20 and rolled a 10. Go for broke, he thought. He put down his last $70 and hit the ten right back. Winning felt good for a change. He tossed in another $20. He felt a surge of luck. One of the guys, Ralphie, looked at him and said, "He's right."

Money flew all over the place. "If I hit a 7 I'm dead broke and out," he thought, but he suppressed it and rolled the dice. Another 10.

He kept rolling and winning. He rolled for 25 minutes. When he finally sevened out, the other guys said, "That's it. That's enough. We've had it." Everybody knew it was time to go home.

He had money stuffed in every pocket. Perspiration soaked his shirt. Everybody was going into the men's room to wash their hands. He hung back until they were done. Then he went in. He pulled the money out of his pockets and counted it.

He counted it again to make sure. Twenties and fifties and hundreds, it added up to $2,150. Not only did he get even, he was up $300.

It was blood money. Never again, he thought. He caught the train to his stop in Bay Ridge. The ride settled his nerves. It was 7:30 when he came down his block. He was four hours late.

She looked stricken when he walked in. She said, "Did you get the snow money?"

He gave her a cool stare. "I told you we were getting the snow money." His tone implied that maybe she hadn't been listening that morning.

"All of it?" she said.

"Of course," he replied. How could she question him like this?

He handed over $1,850. No need to turn over the $300 he won. That wasn't house money, that was gambling money.

He looked at his watch. The Yankees were playing. He'd call his bookmaker. Maybe it wasn't too late to get a bet in.

June 26, 1994

AFFAIR WITH A MERCILESS LADY

They were married almost three years, and she felt truly blessed to have such a wonderful guy. He was always so thoughtful. He drove her to work every morning and picked her up after work in the evening.

"Come on, babe, or you'll be late," he told her as he checked his watch. She was just finishing brushing her teeth. "I'll be right there, hon," she answered. They always spoke nicely to each other. There was never a harsh word between them.

They hurried out of the two-family house—his father lived upstairs—and jumped in the car for the drive to the hospital where she was an executive. "See you tonight. Have a great day trading," she told him, and gave him a kiss on the cheek.

He was a self-employed trader on the floor of one of the stock exchanges in downtown Manhattan. It was awfully good of him, she thought, to drive to his office just so he could give her a ride. It would be so much less stressful for him to take the express bus and read the paper. But he always put her first.

Poor deluded woman. She was blissfully oblivious to his double life. She didn't know he was deeply involved with a cruel and jealous lover—Lady Luck. Instead of heading for the Battery Tunnel to take him to the Manhattan financial district, he shot over the Verrazano Bridge, through Staten Island, over the Outerbridge and down the Garden State Parkway to Atlantic City.

His car was six months old and he had 25,000 miles on it. Since his wife didn't drive she hadn't noticed the mileage. He'd had some disastrous days at Atlantic City. One time he had to badger a casino manager for going-home money after losing his last quarter at the slots. The manager came through with $20. He promptly blew that at another casino.

There the manager refused him going-home money. He had to stop at every toll booth on the Garden State, show his license and registration and fib that he'd "forgotten" his money. The toll takers had heard that lame story before, of course, from scores of Atlantic City losers begging to get home. "Yeah, sure, pally," they guffawed in his face. "You 'forgot' is right—you forgot to quit the slots before you tapped out." At every toll he was humiliated.

This morning he begged Lady Luck for a break at blackjack. The full-throttle drive from Brooklyn took a little over two hours. He rushed into a casino and played cards with a vengeance into the afternoon. Lady Luck smiled for a change. He won steadily. He walked out of the casino with $12,000 and a sigh of relief.

He had desperately needed a good day because of so many bad ones lately. Unbeknownst to his trusting bride, he was deep in debt and so was she. To finance casino-going he had cashed their certificates of deposit and sold a portfolio of stocks and bonds they owned.

His business at the stock exchange was virtually nonexistent since he'd been neglecting it in favor of almost daily forays to Atlantic City. He'd been making withdrawals from their joint savings account at a Bay Ridge bank. The account was down to almost nothing. If she saw the bank book she would get very suspicious.

He pushed the pedal to the metal to get back to Brooklyn in time to deposit the $12,000 before picking up his wife at the hospital. He parked on Fifth Avenue and went into a deli and, although he didn't drink coffee, ordered a large regular to go. He carried the container across the avenue into the bank. He gave the bank book and the $12,000 to a teller with a deposit slip. The teller recorded the transaction and handed back the bank book. He took it and took the top off the container and poured coffee all over it. The bank book was drenched.

"Oops. I seem to have spilled my coffee and ruined my bank book," he said. The teller said, "No problem. I'll make you a new book. I'll just enter your deposit today, OK?"

"Fine," he said, nodding. This was working out just as he'd planned. Now, if his wife looked at the bank book, she'd see only the $12,000 balance and not the numerous recent withdrawals he'd made. Beautiful.

He drove to the hospital and picked her up and they drove home. "He's so reliable," she thought. His father, retired, sitting on the stoop, said, "I feel like making a run down to Atlantic City for a few hours. Want to come along?" He looked at his wife and said, "Dad could use some company. I think I'll go along with him. I put my money in the savings bank. Could you let me have a couple of hundred?" She smiled and said, "Sure. You worked hard all day in Wall Street. You deserve a little relaxation. You two guys enjoy yourselves." She handed him $200.

She went into the house and made dinner for herself and thought, "He's so good, making such a sacrifice to keep his father company. Such a good man I married."

He lost the $200. The next day he drove her to work and then went to the bank and withdrew the $12,000. He drove to Atlantic City and lost it. He hit up the casino manager for going-home money. The manager said no. He did the I-forgot-my-money routine at the tolls again, and the toll-takers mocked him again.

He and his wife spent their third anniversary at a Gamblers Anonymous meeting in Gravesend. He dumped Lady Luck that night. That was eight years ago. They've lived happily ever after. He knows he's blessed to have a wonderful woman who stuck with him. She's grateful for such a good man, and now, a day at a time, it looks like she's finally got the guy right.

September 25, 1994

Having a Super Time at the Pasta Bowl

First he called the principal of the local grammar school. He introduced himself as the manager of the bank down the boulevard. "We're initiating a program to teach children about banking and the value of thrift," he told the principal. "We invite classes in for a tour. We want to make the bank user-friendly to children. Could you and your fourth-graders visit us—say, on Friday at 2 P.M.?" The principal loved the idea.

Next he called the bank and introduced himself to the manager as the principal of the grammar school up the boulevard. "We teach our students to figure percentages by computing interest on bank deposits," he said. "This is the coming thing in education. We'd like to bring a class to your bank to show them the practical application. Could I come by with our fourth-graders at 2 P.M. Friday?" The bank manager said yes, of course, that would be fine.

The caller put down the phone and contemplated his brilliance. "With all those kids in the bank, the manager will cooperate real quick when I pass a note that I got dynamite taped to me and I'm gonna blow everybody up unless he gives me the whole vault," he thought happily. He planned to run straight to his bookmaker and make good his football losses. Then he'd pay off a couple of loan sharks. Then he'd be free.

Oh, don't fret. This caper never got beyond the phone calls. In a moment of grace the desperado who dreamed it up abandoned the nefarious scheme and, instead of robbing the bank, wisely surrendered to Gamblers Anonymous.

His odyssey of recovery from compulsive gambling ("My wife and kids love me today. I go to work. I live a normal life.") was one of several recounted at the Pasta Bowl, where ex-gamblers gathered for mutual support while active gamblers sweated out Super Bowl bets Sunday night. Super Bowl Sunday is get-even day for gamblers who wager millions in desperate hope of redeeming a losing season. Bookmakers and loan sharks, not the Dallas Cowboys, were the big winners. The Pasta Bowl, in a cheery church basement in Staten Island, answers the ex-gambler's prayer to be led not into temptation. Delicious ziti, salad, coffee and cake are consumed with gusto.

I showed up because I love GA guys and their stories. For example, there was the legendary GA member who, in his gambling days, bought a monkey and trained it to descend into a bank's night deposit box, gather up the deposits and scamper up the chute and into his master's arms with the cash.

Recovering gamblers are interesting and entertaining folks. Many are deeply spiritual, the antithesis of their materialistic, self-centered selves when gambling. They speak with real contrition about depredations committed under the compulsion to gamble, and with deep gratitude to the "Higher Power"—GA, to some; God, to others—that has mercifully healed them.

Pasta Bowl speakers spoke of abstaining from betting one day at a time and—the harder part—trying to discern and do God's will in daily living. Making amends to their long-suffering spouses and children was a priority for most of the several dozen men in the room.

Grandiosity assails gamblers. They throw money around and play the big shot. Egotism dogs them in recovery, too. An ego out of control usually results in relapse. A Pasta Bowl speaker admitted that the honor of being asked to address the group had initially filled him with self-importance. He strutted and preened. But anxiety and dread set in as the Pasta Bowl neared, and he came close to deciding to refuse to speak. Finally, he said, he prayed hard for humility. Sure enough, God filled him with calm. "I was nervous when I got up to speak, but now I feel great," he concluded, smiling. The roomful of ex-gamblers applauded. All won big at the Pasta Bowl.

February 3, 1993

FLATBUSH PHILLY'S LAST BET PAID OFF

Flatbush Philly was a waiter like his father. He was a horse player like his father, too. As a kid, he hated horses because gambling took all his father's money and embittered his mother and ruined life at home, but by his late teens Flatbush Philly was a chip off the old block.

"Only wiseguys have it better than waiters," Flatbush Philly told friends. "A waiter works at night. He can go to the track in the afternoon. And when the restaurant is closed on Monday, a waiter can make it to the flats and the trotters, too. Best of all, a waiter gets paid in cash."

Philly, a good-looking guy, had a beautiful girlfriend, Joanne. Stunning. And very nice, too. They met one night when she came into the restaurant with her girlfriends after work. Philly couldn't keep his eyes off Joanne as he served the young women whiskey sours. He was smitten.

They dated. Philly proposed. Joanne accepted. Two weeks before the wedding, he gave his father $20 to take to the track to bet for him on a horse called Royal Joanne. But just as his father was leaving the house for Aqueduct, Philly told him, "Pop, on second thought, give me back my $20."

He made a decision to reform. "I gotta quit gambling. I'm getting married. Joanne's a nice girl. We're gonna save for kids and a house. I don't want to blow all our money on horses."

His father told him he was doing the right thing. "Don't ruin your life like I did," he told Philly.

Philly bought a paper on his way to work the next day and saw that Royal Joanne paid $40 to win. He let out an anguished holler and threw the newspaper up in the air. The pages floated down onto Flatbush Avenue.

But as Flatbush Philly thought about it, he came to the conclusion that lousy luck was positive reinforcement for his decision to quit playing horses. "God is sending me a message," Philly thought.

He and Joanne got married. All was blissful for a while. But he lacked willpower. Putting his toe in the water, he began playing a number every day with a numbers guy who frequented the restaurant where he worked. Some very big wiseguys made the place an informal headquarters. Philly liked them and wanted to be one of them. Police and prosecutors should quit persecuting wiseguys, he thought.

"Big business is full of thieves. The government is crooked. Cops take money. Everybody steals. These Mafia guys are no worse than anybody else," Flatbush Philly thought.

One day he hit the number. All of a sudden he had a pocketful of cash. He resumed playing horses. One of the wiseguys who came into the restaurant for dinner became his bookmaker. Philly liked the idea that a known mobster took his action. It made him feel important. He told his friends who his bookmaker was. They knew the name from the newspapers. "Ohhh," they said.

Before long Philly was involved not only with the bookmaker but with the bookmaker's friend, the loan shark. By now Joanne was pregnant. She was working and they had $2,000 saved. He grabbed the bankbook one morning and emptied out the savings account. It was more important to Flatbush Philly, sick gambler, to take care of his bookmaker and loan shark than to take care of his wife and baby.

"Where's the bankbook?" Joanne asked when she noticed it was missing.

"Well," Flatbush Philly explained, avoiding eye contact, "I got a little jammed up. I went a little overboard playing horses."

Joanne burst out crying.

"Don't worry. I have a solution," Flatbush Philly assured her. "I'll become a bookmaker. They're good people. You'll like them. They're perfect gentlemen. They've got it made. They earn thousands a week without working. We'll be rich. We can buy a house."

Joanne said nothing.

A few times, Philly came close to asking into the mob. He had opportunities when the wiseguys were sitting around the restaurant late at night. But some sane instinct held him back.

Betting and losing gradually were wearing Philly down. The elation of gambling ebbed. Depression replaced euphoria. He found himself crying in bed at night after Joanne went to sleep.

One day he confided in a friend who, he knew, used to play horses but quit. "I'm sick from gambling," Flatbush Philly said.

"You don't have to live like this," his friend told him.

That night, Flatbush Philly and Joanne went to a building on West 16th Street in Manhattan. They met a group of guys and their wives. All the guys were ex-gamblers. They were a cross-section—one had been a cop, another a lawyer, another a college basketball fixer, another—no lie—a bookmaker. There was even another waiter there. Flatbush Philly went into a room with them, and his wife went into a room with the women.

The following night in the restaurant, Flatbush Philly asked the loan shark if he could talk to him privately. They stepped into the kitchen. They were there for a while. The loan shark yelled and cursed at Philly. No one but them knows exactly what was said. Apparently they came to an arrangement for Philly to make payments he could manage until his debt was discharged.

When all this happened, Lyndon Johnson was president and John Lindsay was mayor. The other night, Philly glowed with happiness, and Joanne was radiant, as friends from Gamblers Anonymous and Gam-Anon joined them to celebrate 25 years without a bet for Philly. "I can't believe I ever wanted to be a wiseguy," he said.

March 15, 1992

RUNNING NUMBERS MEANS YOU WALK

A friend of mine takes numbers. An in-law with organized crime connections got him a numbers route 20 years ago after he lost a legitimate job and desperately needed work to support his family.

My friend is well off today. Wealthy, probably. I see him occasionally on his way to play golf. He owns at least one lucrative legitimate business bought with his ill-gotten gains.

His name was in the paper once after he was locked up on gambling charges. The notoriety embarrassed his wife and kids, no doubt. "Once in a while we have to take an arrest. We get bailed out right away," he explained the next time we met. A few hours in jail every few years, maybe a small fine, and some bad press were part of the cost of doing business.

He once described the kind of problem that comes up in his line of work. Seems he was making his rounds one day, collecting numbers on a construction site, when a pair of hard-looking guys approached him and asked, "Who are you with?" He mentioned the name of his boss, and they said, "We're with the 19th Hole"—a gin mill on 86th Street in Brooklyn where mob guys hung out. The numbers play on the construction site was theirs, the pair insisted, and my friend, no tough guy, walked away immediately. Within a few days, his boss and the boss from the 19th Hole had a sit-down to decide who would take numbers at the location. The business was awarded to my friend, and the two hard guys never bothered him again.

As a good citizen, I suppose I should disapprove of all this. I believe that laws should be obeyed, and those who violate them should be punished. And yet I can't condemn my friend with any real conviction, because the truth is that he provides a service: people are going to play numbers, and somebody has to take the action. If playing numbers is a crime, why not lock up the players? Why not lock up all violators of gambling laws?

The answer, of course, is that the jails aren't big enough to hold them. Police estimate that $12 to $15 billion is bet with organized crime in the New York City area annually. Arresting bettors would be comparable to arresting every dope addict—how would the criminal justice system process the hundreds of thousands of suspects hauled in? It's impractical—impossible—to prosecute lawbreakers when they grow so numerous. Prohibition, of course, remains the classic illustration of the futility of trying to enforce laws that lack public support.

My friend is at the very bottom of organized crime. Among those at the top, allegedly, is Andrew Garguilo of Brooklyn, indicted this week for running a bookmaking operation that supposedly netted $86 million a year. Prosecutors identified Garguilo as the biggest bookmaker on the East Coast. He allegedly handled $300,000 a day at locations in Bay Ridge, Bensonhurst and Cobble Hill. The action was placed by smaller bookmakers in the five boroughs and Long Island who were laying off wagers too hefty for them to cover. Authorities described Garguilo as a "made soldier' in the Genovese crime family and said his operation was sanctioned by rival crime families.

"Bookmaking is the cash cow that runs organized crime," declared Brooklyn District Attorney Charles Hynes, whose office got the 45-count indictment of Garguilo. Yet this alleged bookmakers' bookmaker was released without bail after pleading not guilty. Justice Michael Pesce said there was no chance of his fleeing.

Meanwhile, gambling goes on—the early line in the paper yesterday made the Giants 11-point favorites over Indianapolis on Sunday. Anybody who wants to bet the game will have no problem. Makes you wonder what's the point of unenforceable laws.

December 8, 1993

DECRIMINALIZE DRUGS? I'LL DRINK TO THAT

Bernie Bennett, the great press agent, called to tell me where to go to celebrate the 60th anniversary of the repeal of Prohibition.

"Be at Red Blazer Too on West 46th Street at 10 A.M. Friday. The actual anniversary date of repeal is December 5. That's Sunday. I can't promote drinking on Sunday morning. It would be disrespectful. Be there Friday morning and I'll have the regulars lined up at the bar for you to interview," Bernie said.

Watching folks drink unnerves me because I know from experience that if I join 'em I'll fall down, so maybe I'll send a friend, Eddie the Super, who drank during Prohibition and still permits himself a couple of pops now and then.

Not too many drinkers go back six decades. "Could anybody who wanted a drink get one during Prohibition?" I asked Eddie the Super, who was up early tending to tenants' needs. Eddie will be 86 in January and has more energy than most guys half his age.

"Wasn't any problem at all," he assured me.

Sounds like alcohol during Prohibition was like heroin and cocaine today—strictly illegal and readily available.

Eddie's hangout in the '20s and early '30s was Gormley's, a speakeasy in a building on 22rd Street off Seventh Avenue. The steel door had a peephole. Inside was a big room full of people knocking back bootleg booze. After ratification of the 21st Amendment made alcohol legal on December 5, 1933, a sign went up out front. "Gormley's," it said proudly. Just like that, a criminal enterprise became a respectable establishment.

The Gormleys were among the first families of Chelsea. "One of the local bootleggers, Jay Culhane, is supposed to have left $100 million to the Catholic Church," Eddie related. "I used to see his mother walking to Mass."

"What was the difference between drinking during Prohibition and drinking after?" I wondered.

"I don't see there was any difference," Eddie replied.

Consuming alcohol may not have changed too much after repeal, although the quality of the stuff surely improved, but providing it changed radically. Bootleggers ceased shooting each other in turf wars. They put away their guns and became brewers and distillers and distributors. Went from outlaws to taxpayers.

Makes you wonder what would happen if federal laws against hard drugs were overturned just as Prohibition of alcohol was repealed 60 years ago. If states and cities regulated the drug trade as they do alcohol, drug dealers wouldn't have the incentive to shoot each other and innocent bystanders. Besieged cities would enjoy a rest from gunfire.

Gun control is a big issue nowadays. Didn't drugs cause guns and their use to explode? Didn't heroin and cocaine ignite the violence that's escalated to the point where not only drug dealers but desperate addicts—and lately the law-abiding citizens they prey on—routinely go around armed, with deadly results?

And can guns be outlawed any more effectively than drugs? Pardon my skepticism, but I'm unimpressed by politicians who congratulate themselves on antigun legislation.

If Prohibition gave a boost to organized crime, what have laws against hard drugs wrought? Looks like disorganized crime—deadly, random, devastating. Pledges to crush the drug trade have been politicians' boilerplate for 40 years. But government declared a truly wise drug policy 60 years ago when Prohibition was repealed. I'll drink to it. But make mine seltzer.

December 1, 1993

THAT POTBELLY IS A WEIGHT ON HIS MIND

Had lunch Wednesday with a friend who usually orders a big cheesy quiche but on this occasion made do with a turkey sandwich. I remarked that he looked like he'd lost a few pounds since I'd last seen him a month or so ago.

"I went back to OA," he said.

Over the years, I knew, this fellow had been in and out of

Overeaters Anonymous. "That program works well for people who stay with it, but most seem to backslide. Why is that?" I wondered.

"OA is much tougher than AA or NA or GA," my friend explained. "Nobody has to drink or use narcotics or gamble, but everybody has to eat. People in AA don't take the first drink. In NA they don't take the first hit of heroin or coke. In GA they don't make the first bet. It's the first one that triggers the compulsion.

"But food is a necessity. You have to take the first mouthful of food. In OA we tease our addiction three times a day."

That made sense. Maybe it explained all the obesity we see. Is it my imagination, or are more people than ever overweight? Looks that way to me. Food is a problem for an awful lot of folks, obviously. I ride the uptown bus every morning with several immense women. They struggle mightily to hoist themselves aboard. Bus seats aren't big enough to accommodate their girth. They look terribly uncomfortable.

For all I know, they're perfectly happy. I've read a couple of pieces lately in which large people proclaim satisfaction with their full figures and disavow any intention of thinning down. They're obese and they like it and they don't care who doesn't, they say. Big is beautiful.

A reader has to sympathize with them for the embarrassment and humiliation they've suffered over the years from insensitive (and insecure) louts who make fun of their size. Obviously it's terribly painful to have one's physical appearance ridiculed. No one who is called "fatso" ever forgets the hurt.

There's something about surrender to overweight, though, that seems to me to be reckless or defiant or both. For one thing, doctors and insurance companies agree that excess weight can cause sickness and death from diabetes, stroke and heart disease, and is a factor in gall bladder and kidney disorders. Those are facts right out of the *American Medical Association Family Medical Guide*. It's the epitome of denial to disregard such expert opinion.

I read recently that the best way to bring down high blood pressure is by losing weight. My blood pressure went from borderline high to normal when I dieted in the mid-1970s. I avoided taking medication by dropping 10 pounds or so.

I'd love to drop another five pounds, or maybe even 10. Can't seem to shed them, though. Been trying for years to get below 150, where Dr. Imperio insists I belong, but I hover between 155 and 160. An unsightly potbelly protrudes. "I look like a dumpy little old man," I said with a sigh as I stood before our big bedroom mirror the other night, and my wife remarked, "You are a dumpy little old man." A great self-esteem builder, the bride is.

I'm due for my semi-annual checkup with Dr. Imperio in a few weeks, and when I step on the scale he's going to frown and say, "Lose five pounds." I know it.

Most of us worry about our weight. We fight food every day. I admire my friend who's making another try at OA. It takes humility. "I call a woman in the program every morning and give her my food plan for the day. Then I try to stick to it,' he said.

He looks great. OA is working for him. Apparently it works if you work at it. "One day at a time," my friend said, polishing off his turkey sandwich and passing up dessert.

August 27, 1993

Shed Pounds Watching TV? Fat Chance

My desire to eat when hungry is much stronger than my desire to stop eating when full. Am I unique, or do you notice the same tendency in yourself, appetite-wise? I'm always famished come dinnertime and can't wait to attack my plate, yet after sending in a big dinner I'm not quite satisfied. I feel deprived while folding my napkin. Never in my life have I felt a primal urge to get up from the table.

"This may derive from the age-old struggle for survival, with the primary risk to the species historically being death due to famine rather than the danger of excess food," says Dr. F. Xavier Pi-Sunyer, director of nutrition at St. Luke's–Roosevelt Hospital Center in Manhattan.

It's been a long time since famine threatened a Reel. I have a picture at home of grandpa Billy Reel with his big stomach protruding over his belt. My father, Joe Reel, likewise had a large paunch. My potbelly continues the family tradition. The Reel men made a firm decision not to die by starvation. I know I'd rather contend bravely with the danger of excess food.

Still, I'm only six or eight pounds overweight. I often walk 50 or 60 blocks during the day. I walk miles in the park at home on weekends. I never take the car around the neighborhood. I'll walk to the newsstand, the post office, the Italian deli, the bank, the dry cleaner's, and get 20 blocks of exercise doing errands. Walking prevents an obese me. It's enjoyable and requires no willpower.

Obesity is "stunningly high" in the United States, Pi-Sunyer asserts in an editorial, "The Fattening of America," in the July 20 issue of the *Journal of the American Medical Association*. (When observing that the urge to eat surpasses the urge to abstain, the good doctor was referring to folks in general, not to me personally.) The percentage of fat folks shot up over the past dozen years. Data still under study indicate that obesity among children is increasing even faster.

We eat too much and we don't get enough exercise—"an imbalance between energy intake and energy expenditure," in the words of Pi-Sunyer. Sedentary America sits slothfully in front of the TV for four or five hours a day, munching on fatty, salty, sugary snack foods and washing them down with beer and soda. In 1993, carbonated soft drink sales hit $49 billion, more than the gross national product of Chile.

Health-care reform can't succeed if we keep stuffing ourselves. A campaign for moderation in eating is in order. Beefy, jowly President Bill Clinton probably isn't the ideal American to lead by example. Nutritionist Michael Jacobson, head of the Center for Science in the Public Interest, a Washington-based health-advocacy organization, proposes a nationwide "no-TV week" to promote a slimmer, more fit America.

Obesity and TV addiction feed on each other, Jacobson insists. Kids used to play outdoors after school. They ran around and burned up calories. Now they sit in front of the tube, metabolism slowed, and munch junk. A sad irony is that many might prefer to be out playing, but the neighborhood is unsafe or their parents are working and want them in front of the TV with a snack.

It's a vicious cycle of calorie consumption as TV emits a torrent of fast-food commercials and the audience stays hooked. Parent-teacher organizations and civic and church groups ought to organize a no-TV week. If we took walks and played sports instead of passively watching them, we'd see waistlines recede.

July 20, 1994

ECHOES OF O. J. IN TOO MANY MEMORIES

A commotion on the street below his bedroom window awoke a fellow at 2:00 A.M. He heard a smack and a scream. He jumped out of bed. He looked out and saw a woman in a party dress lying on the sidewalk. A man in a dark suit was walking away.

Terrible scenes from his childhood flooded the fellow's mind. His heart pounded. Perspiration poured off him. He began furiously to climb into his clothes. He was about to race down the stairs and out into the street, although he wasn't certain what he would do when he got there—any more than he knew 40 years ago, as a little boy in his pajamas, what he would do when he got from his bedroom to the kitchen where the fight was.

He heard the woman wail. He looked out the window and saw her heading up the block after the man. "Please, Joey, don't leave me!" she pleaded between sobs.

He watched her run after him until they were out of sight. His clothes were soaked, his emotions were a mess. He was as angry at the woman as at the man. He was ashamed of that feeling. He knew it was irrational.

This incident took place on his block in Brooklyn a while ago. The fellow, a good friend, related it to me during a conversation that began with the O.J. Simpson case and proceeded to a discussion of wife-beating. "When I saw the woman chasing after the guy who hit her, I was filled with disgust," he told me. "I have a terrible resentment against men who put their hands on women—and against women who put up with it. I saw so much of it at home when I was a kid."

The O.J. Simpson saga has riveted the nation because, my friend and I suspect, so many of us can identify with a story about violence at home, even though we rarely mention the topic to one another. The shame persists no matter how far back in childhood was the trauma of seeing the old man knock mom around—and maybe seeing her take a swing back. What a terrible dilemma it was for a kid who knew he (or she) was supposed to love both of them.

My friend and I have heard men admit that they used to beat their wives. They always look down or away when they say it. Their shame is visible. Why mention something so vile and degrading? Honesty compels them to tell the truth about themselves, no matter how ugly and humiliating, lest they forget how bad they were and relapse. "I swore I'd never be like my old man, and I ended up worse," these men often say. They saw fathers beat mothers and were repelled and horrified, yet they grew up to do the same to their wives. They talk about it because they've been restored to sanity and know that those who repress the past are condemned to repeat it.

In his tenement in Brooklyn when he was a kid, my friend recalled, there were three families in which the man of the house regularly hit his wife. If the cops weren't breaking up a battle in his kitchen (sometimes they'd let him and his brother wear their hats), they were upstairs dragging Smith off his wife, or downstairs separating the Joneses.

"The expression on O.J.'s face when he was in court reminded me of my old man the day after the cops came the night before," my friend said. "I recognized the look—remorse, shame, denial, guilt, self-loathing, confusion. My mother would give him the silent treatment all day, and then around dinner time she'd say, 'What do you want to eat?' He'd say corned beef or pot roast. The tension was broken. There was no mention of the battle last night. They pretended it didn't happen. A month or two would go by until the next time."

The O.J. Simpson story could provoke a long overdue discussion of the causes and prevention of wife-beating. We shouldn't be surprised if the nation is all ears.

June 24, 1994

SEX EDUCATION: TEACHING VALUES

Public high schools give condoms to kids, thereby encouraging their use. Suppose a condom breaks and the AIDS virus is transmitted. Isn't the high school that dispensed the condom culpable?

"Condoms fail at a rate unacceptable for myself as a physician to endorse them as a strategy to be aggressively promoted as meaningful AIDS prevention," says Dr. Robert Redfield of the Walter Reed Army Institute of Research in Bethesda, Maryland.

He adds: "Having worked with thousands of HIV-positive patients, many of them married, I can say without hesitation that it is intellectually dishonest to promote condoms in any way as a prevention message."

Redfield is quoted in an article in *Our Sunday Visitor*, a Catholic publication. Reading the piece caused me to wonder: How do Catholic high schools handle sex issues? I asked a prominent educator in the Diocese of Brooklyn.

"The foundation of our presentation to kids is values—right and wrong," I was told. "Condoms are a technological approach. Condom distribution is like metal detectors in schools—it doesn't address values."

I won't quote this educator by name to spare him the hostility of condom crusaders. Let them complain directly to me.

"We teach the dignity of the individual person, respecting oneself and the other person in a relationship, and reserving sexual activity for a time in life when both persons are ready to make a permanent commitment, which certainly is not at age 14 or 15 or 16.

"Different schools vary, but somewhere in the curriculum a course in family life or human sexuality deals with sexual activity and its place in personal development. A permanent commitment is the ideal that's held up."

Permanent commitment? Is permanent commitment what we

used to call marriage? Why not call it that? Why the euphemism and ambiguity of "permanent commitment?"

"To be effective with kids you have to understand the world they live in," the Catholic educator explained. "Marriage is certainly the ideal for us. At the same time, we're living in an era in which that ideal is certainly not the rule. The problem is the irresponsible way the adult society deals with sex—the way adults talk about it and live it out. An example is sex in the media.

"There was a time when everybody's mindset was that sex was reserved for marriage. That's not the world kids live in. To pretend that it is risks being perceived by them as not understanding reality. Sexual license is the rule in society. Without giving in to that we have to be cognizant of it."

Our sex-saturated society militates against instilling good moral values in young people. Everything they see around them contradicts a classroom message that stresses self-control and saying no. TV glamorizes sex, trivializes it, treats it as recreation. What chance does a mere teacher have against TV's relentless indoctrination in loose living?

Catholic high school students used to hear a lot about sin. Sex outside marriage was a serious violation of God's will for them. Why not merely deliver that message to kids today and say no more?

"Because it's poor teaching—just as it was poor teaching in 1956, which is why we didn't pay attention to it then. As teachers we have to make students examine what they're doing, examine the values in society and bring them to an understanding of the Catholic ideal.

"It's essential to retain respect and patience with kids. The Scarlet Letter syndrome—self-righteousness and condemnation—creeps into sexual morality in ways it doesn't with other moral issues.

"To contribute to the development of this generation we have to be forthright about our beliefs and stand up for them, but also be aware of the other voices they're listening to and other pressures they're subjected to.

"With issues like condoms and abortion, we can't just say the Church says they're no good and therefore we aren't going to discuss them. We certainly don't encourage them. We try to guide the kids along in their decision-making.

"Sin and guilt are not passé. A religion teacher in a Catholic high school would define sin as harm done to the relationship between man as creature and God as creator. We present an understanding of sin that's realistic and also compassionate.

"Telling a kid that the Church views this or that behavior as sinful is not going to be the last word, believe me. It might be the beginning of the discussion, but it won't be the end of it."

Listening to the educator, it occurred to me that his remarks might upset some Catholics as much as they will exasperate the pro-condom crowd. Some Catholics like to think that Church teaching need only be proclaimed and the faithful will fall in line. That's wishful thinking.

A Brooklyn pastor I spoke with used an anecdote to illustrate how tough it is to call kids to a higher standard. Seems that during a visit to the eighth grade at his parish school he took the opportunity to impart the Church's teaching on sex. He explained to the 13-year-old boys and girls that the Church expected them to abstain from sex until marriage. "They laughed at me," he told me.

A decadent era imperils kids. Society conditions them to disrespect themselves. Catholic high schools are a valuable voice calling them to moral integrity.

February 6, 1994

A Ring of Horror in a Late-Night Call

An old friend called one night a while back. We were very close in the early '60s but hadn't seen each other in years. He sounded depressed and slightly drunk. We exchanged salutations, and then he told me that he had been living with a man and that the man had just died of AIDS.

I was dumbfounded. At a loss for words. I managed to get out some condolences. I knew this fellow as a generous person who had been a very good friend when I needed one. I knew that he had lived a tortured life for many years; he once confided that he'd been sexually abused when he was a boy.

I also knew that he'd married a nice girl in the late '60s. They had a couple of kids. So I was stunned by the news of a man in his life, and stunned again that the man had died of AIDS.

He related that he divorced his wife after he met the man, and they moved to another state. Watching him die slowly had been a harrowing ordeal, he said. I sympathized.

He said he was close with his children. He didn't mention his ex-wife, and neither did I; she seemed too sensitive a subject to bring up. Our conversation was halting, and the fact that he had been drinking made it especially difficult for me.

I felt I'd offered no consolation to my old friend, so a couple of days later I called him back. This time he was cold sober—and the talk was even more strained. Recalling it now makes me uncomfortable. I remember saying that however bad things were for him, drinking wouldn't improve them. He assured me he had no alcohol problem, that his drinking the night he called had been an aberration.

I didn't ask the question that was on my mind and presumably on his: Did he have AIDS, or the virus that causes it? I couldn't bring myself to raise that terrifying subject.

Again, words failed us. Our talk drifted, ending amiably but not very satisfactorily.

This was a year or two ago, and we haven't spoken since. I lost his phone number—or did I throw it away because I lack the courage it would take to deal with my old friend and his plight? He hasn't called again. Although I certainly didn't say so, perhaps he sensed that I disapproved of his leaving his wife and kids to live with a man.

But I would hate myself if I hurt a friend at a desperate time, when he must crave unconditional love.

Oh, what a terrible plague is AIDS. I had pretty much repressed thoughts of my old friend, but was reminded of him by a moving piece in the *New Yorker*. "I have AIDS," begins the essay by Harold Brodkey. It goes on for three stark pages. "From the moment my oxygen intake fell to about fifty percent and the ambulance drivers arrived in our apartment with a gurney and with oxygen for me to breathe, from that moment and then in the hospital until now, I have not had even one moment of physical stability. I am filled off-and-on with surf noises as if I were a seashell, my blood seems to fizz and tingle. I have low and high fevers. I have choked and had trouble breathing." Brodkey writes with dignity, honesty, anger, humor. Read this piece, which ends hauntingly: "Pray for me."

All the news about AIDS is bad. Drug addicts infected by dirty needles continue to pass the killer virus to their partners and children. And the disease is increasing relentlessly among women and teenagers. No cure is in sight, nor is there a consensus about how to preach or teach prevention.

Deadly AIDS defeats us. As for my old friend, the best I can do, it seems, is pray for God's mercy.

June 18, 1993

A Buck a Pack Is a Helluva Whack

Timmy Mahoney quit smoking. Good timing, Timmy! President Bill Clinton wants to raise the federal tax on a pack of cigarettes from

24 to 99 cents. A congressional subcommittee favors an even stiffer hike to $1.49. The increased revenues would help guarantee health insurance for all Americans.

It's ironic that folks whose addiction is killing them are being singled out to subsidize health reform. But it makes sense to make people pay dearly for their bad habits. Society ought to get something out of them before they pass on to the great tax haven in the sky. It costs $24 billion annually to take care of people who get sick from smoking, according to Representative Michael Andrews (D-Texas), a crusader in Congress for a higher tobacco excise tax. Smokers should pick up as much of the tab for themselves as possible.

My friend Timmy, a retired truck driver, smoked a couple of packs a day for 50 years. "Over 400,000 cigarettes—I figured it out one day with an adding machine," he was telling me. "I'm off 'em 30 days. I stayed in the house the first three days. I knew if I went out I'd buy a pack. I still get the urge, but it's less and less. Every day I don't smoke I put $4 in a jar. I got $120 in the jar."

Timmy's breathing easier. His lungs have cleared up. "When I lay down to go to sleep at night, I'd start wheezing," he said. "My wife said she noticed I don't wheeze anymore."

Timmy's incentive to kick the habit was the news last fall that President Clinton hoped to fund health care reform with a 99¢ sin tax on cigarettes. "A buck a pack is a helluva whack. I'm gonna have to quit these damn things," I recall him telling me at the time. He was inhaling a Salem as we spoke.

So score one success for health-care reform even before it's been debated fully in the nation and Congress. Clinton's proposed gouge has already had the salutary effect of getting Timmy off the killer weed, as it's aptly known. The Public Health Service's Office of Disease Prevention says that 19 percent of all deaths in the country in 1990—400,000 of them—were linked to the use of tobacco.

And Timmy's positive experience in just one month demonstrates once again what we all know—not smoking improves health and saves money. I had a sore throat for seven years that went away within weeks after I put Camels down for good.

Smoking has been out of style for years. The habit is heavily stigmatized. Smokers know it makes them feel lousy. So why do they do it? They're addicted. Nicotine is a drug. It took me literally years of trying to finally get smoke-free, which I managed to do some years ago. "If I ever go back to smoking I'll never quit again. It's too hard," Timmy said. Amen.

What if the nation's 46 million cigarette smokers all got smart and quit like Timmy? The percentage of adults in the U.S. who smoke has declined steadily from a high of 46 percent in 1964 to 27 percent now. Should the trend continue—and it probably will as smoking is restricted by laws like the proposed Smoke-Free Environment Act that would ban it in public buildings—Clinton and Congress would have to find another source of revenue to pay for health insurance for everybody.

How about federal taxes on fatty, salty, sugary foods that cause heart disease, which consumes many billions in health-care costs? Soft drinks, potato chips, ice cream, cookies, candy and meat are top sellers in supermarkets. Fast-food restaurants prosper by pushing high-cholesterol burgers and fries. Why not slap excise taxes on these items to pay for health care and discourage their consumption, in favor of more nutritious pasta, fruit and vegetables? Let Clinton lead the nation by reforming his own eating habits. He could join Timmy Mahoney as a role model.

March 25, 1994

It's Not So Easy to Just Say No

I drink too much coffee. I'm drinking a tall container, black, no sugar, as I write. Cost me 92 cents at the luncheonette in the lobby. That's a ridiculously high price for a container of coffee, even a tall one, but it's what a lot of places charge these days. I paid up and shut up like a typical caffeine addict, which is what I am.

My doctor told me not to drink coffee because it raises my blood pressure. And it affects my nerves for the worse, as I've known for years without the doctor having to tell me. Coffee makes me nervous. Caffeine is a stimulant. That's why I like it. Stimulation is one of my favorite things.

Last month I was tapering off coffee nicely, down to just one cup after breakfast and another after lunch. My wife doesn't make coffee after dinner, and I'm too lazy to brew a pot for myself. So a mere couple of cups a day was my ration for most of December. I was proud of my self-discipline.

Alas, I couldn't maintain such a strict regimen. On vacation the week after Christmas, I spent three days and nights at an inn. Coffee flowed freely at all meals. "More coffee, sir?" I kept hearing, and, of course, I kept saying, "Yes, thanks." In the years when I drank alcohol I never said no to a drink unless I misunderstood the question. Now I'm the same way with coffee. Asked if I want a cup, I always say yes. Can't say no.

Can't say no. Can you identify? My theory is that the inability to say no (to coffee, alcohol, tobacco, chocolate cake, etc.—substitute the temptation that applies to you, dear reader) is at the root of most of life's problems.

I pay very little attention to politics because no politician ever did anything that made me as jumpy as I get after a fourth or fifth cup of coffee. How I feel on a given day depends more on my coffee intake than on anything done or left undone by the president, the governor or the mayor.

If coffee is bad for my nerves, why do I keep drinking it? Why don't I just quit? Well, I've tried. I drank no coffee for a whole week last October. Not a drop. Sacrifice wasn't required the first two days because a stomach virus made it impossible for me to eat or drink anything at all for 48 hours. Withdrawal from caffeine caused me a terrible headache to go with the stomachache from the virus. After the virus subsided, I had to be very careful about what I consumed for a few days, so I stayed off coffee because I was afraid it would be too hard on my tender stomach. Before I knew it, I was caffeine-free for a week.

Beautiful. I slept like a baby at night and was serene all day, with nerves as calm as a Grandma Moses landscape.

Alas, it didn't last. The truth about me is that I have no willpower (except when my will is to do something that's bad for me, in which case my will is quite powerful). After seven days, I got a strong urge for coffee and promptly submitted to it. Walked right into a deli and bought a big container, black, no sugar. And I was hooked again.

That backsliding reminded me of years ago when my addictions were alcohol and tobacco. Every so often, I'd manage to get off booze and cigarettes for a few days. I'd congratulate myself for heroic abstinence. Then I'd get an urge for a drink or a smoke and say yes to it. "One won't hurt," I'd tell myself. But, of course, one was too many and a case and a carton weren't enough.

Many folks nowadays have a terrible time saying no to food. Compulsive eating afflicts a lot of us, obviously. An obesity epidemic is evident. All the overweight people attest to it. There's no way to hide a food addiction; if you've got one, people can tell by looking at you. A good friend of mine went to Overeaters Anonymous several years ago and, a day at a time, lost weight steadily for months until he'd shed 100 pounds. "It's tough because I tease my addiction three times a day," he told me at the time. "You have to eat to live. But in OA I'm eating moderately at breakfast, lunch and dinner, with nothing between meals." I saw this fellow the other day and it looked to me as though he's regained the 100 pounds and then some. I didn't want to ask him because it was none of my business and I'd hate to embarrass him, but obviously he dropped out of Overeaters Anonymous. He couldn't keep saying no to stimulants in the form of second helpings, I suppose.

A lot of us made New Year's resolutions, but resolve to quit or control compulsions seems unsustainable with all the temptations presented by the pro football playoffs. How can anybody stop overeating, drinking, smoking or anything else with all the damn games on? TV sports and commercials stimulate urges for more stimulants. Years ago, I used to drink one beer after another and smoke one cigarette after another while I watched games on TV. I thought I was a sports addict who enjoyed a beer and a smoke. Actually, I was a beer and smoke addict who enjoyed a game. If I watch football this afternoon and there's coffee nearby, I'll want to gulp it down until I'm so hyper I could return a kickoff.

After finishing the first container of coffee, somewhere around the middle of this column I took a break and went out and got another one. Couldn't resist the craving. One column, two coffees. No good. Relief from compulsions is possible, of course. Many former sufferers testify that prayers helped heal them. They counsel humility—don't rely on your willpower, they say, but on God's willpower. I believe them. Too bad 92 cents won't buy a container of humility.

January 15, 1995

"NO" Isn't a Warning, It's an Answer

I used to hide in the garage, where my sons wouldn't see me, to smoke cigarettes. They were in the early grades of public school at the time, and they learned as part of the school curriculum that cigarette smoking was hazardous to health.

They told me bluntly I shouldn't smoke. "It's bad for you, Dad," they said, their little faces quite serious and slightly reproachful.

Cigarettes could kill their father, they knew from school. I felt terribly guilty lighting up in front of them. I cursed my lack of willpower and slunk to the garage for a nicotine fix.

After a year or two of sneaking smokes I managed to quit, breaking a heavy 20-year addiction. There's no doubt that pressure from the kids, and the discomfort of pacing and puffing in a chilly garage, hastened my abstinence from tobacco.

What reminded me of this was the big story in the paper about the Board of Education voting to require all AIDS educators in the city's public schools to sign an oath that they will emphasize abstinence from sex over reliance on condoms to prevent the disease.

I thought the board's decision was excellent. Courageous. Cogent. Maybe not politically correct, but surely it has everything else to recommend it, including common sense. Can't imagine how anybody could cavil.

Would you want your kids taught in school that it's okay to smoke cigarettes with filter tips to decrease the likelihood of contracting cancer, emphysema and heart disease? Of course not. You'd want the teachers to tell them to shun cigarettes, period. Half-measures won't defeat fatal diseases.

Absolutes are important, particularly to kids. Children and adolescents should be told forthrightly to say no to sexual relations, which would be bad for them even if they used condoms. AIDS is by no means the only reason for kids to postpone sex until they're adults. Vitally important spiritual and emotional considerations militate against sex too soon. Adults shouldn't be afraid to say so. Mayor Dinkins and Schools Chancellor Fernandez and other putative grownups who push condoms for kids ought to be ashamed of themselves.

Will some young people ignore a righteous message even if they hear it loud and clear in school? Will they have sex anyway and expose themselves and others to AIDS? Sure. After years of anti-tobacco propaganda, some kids smoke cigarettes. Some use cocaine, knowing an overdose can be deadly. Some abuse alcohol despite having heard in school and even seen at home that alcoholism destroys life. Some drink and drive. Deaths result.

Self-indulgence can be fatal. Does that mean we should sanction it with a warning to be careful? Admonitions against immoral and self-destructive behavior frequently go unheeded. That's no reason to capitulate to decadence. Rather, let's demand self-discipline, self-restraint, moral purpose. The very highest standards—what's best for body and soul—should be held up to young people to emulate. Don't toss them rubbers and say good luck. Is that any way to treat a kid? What if the rubber breaks?

Many of us grew up in a time when the consensus of opinion held that sex before marriage was wrong. This was the message from pulpit and media alike. Not everyone behaved accordingly in the backseat of the car, but many did. The old-fashioned approach kept promiscuity under control.

So-called sexual liberation—if it feels good, do it—made AIDS an epidemic. Sexual repression was vastly preferable. Let's restore it without apology, beginning in the schools.

August 21, 1992

Chapter Five:
These Modern Times

A Dad Gets a Second Chance

The happiest guy in Queens is a new grandfather I know. He bursts with joy when he holds his 8-pound, 22-inch grandson. He never held his daughter, the baby's mother, when she was a baby. He was out of the house and out of her life before she was born. Gratitude overwhelms my friend when he considers how he got a second chance to be a loving father—and, now, a grandfather.

He and his wife broke up when she was eight months pregnant with their daughter. His drinking had cursed their marriage. She wanted him to stay for the baby's sake, and he said maybe they could make a go of it, but that was the booze talking. He flew to El Paso, crossed the border and got a quickie Mexican divorce.

A month later their daughter was born. He didn't go to the hospital. He was in some joint in Woodside, drinking. Over the next 17 years he saw her and his daughter three or four times, never for long. One Saturday afternoon he came out of a gin mill, the sunshine hurting his eyes, and they were in a car at the curb. He looked at them. They looked at him. He kept moving.

His life changed when he sobered up eventually. His ex-wife heard about it but wasn't impressed. His daughter was curious, though. By now she was 17, and she had always wondered what her father was like.

His phone rang one night. "Daddy?" she said. It was a miracle, but he wasn't surprised. He had attended a Cursillo, a religious retreat, two weeks earlier in Brooklyn, and had confessed his sins and humbly asked God to forgive him, and for the first time in his life he came to believe that God loved him. So he was expecting a miracle.

"Yes, this is your daddy," he said. And she said, "I'd like to get to know you." His heart leaped. She asked if they could get together. He said sure. They made a date for dinner the following Sunday at a diner on Northern Boulevard in Bayside.

He put down the phone and went directly to a reunion of his Cursillo group, which happened to meet that night. He told his sponsor, a veteran of the retreat movement, what had happened. He could hardly contain his excitement. His sponsor warned him not to get carried away.

"How old did you say she is?"

"She's 17," he said.

His sponsor nodded. He knew something about 17-year-olds. "Don't take this the wrong way, but she's probably calling because she's having problems with her mother, not because you're such a wonderful guy."

His heart sank. He felt deflated. His sponsor put a hand on his shoulder. "Here's what you do: Go to the diner and meet her for dinner. If she starts bad-mouthing her mother, tell her you don't want to hear it. Tell her that while you were running to bars for years, her mother loved her enough to stay with her and raise her. And tell her it looks to you like her mother did a wonderful job."

He nodded, but he knew he could never utter those words. He was sure he had too much pride to be humble.

On Sunday he drove to the diner, his heart in his throat. To meet his daughter after so many years was the fulfillment of a dream and also the most anxious moment of his life. What would they talk about? Would his face burn with shame when he apologized for abandoning her literally before she was born?

She was as lovely as he knew she would be—his wife had been a beautiful young woman. "Hello. You look good," he told her. She smiled and blushed. He smiled and blushed. God, he thought, it's hard to talk to a female if you don't have a few drinks in you. But he knew he had to do it sober.

The conversation was a little awkward but not too bad. Halfway through dinner she said something negative about her mother. He cut her right off. "I don't want to hear it. While I was running to bars for years, your mother loved you enough to stay with you and raise you. And it looks to me like your mother did a wonderful job."

How did that come out? Must have been the grace of God, he thought. As soon as he said it he realized every word was true.

The dinner was a reconciliation. They've had many lunches and dinners in the half-dozen years since. It's been a wonderful relationship, but difficult emotionally for him at times. Whenever he thought of all her birthdays and Christmases he'd missed during her first 17 years, and all the other times he should have been a father to her but was absent, guilt overwhelmed him. "How can I ever make amends to her?" he often asked his sponsor, who always replied, "Just be the best father you can be today. That's all God expects of you."

God and his daughter forgave him, but his ex-wife is taking her time. Her resentment is deep-seated, and not unfounded, he must admit. She didn't want him at the wedding when their daughter was married a few years ago. So he stayed away. It hurt terribly not to be there.

When the baby was born the other day, he ran to the hospital as soon as he got the good news. His ex-wife was sitting in the room with his daughter. "Hi. Congratulations, grandma," he said to her. He chatted with his daughter and then went with his son-in-law to look at the baby. On the way out his ex-wife said good-bye in a nice way. He wasn't going to get his hopes up too high, but he prayed they'd all be together at the christening. Nothing is impossible with God, he knew.

February 5, 1995

NEW YORK'S NO. 1 PROBLEM

A friend's recent visit to a Bushwick elementary school, and his niece's ordeal as a teacher in a Jamaica junior high school, gave us something to talk about over coffee the other night.

"The elementary school was an oasis in a disaster area," my friend said. "It was a public school, but it reminded me of the parochial school I attended in Flatbush years ago. The kids wore uniforms. I didn't know public school kids wore uniforms, but these kids did. They looked spiffy. They obviously had pride in their appearance.

"Driving to the school I was shocked by the condition of the neighborhood—abandoned buildings, stripped cars, streets filthy with litter, guys hanging out on corners. A picture of urban blight. You could tell it was a part of Bushwick with plenty of unemployment and drugs. A very depressed place.

"I parked and went into the school. What a contrast! I was greeted at the door by two smiling kids who took me to the principal's office. She had invited me to review a presentation the kids were giving. I complimented her on the condition of the school—the hallways were quiet, everything was immaculately clean, the atmosphere was conducive to learning. She said she was a strong supporter of old-fashioned education.

"The teachers brought their classes one at a time into the auditorium. Very orderly. No pushing or shoving or loud talk. The principal addressed them and the kids listened attentively. She was the only person in the room talking.

"They stood and sang the National Anthem and recited the Pledge of Allegiance. Then the show went on. It was about Irish culture in America. There were no Irish kids in the school, but the black and Hispanic and Asian kids did a first-rate job performing songs and dances and scenes that portrayed Irish-American life.

"I was tremendously impressed. These were bright, attractive, respectful kids. They put on a terrific show. They were gracious hosts. I felt the greatest respect for the kids and faculty and staff, and also for the kids' parents, who obviously raised them well."

He paused to sip his coffee. His brow furrowed. He looked grim. I sensed what my friend was going to say next, and I was right. I've come away from schools in places like Bushwick with the exact same sentiments.

"What worries me is: what's going to become of those kids?" he said. "They were lovely, polite, intelligent, innocent, full of potential. Yet I left the school and drove away from that devastated neighborhood with a terrible sinking feeling that the kids were doomed to be dragged down by a horribly degraded environment.

"The thought of those beautiful kids ending up on drugs or in jail or on welfare or having babies out of wedlock 10 years from now put a pall over what should have been a very hopeful and heartening day."

I nodded. "I've had exactly the same experience," I told my friend. "I don't like to think about it. I don't believe I've ever written a column about it because I hate to ruin the readers' day. I try not to succumb to despair. It's depressing to think kids have no chance in life, that they're condemned to failed lives.

"I'm not cynical or pessimistic by nature. I like to be hopeful. But I can't escape what looks to me to be the awful truth: conditions in neighborhoods like Bushwick are so bad that kids have virtually no chance of surviving. It's awful to think this, and I don't like myself for thinking it, but it's the way I feel. I sure hope I'm wrong."

My friend nodded. "My niece teaches in a junior high school in Jamaica, and she was telling me that in two years she's had two kids threaten to kill her. The kids are almost impossible to control, she says.

"When a kid gets really out of hand, she calls the home to report the problem to the parents. The mother always tells her the same thing: 'I can't do anything with him. I was hoping the school could straighten him out.' My niece says she feels sorry for the mothers because the kids don't mind them any more than they mind her. They're as bad at home as at school."

I finished my coffee. "We know what the problem is—no father in the house," I said. "The absence of fathers is killing the city. It's killing cities across the country. Kids are fine until they get to be 12 or 13. Then they become just like we were when we got to be 12 or 13—rebellious, sassy, looking to impress the girls."

"The difference," my friend said, "is that we had a father at home."

I nodded. "Exactly. I was afraid of my father. And he never laid a hand on me. He never had to. His presence in the house was enough to prevent me from getting too far out of line. A father is the most affective deterrent to bad behavior by boys. Kids born out of wedlock or who've had their lives disrupted by divorce are far more likely than kids in two-parent homes to live in poverty, drop out of school, get pregnant as teenagers, turn to drugs, go to jail. More than 70 percent of kids in state reform institutions are from fatherless homes. When the out-of-wedlock birth rate and divorce rate exploded, so did juvenile crime, child poverty and poor performance by kids in school."

We finished our coffee. We sat and said nothing. A shortage of responsible fathers is the number one problem in New York. No doubt about that. But we sure didn't know what to do about it. How to restore the two-parent family? That was the question. The future of inner-city children—millions of good kids like those my friend saw at that splendid school in Bushwick—depends upon finding the answer.

March 27, 1994

A DAY'S WORK: FROM BARFLIES TO FIREFLIES

I wonder what it would be like to retire to a rural refuge far from the din and dirt of the abrasive city. A friend, Charlie Clarke, did just that five years ago, after tending bar for 43 years at the Third Avenue saloon established by his uncle, P.J. Clarke. "How's Harpurville?" I asked Charlie over the phone. "Got much of a crime problem up there?"

"Had a major case just the other day," Charlie reported. "The cows at the dairy farm next to my spread broke through the fence. They milled around out on Still Road for an hour. It was anarchy."

Harpurville is 20 miles east of Binghamton, upstate New York. Charlie and Peg, his bride of 48 years, love the tranquillity of upstate after so many busy years down here. Charlie, one of six boys, was born over his uncle's place in 1921. He and Peg raised their seven kids in Seaford, on Long Island. They moved back to Manhattan and lived for a decade before retiring to a 60-acre tree farm in Harpurville. Their son Pat, a local builder, uses the trees for lumber.

"What do you do all day?" I asked Charlie. I was interested because the thought of retirement has begun to appeal to me, especially after a three-day weekend during which I enjoyed idleness to the fullest. It was a struggle to get going yesterday. I wanted to stay lazy but had to bestir myself to put words together.

"Peg and I are writing a book," Charlie said.

Hmm. Here I was wishing I could retire so I wouldn't have to write anything, and my retired friend Charlie was at the typewriter first thing in the morning.

"Actually, I talk and Peg types," Charlie said. "It's hard work. I ransack my memory for the highlights of all those years behind the bar. Celebrities came into Clarke's all the time, but the only one who ever got an ovation from the customers was Judy Garland. It so happened Jake LaMotta, the former middleweight champ, was holding court at the bar that night. Jake was very big at the time. And Judy Garland was very big, too, of course. She came through the door and moved past the bar and the customers spontaneously broke into applause. Jake wanted to get into the spotlight, so he stepped away from the bar to greet Judy. He threw his arms around her. She gave him a hug and said, 'How nice to meet you, Rocky!' She thought Jake was Rocky Graziano. Judy swept into the back room. Jake slouched back to the bar. He shook his head and told me, 'How soon they forget!' "

We laughed and Charlie said, "Jake was right about that. Two weeks after I retired, an old friend came into Clarke's looking for me. He didn't know I'd retired. 'Where's Charlie?' he said. And the bartender said, 'Charlie who?'"

Charlie told me that he and Peg get up early in the morning and have coffee. No, they don't eat a big breakfast. "When you get older you don't eat much," Charlie said. "You know the old story—by the time you can afford steak, your teeth are gone." They keep busy doing chores around the house. And he's cultivating a big flower garden. "The local paper ran a picture of it," Charlie said proudly. "All those years behind the bar, I never thought I'd be raising geraniums." For a few years he volunteered in the detox unit of a Binghamton hospital—Charlie is a certified alcoholism counselor—but gave that up because he got the impression the paid employees thought he was a threat to their jobs.

"Peg and I don't just sit around. We keep the bones moving. Sometimes we go to the doctor's office even if we aren't sick, just to read the magazines. Do we miss anything about New York? Yes, we miss New York humor."

That's what I'd miss, too. Charlie's kept his wit in the sticks.

Rather than retire and go rustic, I'll stay put and pass the laughs along.

September 7, 1994

WHERE EVERYONE'S A MINORITY

It occurred to me on the subway that I'm a minority. I should have realized sooner that white folks no longer compose a majority of the city's population. Guess I wasn't paying attention.

My friend Des and I boarded the downtown express at 86th Street and Lexington Avenue at about 9:45 Monday night. The car was maybe a quarter full. We sped toward 59th Street.

I looked around at fellow passengers. The entire rainbow coalition was there. Des and I were the lone middle-aged white males. The rest of the faces were black, brown, yellow.

Des grew up in High Bridge in the Bronx when the neighborhood was all Irish and Jewish. Is there an Irish-American or Jew left in High Bridge today? I'd be surprised. Des, 54, currently resides on East 58th Street. And he has a house in the Hamptons.

Des got off at 59th Street to go home. I stayed aboard, a minority of one.

You know, the subway is irresistible, a spectacularly efficient form of transportation. I hate to pay a taxi fare. A cab is an awful waste of money (and gasoline) when you can get where you're going faster and cheaper on the train. New York and automobiles are irreconcilable.

Of course, a cab is probably safer—unless you're a cabbie. But I still like to take my chances on the subway because it's such a bargain for $1.25. And subway crime has declined sharply for a couple of years, which is very reassuring. You feel as though the odds are more in your favor all the time. If New York manages to rise again, the renaissance will be thanks to a mass-transit system that's a wonder.

Anyway, Monday night, I hurtled downtown to Bowling Green. A young black couple with two little kids sat opposite me. Everyone in the car—black, Hispanic, Asian and a white fellow with a briefcase who got on at Grand Central—appeared weary after a long, hard day.

I'm a little claustrophobic, and I always worry that the train will stall between stations. It did briefly a couple of times, causing me to pray for relief from anxiety. Nothing promotes reliance on God rather than self like an onslaught of claustrophobia. Claustrophobes should be allowed to ride the subway for half-fare.

And I was a little uneasy as a minority, too. I've lived in New York for three decades, and I was accustomed to being a member of the majority. Haven't quite adjusted to minority status. Is this bigotry? I hope not. I think it's being human.

My stop was Bowling Green. Took a mere 25 minutes from 86th Street. I sloshed down to the ferry in pouring rain, about a five-minute walk.

Cruised to Staten Island and boarded a bus to my neighborhood. Passed a number of delis and convenience stores along the way. They were manned by people who used to be the minorities in New York until I replaced them. The stores were open despite the heavy downpour. You have to be to prosper in the land of opportunity. Some stay open 24 hours a day.

Got home in time to catch the end of the Reagan speech while my feet dried. The former president talked about what a great country America is. He laid it on pretty thick about the shining city on the hill, beacon of hope to all races, creeds and colors.

But you know the old man had it right? The whole face of New York has changed. It took years, including the Reagan-Bush years—and now we have a brand-new population of immigrants with black and brown and yellow complexions running stores and neighborhoods.

It's different, and it makes me feel slightly insecure sometimes, but we sure do welcome newcomers from everywhere.

I was going to write about politics today but decided against it; everything about politics has already been written. Instead, I will quote a conversation with the young guy at the newsstand in the Staten Island ferry terminal who always gives me a big smile and a "Have a nice day!" when accepting my 35 cents for *New York Newsday.*

"By the way, what's your name?" I asked him yesterday.

"Rocky," he said. We shook hands. "That's what they call me. My name is Rakesh."

"Where are you from?"

"India."

"How long are you here?"

"Two years."

"Your English is very good."

"English was my favorite subject in school."

"What hours do you work?"

"I get here at 4 A.M. Usually I work to 2 P.M., sometimes to 4."

He beamed. Rakesh was proud to toil 10 or 12 hours a day to succeed in the land of opportunity.

The more I think about it, I have to say it's an honor to be a minority here. It's just an honor to be here, period.

August 19, 1992

THE GOOD LIFE'S NOT SO GOOD

Brooklyn Bea and I are the same age—55. We think alike and identify with each other. Bea, who grew up in East Flatbush and lives in Mill Basin, appreciates life's ironies and absurdities.

"Ever notice," Bea observed recently, "that now that we're older and the kids are grown and we're able to afford some nice things, they don't satisfy us like we thought they would?

"For example, when I was a young woman I wanted contact lenses. I was sure they would improve my appearance. But they cost a lot more than glasses. I felt they were too much of an extravagance.

"Now I can easily afford contacts, and I've got them—but I've also got big bags under my eyes. My husband, Charlie, says I look better in glasses."

Bea and I laughed. It's a great relief in middle age, we find, not to take ourselves too seriously. A person past 50 can poke fun at his or her appearance, shortcomings, eccentricities, etc. We don't have to keep up the old image anymore. It's too late to impress anybody.

"No contact lenses for me. I'd forget where I put them and never find them," I told Bea. "Contact lenses are too small to locate after you've left them on the arm of a chair in the dining room as you passed through from the living room to answer the phone in the kitchen. I do that all the time with my reading glasses. When I get off the phone I say, 'Now where the hell did I put my glasses?' It's no big problem—I know I'll only have to search for a minute or two before they turn up on the arm of the chair. But imagine searching for contact lenses. I'd spend half my life crawling around on my hands and knees."

Bea gave me a funny look. "What are you talking about? If you wore contact lenses, you certainly wouldn't remove them when you answered the phone."

Hmmm. That was true, come to think of it. "Yeah, you're right, Bea," I said, sighing. "I forgot about that. I forget a lot. I also talk a lot without making any sense. This began to happen after I turned 50."

The so-called good life can be more trouble than it's worth, Bea remarked. "Charlie and I were thinking of buying a new car. We could buy a fairly expensive model, but we decided against it because a luxury automobile nowadays presents too much of a temptation to car thieves. You have to go through so much aggravation with the police and the insurance company if your car is stolen. You don't have any peace of mind when you own a luxury car. Even if it doesn't get stolen, you worry all the time that it will. And you worry that you might get carjacked."

I nodded. "Drive something old or beat-up, and carjackers will assume you're broke and give you a pass. Under no circumstances would I own a flashy automobile even if I could afford one. A year ago we bought a Saturn. One reason was because we figured the Saturn wasn't sleek enough to appeal to car thieves. Our second car is a 1982 Toyota. If I'm going to a bad neighborhood I always take the Toyota. I don't give a damn if it gets stolen."

The conversation jogged Bea's memory. "I remember when we could only afford one bottle of liquor," she said. "When company came we hoped they wouldn't drink too much because it would be embarrassing to run out. Now we have a whole liquor cabinet full of Scotch and bourbon and rye and vodka, and when company comes, hardly anybody drinks. Maybe they have a glass or two of white wine and that's it."

"A good load would kill me," I had to admit. "I might survive the drunk but I couldn't survive the hangover. I remember ferocious hangovers. I quit alcohol because the shakes and sweats and fears and remorse were unbearable. Staying sober is so much easier than drinking. And so much cheaper. I often think how ironic it is that when I drank I couldn't afford it, and now that I can afford it I can't drink."

"Ever think of resuming your drinking career?" Bea wondered.

I shook my head. "Nope. A pickle can never go back to being a cucumber."

Bea smiled. "Speaking of drinking makes me think of eating. Years ago we never went out for dinner. I cooked on an old stove at home. The oven didn't work right. Now I have a modern kitchen with a microwave and a self-cleaning oven, and we often go out for dinner. And every time we go I get indigestion."

"The other night I ate in style at Peter Luger in Williamsburg," I told Bea. "Delicious steak. Big portions. But I can't eat a big meal anymore without suffering. The next day I was logy and had a headache from overdoing it."

"Charlie and I saw Alan King perform at Westbury," Bea put in, "and he said that when he was a boy growing up in Williamsburg he used to put his face to the window of Peter Luger and look at the swells eating steaks and dream about being able to afford to have dinner there some day. Now, he said, he could afford to buy Peter Luger but he can't eat there because the food is too rich."

The topic of food reminded us that we'd both like to lose some weight. "I'd buy one of those exercise videos but they only discourage me," Bea said. "The models who star in the videos all weigh 110 pounds. And when you go to a gym to take an exercise class, the instructor is always so slim. I look at them and I feel like an elephant in a china closet."

I nodded and said, "If a video producer ever needs a male model with a bony chest, skinny arms, a potbelly and no rear end, I'm available."

The last laugh was on me, but Bea had the last word. "It isn't easy getting older. But thank God we're alive." Amen.

May 8, 1994

IT'S A TOUGH JOB—NOW TRY TO KEEP IT

The bus was packed yesterday morning. Standing room only. First time in a while. Summer vacations are over, Labor Day came and went, and folks fortunate enough to have jobs went back to work.

Work. What a drag. But there's one thing worse: unemployment. "I don't like my job, but I'm sure grateful to have it," a friend said with a sigh the other day. The next day another friend passed the same remark. A lot of folks probably feel that way. Their jobs are neither intellectually stimulating nor spiritually fulfilling, but the bread they put on the table fills the stomach, and that's no small consolation in our precarious economy.

Quite a few middle-aged women, I noticed, were aboard the bus to catch the 6:40 A.M. ferry from Staten Island to Manhattan. They looked like they'd much rather be home in bed than on the way to a day's toil at a word processor in a stuffy office for a modest wage. No doubt some of them had little choice. They had to go to work to make a living.

Maybe their husbands had lost their jobs. New York State has lost 562,500 jobs since May, 1990. The rest of the nation gained 1,043,500 jobs during that same period. High taxes here discourage enterprise.

Many of the jobs lost were good ones at big corporations like IBM and Eastman Kodak that shed employees to cut costs and keep lean in a brutally competitive economy. Middle-aged men (and some women, too) earning substantial salaries were let go because they were a drain on profits. Their work might have been good, but they made the bottom line look bad.

One such victim came by for dinner the other night. He was an executive at a major insurance company for 23 years. A few years ago the company began trimming employees. He shrugged off the downsizing at first, feeling invulnerable, but insecurity set in as colleagues all around him got the ax. One fateful day the boss called him in and told him he was finished, too.

He's been looking for a job. Sending out résumés, making calls. Many of his calls, he said grimly, go unreturned. He does some consulting work for a small company in New Jersey. He visited my house on the way home from there. "A few weeks of consulting work a year won't pay the bills," he said matter-of-factly. "Companies are cutting back on consulting to save money, so I can't count on it."

I didn't want to be nosy, but I wondered how he was surviving. This fellow always made a good living and never dreamed that in his most productive years he'd find himself unemployed—and with no prospect, apparently, of ever working again. A terrifying situation. Did he at least get a pension? "Yes, but it's greatly reduced. I needed 30 years with the company to get a full pension."

He has a mortgage. He has a daughter in college. His wife works, but her job was intended to help out with tuition bills, not to support the family.

He wasn't complaining, he was just telling it the way it is. And it was scary. How many middle-aged men with decades of executive experience find themselves reduced to wondering how long they can hang on before they have to sell their homes? And then where will they live? Imagine the toll this takes on their self-esteem. Imagine the fear of the future they and their wives and kids feel.

By the beginning of the '90s, the typical executive worked three hours more per week and took 20 percent fewer vacation days annually than in 1979. Fear of losing your job and, perhaps, losing your home makes for motivation on the assembly line or in the executive suite.

"I don't like my job, but I'm sure grateful to have it." If folks are unhappy at work but happy to be working, the paradox is perfectly understandable.

September 8, 1993

BUT FOR THE GRACE OF A STRANGER . . .

A poignant scene unfolded on lower Broadway the other evening rush hour. A seriously disabled young man in a wheelchair waved a piece of paper at passersby. The disability made him mute, and his body writhed in contortions as he tried to attract someone to stop. Scores of downtown office workers bound for buses and subways hurried past him on a corner at Broadway and Fulton Street.

It was freezing cold. Only thin jeans covered his scrawny legs as the young man in the wheelchair spastically waved for help. A middle-aged woman spotted him and stopped. The crowd surged past them. She leaned down and spoke to him, but he was unable to reply. He awkwardly pushed the piece of paper at her. She reached into her bag and brought out glasses and put them on and read it.

The woman studied the piece of paper. She thought about what to do. She stood still as commuters bundled up against the cold streamed by. After a minute or so an empty cab stopped at the light on Broadway. She went over and stuck her head in the passenger window and said something to the cabbie. He pulled to the curb and got out. He and the woman pushed the young man to the cab and lifted him in. The cabbie opened the trunk and loaded in the wheelchair.

The woman reached into her pocketbook. She slowly took out a bill. She heaved a sigh.

A man who had been observing the scene stepped forward and asked her, "Where is the young guy going?"

"The piece of paper gave an address on Seventh Avenue in Greenwich Village," the woman said. She clutched a $20 bill. "I told the driver I'd pay $20 if he'd take him there and help him inside." She looked at the young man in the cab staring vacantly at her, and she said plaintively, "He was so sad in his wheelchair, I had to stop."

The cabbie closed the trunk, and the woman reached out to hand him the money. "No, I've got it," the man said. He came out with his wallet and handed the cabbie $20. The woman looked at the man and said, "Thank you."

The man nodded. As he hurried away he said to a friend, "I couldn't live with myself if I didn't pay the cab fare. I saw the kid in the wheelchair before she did, but I didn't want to get involved. Too much trouble. I crossed the street. I happened to look back and there she was. Thank God for that woman! The kid could have sat there all night and frozen to death."

Several days later the friend, who had witnessed the same scene and not intervened, is still pondering that slice of New York life:

What was the young fellow doing at Fulton and Broadway on a dark, cold night? How did he get there? Who left him with nothing but a piece of paper bearing an address? How could anyone be so irresponsible? When the cabbie got the young man to the destination, was anyone there to take him in, or did the cabbie have to leave him on the sidewalk?

Why did so many New Yorkers ignore the young man's plight? He was truly pitiable, obviously incapable of taking care of himself, desperately if silently crying out for help, and yet hundreds, perhaps thousands, of passersby gave him no more than a glance. Can such callousness be explained? Is it the inevitable result of more than a decade of seeing, every day, down-and-outers and lunatics sprawled on sidewalks, sleeping in subways and wandering the streets?

What happens to those who care so little for the poor and sick? Will God have mercy on us?

The woman who stopped to help the young man in the wheelchair was a good Samaritan of the sort celebrated in the New Testament. A guilty bystander paid $20 to assuage his shame. Perhaps she will pray for all of us.

January 29, 1993

HARD FAITH IN THESE DEMANDING TIMES

Even his harshest critics would be disappointed if Pope John Paul II relented and made the Catholic faith easy for followers.

"Abortion? Have an abortion if you like. Make your own decision. It's up to you if you want to kill the baby. No pope or church should lay a guilt trip on you. Who am I to say that life is better than death?"

Suppose John Paul II proclaimed that nonjudgmental message. Would Catholic-bashers applaud his surrender of standards? Probably not. Naysayers need standards to scorn and authority figures to hate, after all. A pope who made abortion optional would leave them speechless.

The Catholic Church is often called upon to liberalize its demanding doctrines. Relaxing the rules would fill churches with worshipers and seminaries with future priests, say prophets of innovation. Their advice ignores the decline of mainline Protestant denominations that followed the path of least resistance only to end up with more empty pews. Suffice it to say that if the Archbishop of Canterbury showed up in Colorado, crowd control would be no problem.

But the Pope of Rome, preaching personal responsibility, self-discipline and sacrifice, drew hundreds of thousands to Denver, and millions more watched on worldwide TV. The bright faces and loud cheers of his youthful audience indicated that the Catholic Church, despite undeniable problems, possesses exuberant faith, hope and charity as it heads into its third millennium.

World Youth Day ceremonies in Colorado presented the pope

with a perfect platform to revise and modernize Catholicism—if he had chosen to heed surveys showing him out of step with the American laity and the larger society. Newspaper and magazine stories published on the eve of his arrival recycled the old news that many Catholics disagree with some church teachings, particularly the difficult ones having to do with sex.

But rather than capitulate and repeal sin, the Holy Father urged old-fashioned prayer, charity and reliance on God to combat temptation. He told young people in Denver: "Drug and alcohol abuse, pornography and sexual disorder, violence: These are grave social problems which call for a serious response from the whole of society ... But they are also personal tragedies, and they need to be met with concrete interpersonal acts of love and solidarity, in a great rebirth of the sense of personal answerability before God, before others and before our own conscience. We are our brothers' keepers!"

Reject permissiveness. Repudiate the false morality of modern society. Defend, protect and cherish life, which is God's first gift and the fundamental right on which all other rights are based. Exercise charity in word and deed, always obeying St. Paul: "Do not be overcome by evil, but overcome evil with good." The victory of grace over sin leads to peace and reconciliation. Build an authentic civilization of love.

Thus did John Paul preach, and he implored young people to keep the faith by giving it away: "Do not be afraid to go out into the streets and public places like the first apostles who preached Christ and the good news of salvation in the squares of cities, towns and villages. This is not a time to be ashamed of the Gospel. This is the time to be proud of the Gospel. It is time to preach it from the rooftops."

Rather than accommodate poll findings that favor a soft, comfortable Catholicism, the pope sought to rally an army of evangelists to carry the cross for a hard faith. Whether young Catholics will accept the challenge remains to be seen. Thanks to their unbending, truth-telling Holy Father, they won't labor under the delusion that grace is cheap.

March 13, 1994

SACRIFICE MONEY INSTEAD OF CHILDREN

My three kids attended public elementary school. We could have afforded parochial school—tuition was modest then—but the local public school offered education just as good if not better. We felt we could provide religious training at home.

This was 20 years ago, and at that time, in a typically middle-class New York neighborhood such as ours, there was a basic moral consensus, a common sense of right and wrong that was shared by just about everybody—Protestants, Catholics, Jews, nonbelievers. Whether a kid went to public or parochial grammar school, he or she was exposed to other children who were raised with pretty much the same values.

If we were parents of kids starting school nowadays, though, given the turmoil in public education and the erosion of moral values, we would make a different decision. Has our neighborhood changed? No. But because a return to traditional religion is the only hope for a society on the skids, we'd want a parochial school education for our children to reinforce the faith taught at home. Under siege from secular forces, religion demands loyalty. We'd support parochial education with the conviction that the salvation of society as well as souls was at stake.

The decision would be costly. Kindergarten tuition is $1,200 and first grade is $1,560 at our parish school. Many families are priced out. As tuitions have risen over the past 20 years, Catholic elementary school enrollment has plummeted—from 120,000 to 55,000 in the Diocese of Brooklyn, which includes Queens, and from 51,000 to 39,000 in the Diocese of Rockville Centre.

Children are in jeopardy as society comes apart. A just-published Carnegie Foundation of New York report shows the quality of life for kids deteriorating due to poverty, broken homes, teenage pregnancy, poor medical care and parents too busy or distracted or irresponsible to care for them. Kids suffer mainly from lack of love. Love is faith's first imperative. In 1960, the Carnegie report noted, 1 percent of children under 18 experienced the divorce of their parents. In 1990, the figure was 50 percent.

A 12-minute video, *Take a Step in Faith,* offers a vision of a life of love for kids. A single mother of two young boys is shown walking them to school. She speaks of the obligation to educate kids in schools where they learn to believe in a loving God as well as reading, writing and arithmetic. Prayer, she says, is paramount—for kids and for adults. "It works," she says, smiling.

Her boys attend a parish elementary school with an enrollment of 600 children. The school is tuition-free. When they graduate, they can attend a nearby Catholic high school and the parish will pay the $3,000-per-year tuition, as it currently does for 90 boys and girls. The bishop and the pastor appear on the video to describe how the parish raises the money for education—and for dozens of other valuable programs for kids and adults, particularly the needy. Every churchgoer is asked to contribute a "sacrificial gift" to the Sunday collection. Many do, donating from 2 to 5 percent of their gross income to the church. The weekly collection averages $42,000.

The parish is Christ the King, in a middle-class section of Jacksonville, Florida, in the Diocese of St. Augustine, headed by Bishop John Snyder, formerly of Brooklyn. Many parishes in the diocese have adopted so-called sacrificial giving. On the video, Bishop Snyder urges giving until it hurts so that children can grow in faith, hope and charity.

God bless Bishop Snyder. His message, widely heeded, could redeem not only churches but the nation.

April 13, 1994

Chapter Six:
Halls of Fame
••••••••••••••••••••••••

THE QUIET KID IN THE HALL OF FAME

There was a quiet kid in Holy Rosary on Chauncey Street in Bedford-Stuyvesant who picked up a basketball in the parish gym and seemed to know what to do with it.

He didn't excel at the game right away. He couldn't play constantly like some kids do because he had to work after school. His father had died when he was 5 years old. He and his two brothers and two sisters were raised by their mother. The family lived on Reid Avenue between Hancock and Halsey Streets.

He was an altar boy. He looked up to the parish priest, Father Tom Mannion, who encouraged sports as a constructive outlet for kids. Father Mannion personally put up backboards to transform the Holy Rosary auditorium into a gym.

The quiet kid played several nights a week for PAL and CYO teams at Holy Rosary. This was after delivering groceries for a vegetable market in the afternoon.

He was a graceful but unspectacular player—not a great leaper, but fluid and efficient. He seemed to pass always to the right teammate at the right time. And when he shot the ball it floated up like a feather, bounced softly on the rim and, more often than not, fell through the hoop.

He carried himself with a special dignity. He was polite and quiet-spoken. He seemed older than his years. While still in high school, he ran the vegetable department for a supermarket on Reid and Halsey. The store manager, Alma Thomas, put him in charge because he was so mature.

He played pickup games at Madison Park on weekends. The competition was keen. Tracy Lee played at Madison Park, Jake Jordan, Jimmy Daniels, George Jackson—great playground talents.

The best player in the neighborhood happened to be the quiet kid's best friend, Tommy Davis. They were friendly foes. The quiet kid played for Holy Rosary, Tommy for St. Phillips Episcopal. Tommy was all-city at Boys High. Tommy Davis was to become a great major league baseball player.

Tommy kept after the quiet kid to try out for the team at Boys. Tommy went to Father Mannion. "Father, you gotta get him to try out."

So the quiet kid did in his senior year, and Boys' coach Mickey Fisher made him a starter. He graduated in January, so he played only half a season. His best game was against Thomas Jefferson with Tony Jackson, who went on to star at St. John's. The quiet kid scored 20 against the Jeffs. Very impressive.

No college showed interest, though. The quiet kid was a good student, but college was out of the question without a scholarship. So Father Mannion wrote to a priest he knew at Providence College recommending the quiet kid to the school in Rhode Island.

The Providence coach at the time, Joe Mullaney, a Manhattan native with a keen appreciation of New York talent, came to visit, but no scholarship was offered immediately.

By now it was spring. The school season was over. The Flushing YMCA sponsored a prestigious post-season tournament. Tommy Davis played for the Gems, one of the top teams. He persuaded the quiet kid to try out for the Gems. The quiet kid was cut. Not good enough, the coach said.

Most kids would say, well, that's it, game's over, time to join the Army. Not the quiet kid, though. All the years of discipline and hard work, of serving Mass and bagging groceries and studying, had stored up confidence, motivation, determination.

He and other kids cut from the Gems formed a team, talked their way into the Flushing Y tournament—and won it! In the championship game the quiet kid scored 36 points.

Providence coach Mullaney's father was at the game. He sent his son a press clipping. A scholarship offer was forthcoming within days.

The quiet kid went off to Providence to become probably the finest player ever to wear a Friars uniform. After graduation he played in the National Basketball Association with the St. Louis and Atlanta Hawks, and established himself as one of the great guards of all time.

He did it all effortlessly, it seemed. Elegant was the adjective to describe him, on and off the court.

Today he coaches the Cleveland Cavaliers and makes his home in Seattle, Washington. A devoted husband and father of three grown children, he is known for commitment to family and religious faith. He and Father Mannion, retired from the Diocese of Brooklyn and serving a small parish in Oregon, still keep in touch.

He's eternally grateful to his mother, Henrietta—she now lives in Queens with his sister Mary and her husband, John Roquemore—for the loving, caring, disciplined upbringing she gave him and his brothers and sisters, all of whom are doing well.

He's proud of boyhood pals from the old neighborhood who made good—Al Lewis, a prominent Brooklyn businessman, and Al Waldon, a Queens state senator.

He never fails to thank Brooklyn, a character-building place to grow up.

He comes in from Seattle to be inducted into the New York City Basketball Hall of Fame at a dinner at Harry's at the Woolworth Building. Inducted with him will be, among others, Nat Holman, Red Holzman, Tiny Archibald and Bobby Wanzer. Last year's first class of inductees included Kareem Abdul-Jabbar, Connie Hawkins, Dick McGuire, Bob Cousy and Billy Cunningham.

He belongs with the best, does the quiet kid from Holy Rosary who became a great player, a credit to Brooklyn, a role model's role model—Lenny Wilkens.

September, 22, 1991

A HALL OF FAME THAT COUNTS

A mere 47 years after he led the league in scoring in basketball, Marty Bannan of Brooklyn will be inducted into the citywide Catholic High School Athletic Association Hall of Fame. Marty deserves the recognition not just for his accomplishments on the court as a schoolboy but also because he forsook the game he loved to pursue a larger purpose. At age 17 he turned down a basketball scholarship to St. John's University and entered the seminary. And today he's still Marty from Williamsburg to old friends, but those who wish to stand on ceremony may call him Monsignor Martin Bannan.

Said no to big-time college basketball because he preferred the priesthood? Really? No kidding?

"When I was pastor of St. Ephrem's in Bay Ridge," Marty reminisced the other day, "my associate pastor, Father Joe Grimaldi, gave a talk one day to our parochial school eighth graders. He asked those who felt they might be called to religious life to consider it. He used me as an example. He told the kids, 'Look at Monsignor Bannan. He could have played basketball for St. John's, but he gave that up to become a priest.' And one of the kids piped up, 'What did he do that for?'—like nobody in his right mind would make such a dumb decision. When Joe got back to the rectory and told me, we roared.

"But the truth is I've never had any second thoughts. One of the great influences of my life was my coach at Cathedral High School, John Crane. I made all-city as a junior, and in the fall of my senior year before the season began he called me out of physical education class one day and said, 'Marty, I want you to know something: If basketball gets in the way of your studies, it's all right with me if you choose not to play.' That came completely out of the blue. Not playing had never entered my mind. He said, 'What's most important is your goal of the priesthood.' That made a deep impression on me to this day. John Crane put basketball and its place in my life in perspective.

"I had a good senior season. I can't remember if it was 16 points or 18 points a game, but I led the CHSAA that year, 1947–48. I had a good outside shot. I'd love the three-point shot today. And I was versatile and even played the post sometimes and put up hook shots and made a few. Does this sound vain? I hope not. Anyway, Kentucky contacted me, and Fordham, and St. John's. The possibility of playing in front of 18,000 fans at Madison Square Garden was something to think about. I had to decide what I was going to do— accept a scholarship to play college ball or go on to Cathedral College to study for the priesthood, which was my goal since I was in the third grade at Transfiguration in Williamsburg.

"So I went for advice to Father John Healey, a great man, may he rest in peace, who was athletic director at the prep. 'What if your knees go bad?' he said. Funny thing is, later in life they did. I've had some knee problems. Finally he said, 'Why don't you go on to Cathedral College for your freshman year, and then if you decide you want to transfer, we'll get you into anywhere you want to go.' That sounded reasonable. I went to Cathedral and never looked back.

"Something reassuring happened. The spring after my senior season at the prep, and again after my freshman year at the college, I played post-season games for St. Agatha's parish. Three St. John's players, Bob Zawoluk, Jack McMahon and Ron MacGilvray, were on the team. The post-season competition was tremendous in those days. We beat the Seton Hall freshmen with Walter Dukes, one of the first great 7-footers. In two years we never lost a game. I held my own pretty well, and I remember thinking, 'I can play with these guys. I'm as good as they are.' And that was very satisfying. I had nothing more to prove as a basketball player.

"I'm grateful to have come along and played when I did, when the pressure on young players wasn't as intense as it is today. Kids are pushed too hard in sports nowadays. They start too young, and they have to grow up too fast. Some colleges use the kids but don't help them to grow as young people and see the fullness of life. There's exploitation of poor black kids.

"Don't get me wrong, though—I love the modern game. The

players are enormously talented, far superior to my era. The way they shoot the ball! I love this time of the year, March Madness. I think it's the most exciting time in sports.

"What would I tell that eighth grader at St. Ephrem's who thought I was crazy to pass up basketball for the priesthood? I'd tell him I've never once doubted that I made the right decision. I'm 39 years ordained, half of them as a parish priest and the other half in administrative work in the diocese. I was director of the CYO. I was a vicar. Now I'm assisting Bishop Thomas Daily in personnel matters, recommending priests for assignments in the diocese.

"Recently I was talking to a group of seminarians and I told them that one of the great joys of the priesthood is the affirmation we get. Don't expect a letter from the bishop or a pat on the back from the pastor every time you do something, I told them. Don't look for rewards. But affirmation will come from the people we serve. People are very grateful."

Marty's induction into the CHSAA Hall of Fame is an appropriate honor for one of the most respected and admired men in Brooklyn. Old schoolboy stars tend to fade away and be forgotten. It's gratifying to contemplate one who became a monsignor.

March 19, 1995

Too Many Losers Beneath the Boards

The *New Yorker* profiles Harlem high school basketball meteor Felipe Lopez (full-page photo by Richard Avedon), and *Harper's* dissects the hard lives of three Coney Island schoolboy stars, in editions now on newsstands. That such prestige publications would devote so much space to the inner-city game testifies to its appeal as sport and sociology.

"Who's that attractive woman you were gabbing with in the bleachers behind the Rice bench?" I asked my pal Tom Konchalski as we walked out of Alumni Hall at St. John's University after the Catholic high school tournament semifinals last week. St. Raymond's beat LaSalle and Monsignor McClancy topped Rice.

"That's Susan Orlean of the *New Yorker.* She interviewed me about Felipe," replied high-school superscout Tom, whose evaluations of players are highly regarded by college coaches nationwide.

"Tom, you're big-timin' me! I can remember when the only writers you knew were me and Bill Travers," I said, referring to the former *Daily News* high school sports scribe.

Basketball has transcended sport to become a culture that intrigues social critics. The game enriches colleges, sneaker companies, pro franchises, ad agencies, TV networks and newspaper writers. A fresh supply of skywalkers from the nation's ghettos is required annually so that white guys who can't jump can get paid.

Orlean writes like leaper Lopez of Rice plays—with dazzling grace. She limns Felipe's winsome personality as deftly as she describes his pogo-stick spring. ("Felipe's got hop," as hoop aficionados put it.) But the most fascinating passages describe his life as a Dominican immigrant in the South Bronx who commutes to the venerable Christian Brothers academy on 124th and Lenox in Harlem. It's a revelation to meet this talent-blessed young fellow who treads mean streets with cheerful certainty that in a few short years pro basketball will make him a multimillionaire and worldwide household name in the Michael Jordan mold.

Not so optimistic are the 20 pages the current *Harper's* devotes to a trio of Coney Island schoolboys who played for Lincoln High during the 1991–92 season. In this grim diary, author Darcy Frey takes readers into the deadly housing projects the young men hope desperately to escape to play for golden colleges like North Carolina. Beaten down by the material and spiritual poverty of a lethal slum, handicapped by poor schooling that dashes college hopes, haunted by the sight of former playground legends defeated by drugs, they struggle to get out of Coney Island but their struggle seems doomed to failure. And greed and envy inevitably corrupt their once-pure love of the game.

Frey writes: "Here they are, playing by all the rules: They stay in school—though their own school hardly keeps its end of the bargain. They say no to drugs—though it's the only fully employed industry around. They don't get into trouble with the NCAA—though its rules seem designed to foil them, and the coaches who break the rules go unpunished."

So-called March Madness—the NCAA tournament to determine the collegiate men's champion—got under way yesterday, and millions of us will follow the bouncing ball. What is naggingly overdue is a fair deal for the poor kids from the projects. Colleges prosper mightily from their talent and sweat; student applications and alumni donations increase with a winning season. Ticket sales and TV contracts mean big money for everybody but the players. Only the elite like Felipe will get to go pro and cash in.

The NCAA ought to make an issue of this injustice. Basketball must value the young men from the ghetto who make the great game happen.

March 19, 1993

OUR LOVE FOR THE KNICKS IS COLOR-BLIND

When the Knicks started five black players for the first time in the late 1970s, a skeptic asked the president of Madison Square Garden at the time, Sonny Werblin, if New York fans would accept an all-black team.

"They will if we win," said Sonny, terse realist and good guy. Sonny, may he rest in peace, had the right idea: No quotas, no affirmative action, no white faces merely for show. Just win, baby.

New York's love for today's Knicks, battling the Chicago Bulls, is color-blind. That's progress. The Knicks of my youth employed one black player, Nat "Sweetwater" Clifton. He had played for the Harlem Globetrotters and displayed flashes of their showboat game. He'd grasp the ball with one hand and push it toward an opponent, teasing, then pull it back. "Ohhh!" the crowd would gasp, marveling at the massive mitt with which Sweets held the ball like an orange. He was a good player but was regarded more as an entertainer.

If memory serves, the only other black players in the league back then were Chuck Cooper of the Boston Celtics and Earl Lloyd of the Syracuse Nationals. The dynasty team of the '50s, the Minneapolis Lakers, was white as a Minnesota snowfall. They even had a substitute guard named Whitey Skoog, who helped Slater Martin and Pep Saul feed the ball to George Mikan, Jim Pollard and Vern Mikkelsen. (I'm showboating a little bit myself—those names just jumped to mind after 40 years.)

Was the shortage of black players a sign of the racial discrimination of the times, or were there only three blacks talented enough to compete in the National Basketball Association? The latter explanation seems unlikely, considering how blacks have come to dominate the game today, a development that met with resistance. There used to be an inside joke among coaches: "How many blacks do I play? I play two at home, three on the road and four when we're losing."

Ouch. A story like that hurts. Blacks have a right to be angry. How many black kids in high school or neighborhood leagues got cut by a white coach who preferred his own kind? Probably a lot.

Maybe the tremendous popularity of pro basketball is a tribute to the progressive approach to race relations the sport came to adopt. Two of the greatest white players were, for a time in their careers, sixth men on teams that started five blacks. I'm thinking of John Havlicek of the Celtics and Billy Cunningham of the Philadelphia 76ers. Their contribution off the bench was valued more than an integrated starting lineup. Skin color was subordinate to success. Just win, baby.

The Knicks were fortunate to have a hero with a savvy head and a huge heart who happened to be black—Willis Reed. Nowadays, when they need a basket and no fooling about it, the Knicks go to Patrick Ewing the way they went to Willis in the championship seasons of the '70s. Willis was not only a great player but a great leader.

Some people might have predicted that black dominance of basketball would cause white kids to lose interest in the game. That sure hasn't happened. Seems like every suburban driveway has a hoop up. Rural driveways, too. And girls, black and white, are into playing basketball as never before.

A skinny little white kid who loves the game can dream of being the next Bobby Hurley, the Duke all-American who'll become a multi-millionaire when he signs a pro contract shortly. Of course, Bobby didn't get good in any suburban driveway, but by going head-to-head against black kids on gritty Jersey City playgrounds. The toughest competition brought out the best in him.

Rarely but occasionally you'll hear a reactionary (redneck?) whine, "The Knicks oughtta play a white guy or two. Let's have some affirmative action!" Nobody pays the slightest attention to such nonsense. Just win, baby.

May 26, 1993

A FATHER'S "INTEREST" IN SON'S GAME

Reading the paper on the way to work, I rest my eyes for a moment and eavesdrop on two fellows who sit together every morning and spend the commute talking about their eighth-graders' progress in sports.

The pair are in their mid-40s, I'd estimate. By dress and demeanor they appear to be successful businessmen. But do they prepare for the day's work by digesting the *Wall Street Journal* and discussing market trends? Nope. The topic is how their kids are doing in parish league hoops. "'Flash in the paint! Flash in the paint!' I tell my Richie. But he doesn't listen. He wants to hang on the perimeter for a jumper. 'You won't get a pass unless you flash in the paint,' I tell him. But he ignores me," Richie's father laments. He drains his container of coffee and sighs.

The other father nods. He knows how Richie's dad feels. His son doesn't listen, either. That's the trouble with the world: 12-year-olds ignore their fathers. Every boy would grow up to be an NBA player if only he paid attention to his old man.

"My Kevin got burned on defense. The kid blew by him every

time," Kevin's father put in. "After the game I took him for pizza. I told him, 'Kevin, the kid you were guarding, or were supposed to be guarding, beat you off the dribble all day. He always went to his right. He obviously can't dribble with his left hand. So you gotta overplay him to his right.' I hope Kevin listened. We play that team again Saturday. Monday I'll let you know if he listened."

These guys talk Little League baseball in the spring and summer, kids' soccer in the early fall and now church league basketball. Sports leagues for kids keep them off the streets. They keep the kids' fathers off the streets, too. By identifying with their kids' moves on the court, dads can be young again.

Listening to the fathers brings me back. I went through the whole sports thing with my kids, who are grown now. I remember my preoccupation with Little League baseball in the 1970s and with CYO and high school basketball and soccer in the '80s. My wife and I went to a dozen or more games a season. When a son played high school basketball, I was at all his games—alone. The tension and excitement of the competition caused Mrs. Polonia's pulse to race and her face to redden. Apoplexy appeared imminent. The emotional toll was too much for her, so she stayed home.

The most fun we had was when our daughter played jayvee basketball and varsity soccer in high school. She made the jayvee basketball team because the coach needed a willing worker for practice. She rarely got into a game but cheered her teammates lustily from a seat on the bench. She sincerely hoped the girls who played ahead of her did well. She never secretly rooted for them to miss their shots so the coach would pull them out and put her in. One time her team had a big lead so the coach gave her a chance in the final seconds of a game. An offensive rebound fell right in her hands. Startled to find herself with an open shot, she glanced at her teammates to get an indication if they thought she should shoot it. They looked at her as though thinking it over. By the time she finally decided to fire away, a defender got a hand in her face and she put up a brick that banged off the rim. The buzzer sounded to end the game. She and her teammates ran off the court happily.

"Too bad our daughter missed her only shot of the season," I told my wife as we stood up in the stands with the other parents. We laughed. We really didn't mind at all that she'd missed. What was important was that she'd played and had fun.

She was a good soccer player and started for three years on the varsity. But the better she got and the more the coach and her teammates relied on her, the less fun she seemed to have. That was the way my wife and I saw it, anyway. When excelling and winning become more important than playing for fun, sports are an ordeal for many kids.

I never pushed my daughter in sports. I was pleased that she played, but didn't care how well. I was a typical chauvinist father: I pushed my sons. Oh, I didn't traumatize them. Nothing that bad. But I subconsciously hoped to recapture my youth through the male offspring. So I spent a lot of time playing catch with them when they were little and shooting baskets with them as they got older. I coached them incessantly. "Remember to keep your elbow in when you shoot the jumper," I repeated a few thousand times. In the back of my mind lurked the thought that I would share in the glory if they became good players. I doubt I was unique among fathers in thinking that way. I detect hints of paternal grandiosity in the voices of the fathers I overhear during the morning commute.

My sons turned out to be ballplayers of about the same caliber as their old man had been when their age. No pro scouts or even college recruiters beat a path to our door. I never got to be the puffed-up father of a sports hero. That's just as well, because no doubt I'd have been insufferable.

Overhearing fathers review and evaluate their sons' budding (they hope) athletic careers during the morning commute, I sometimes get an urge to pipe up: "Don't make a big deal out of your boys' ballplaying. Be as happy when they miss a shot as when they make one. If the kid your guy is guarding goes by him for a basket, so what? If the coach takes your son out of the game, root for the kid who replaces him. It's wonderful that your boys play ball. How well they play is insignificant. All that matters is that you love them and they know it."

They'd probably tell me to mind my own business. But they'd have heard the truth.

November 6, 1994

When Scoring Isn't Just a Game

I was dismayed to read that Kenny Anderson has fathered children by two women and lives with a third. The 23-year-old pro basketball star is looked up to by millions of boys. Too bad he falls short as a role model.

His irresponsibility weighs on Anderson, a graduate of Archbishop Molloy High School in Queens. "I'm not a good father because I don't see them. It really bothers me a lot," he said of his little girls in an interview.

A troubled conscience is good if it motivates a change in behavior. The woman who shares Anderson's palatial New Jersey home is reported to be his fiancée. If so, he ought to marry her. The New Jersey Nets pay Kenny close to $3 million a year. He should settle down before it all goes for child support.

I make these comments uneasily. Remarking on the moral shortcomings of others is distinctly out of style. Defenders of Kenny Anderson will remind me to be tolerant, to live and let live, to judge not lest I be judged. I hear them. But the truth must be heard, too: Making babies while refusing to be a loving father is disgraceful.

I don't know Anderson personally, but I have friends who've known him well for years, and they assure me he's a fine young fellow. It's quite possible to have disorderly relations with the opposite sex and still possess many good qualities. I'd love to see the best come out in Kenny, who's in the spotlight as the Nets visit Madison Square Garden to meet the Knicks in the opening round of the pro basketball playoffs tonight. He has a chance to be the greatest guard ever to play the game, and I hope he achieves that stature. But what does it profit a man if he gains the whole world and loses his immortal soul? That's a good question, maybe the best question ever posed.

Unless he reads this, Anderson probably won't hear any criticism of his loose living. He grew up and lives in a permissive society that shrinks from moral judgments. It wasn't always thus. Those of us of middle age can remember, for example, when Brooklyn Dodgers manager Leo Durocher paid a high price for low morals—he was suspended from baseball for a year.

A relentless womanizer, Durocher carried on a public affair with movie star Laraine Day, and they married before a divorce she was getting was final. The moral turpitude of ex-altar boy Leo the Lip shocked Catholic Church officials. On March 1, 1947, Father Vincent Powell, director of the Catholic Youth Organization of Brooklyn, announced a boycott of the Dodgers. Durocher, the priest said in a public statement, "is undermining the moral training of Brooklyn's Roman Catholic youth. The CYO cannot continue to have our youngsters associated with a man who represents an example in complete contradiction to our moral teachings."

That wasn't all. According to the baseball book *The Era–1947–1957* by Roger Kahn, U.S. Supreme Court Justice Frank Murphy, a prominent Catholic, telephoned Commissioner of Baseball Albert "Happy" Chandler and warned him that unless Durocher was disciplined, the boycott could go beyond Brooklyn. Murphy threatened to advise CYO leaders in dioceses across the nation to prohibit kids from attending major league games.

On April 9, Chandler suspended Durocher for the balance of the '47 season. On April 11, the Brooklyn CYO. called off its boycott.

A revolution in public attitudes has happened since then, obviously. A modern religious leader who proclaimed a boycott to punish wayward public behavior would be denounced as a moral despot. A boycott wouldn't work, anyway. Folks look forward to the NBA playoffs, and they shouldn't be deprived. But Kenny Anderson should know that no matter how well he plays, he's a big disappointment.

April 29, 1994

POLITICAL FOOTBALL? PUNT FOR REAL THING

Guess I never grew up, thank God. At the height of the mayoral campaign I should be interviewing politicians, but high school football people are so much more interesting.

More truthful, too. I asked Jamie Prosser of Marine Park, the tight end and safety on the Xavier High School team, how much he weighs, and he replied:

"Roster weight or real weight?"

Good quip for a 17-year-old. "The truth," I demanded.

"About 165," Jamie admitted.

The roster lists co-captain Jamie at 175. That's supposed to scare the opposition! Can you imagine a tight end who weighs 165? Tight ends should go about 185 and stand 6–2. Jamie is 5–10.

"When you played schools like Cardinal Hayes and Nazareth this season, how much size did you give away to their defensive ends?" I wondered.

His opponents were over 6 feet and 200 pounds, Jamie replied. Ouch!

Xavier was winless as we spoke, having lost its first four games, and may not yet have won as you read this. Last year's team, on which nimble Jamie, an able tackler, played defense only, went 6–4, a good year. Jamie got used to winning.

All 11 offensive players on that squad graduated, however, and Jamie was pressed into service as a blocker and pass receiver this season. He accepted coach Dennis Tobin's decision to make him a two-way player. No complaints. Football is a team game. The coach makes the decisions. The team comes ahead of the individual. That's football. If you don't like it, don't play. Simple as that.

"Last season, when you were winning, that bus ride to Red Hook every afternoon was a lot more fun than this year, I imagine," I said. Xavier is on West 16th Street in Manhattan. There's no place for football nearby, so the squad buses to Red Hook to practice on a makeshift field there.

Jamie begged my pardon. "Practices are fun," he told me. "The morale of the team is good; we're having fun—or as much fun as you can have when you're not winning. As co-captain, sometimes I feel sort of guilty that we're losing. But we've been getting better. We lost to Nazareth, a good team, 22–7, but we played well. We're a young team with a lot of juniors. The important thing is we're improving. Losing hasn't pulled us apart. We're very close as a team."

Listening to Jamie was refreshing. His words affirmed the values that make sports meaningful—the joy of playing, love of the game, teamwork, dedication, selflessness. And he's a student first, a football player second.

There are plenty of good high schools in New York, public and private, and Xavier is one of the best. "We lost four guys when progress reports came out last week," Jamie said. Their classroom performance was unsatisfactory, so they were off the football team. That's the way it is at Xavier, where the Jesuits, God bless 'em, uphold academic standards. Ought to be that way at every school and college.

Jamie, who lives on Madison Place, described his typical day. His alarm goes off at 6:30. The B-2 bus takes him to the Kings Highway station, where he catches the train to Manhattan. He arrives at Xavier in time to gab with friends in the cafeteria for a few minutes before his math class, introduction to calculus, at 8:25.

The school day also includes classes in Spanish, religion, history and English literature.

"What are you reading in English?" I wondered.

"The *Iliad*," said Jamie.

"Who wrote that?"

"Homer," Jamie said.

"Homer wrote a good epic Greek poem, but could he have cranked out three columns a week for an Athens tabloid?"

Jamie probably wondered: What's this wacko talking about?

After classes and several free periods for study, the Xavier school day ends at 2:30. Jamie and teammates go to the locker room and dress for practice. A bus hauls them to lower Manhattan and through the tunnel to Brooklyn. They're on the field in Red Hook at 3:30. Two hours or more of arduous drills follow.

After practice, Jamie usually gets a ride home from his or a teammate's parents (quarterback Matt Hickey and safety Rob Gallagher live in Midwood). If not, it's back to Xavier on the bus and then to Marine Park via public transportation. After dinner, homework concludes a long, demanding day.

A regimen such as this prepares a young fellow for the future, whatever it might bring. Good to know Brooklyn is producing guys like Jamie. Ne'er-do-wells are all too visible, but the Jamies are out there, too, making something of their young lives, devoted to doing the right thing.

Coach Tobin, who grew up in Bay Ridge and played quarterback for Xavier a decade ago, agreed with Jamie's assessment of the team. "Morale is really good. The kids aren't happy losing, but they aren't down on themselves. Last year, when we were winning, I tried to build on wins, using success to motivate. This year I'm telling them after losses: Put it out of your mind, don't let it get you down, focus totally on this week, take one game at a time."

Good thoughts, good advice, good coaching in life as well as football.

I hope Xavier wins some games this season, but lessons learned in defeat will benefit the players more than victories. The wisdom of Coach Tobin's words will come back to them decades from now.

October 24, 1993

THE BIG BATS ARE REALLY A BUNCH OF BORES

Let's think the unthinkable: Suppose the Yankees moved to New Jersey. I've thought about it and decided it wouldn't matter.

The Giants and Jets moved to New Jersey. New York is still standing. So let the Yankees go, too. When bumptious George Steinbrenner threatens to take his ballclub to Bergen County or wherever, the rest of us should just shrug.

If Governor Whitman and New Jersey legislators wish to spend hundreds of millions of Garden State dollars to build a ballpark for Steinbrenner, we won't mind. New Yorkers could patronize the Yankees by crossing the Hudson for games now and then, just as many support the Giants and Jets.

But, you say, what about tradition? Isn't Yankee Stadium the venerable House That Ruth Built?

Times change, and we mustn't be slaves to nostalgia. The current Yankees have no stars in the tradition of Bronx Bombers like Ruth, DiMaggio, Berra, Mantle, Maris and Jackson. When only 22,000 fans showed up at the stadium for the Fourth of July game against Oakland, Tony Kubek, former shortstop and cable TV announcer for the Yankees, remarked to reporters, "We drew 76,000 for a double-header on the Fourth of July in 1961."

But Mickey Mantle and Roger Maris were clouting homers at a record-setting pace for the '61 Yankees. On the mound was Whitey Ford. Consider the current dull crew in the Bronx. The big bats are bland Wade Boggs and no-charisma Paul O'Neill. The ace of the pitching staff is colorless Jimmy Key. Such faceless fellows may be in first place, but they don't compel huge crowds to come see them. Mayor Giuliani, desperate to mollify Steinbrenner, asked too much when he implored this week, "There's no question what New Yorkers have to do is show up for a lot more Yankee games."

I don't see why. Players and management lament lower-than-expected attendance, yet often they seem bent on alienating fans. "I think we should get a little more support," Yankees outfielder Luis Polonia whined the other day. Yet for months major league ballplayers have threatened a strike later this season that would doom the playoffs and World Series. If I were still a baseball fan, I'd infer from strident strike talk that ballplayers didn't need my support. And my impression that baseball cared nothing for me would be confirmed by the prediction of Chicago White Sox owner Jerry Reinsdorf recently that if players walk out, big league baseball might not resume until sometime in 1996.

In other words: Fans be damned. They should get the hint sooner or later. Maybe lackluster attendance at the stadium lately suggests fans in New York, where trends are set, are beginning to feel expendable.

Steinbrenner wants the city to build him a new ballpark or pay for expensive construction projects to improve access and accommodations at Yankee Stadium, but we should ignore him. What makes his welfare our responsibility? We don't build a store for Macy's or Bloomingdale's. Besides, despite Steinbrenner's constant poor-mouthing aimed at blackmailing us into subsidizing the Yankees, they're doing just fine. They drew 2.4 million fans at home last year, fifth-highest attendance in club history. And their TV revenues are astronomical: MSG-TV is paying the Yankees $486 million from 1989 through 2000.

The Yankees should be proud to call New York home, and satisfied to play in the Bronx. If they're not, we'll make do. It's beneath our dignity to beg them to stay. Let Steinbrenner con Jersey into bankrolling him. It would be a relief, come to think of it, to bid greedy George good riddance.

July 8, 1994

Chapter Seven:
Himself
·················

HAIRY-CHESTED AT THE CHECKOUT COUNTER

My wife, Mrs. Polonia, who holds a job and also keeps our house and cooks our meals, sends me to the supermarket to shop on Saturdays, and it was there that I made the decision to join the men's movement.

A stout, blue-haired woman in tight pants pushed in front of me on the checkout line. I was going to say something, but she stared me down. I turned away, wimplike. She sneered. The checkout lady snickered.

That did it.

"I need to get in touch with my primitive masculinity and re-capture old-fashioned male self-assertiveness, so I'm joining the men's movement next week if you don't mind," I announced as I lugged bags of groceries from the car into the kitchen.

Mrs. Polonia was washing out the coffeepot. I went on quickly, "I need to bond with fellow males, communicate, reveal emotions, share intimacies, talk about—you know—feelings."

Mrs. Polonia scowled and said, "Didn't they have any paper bags at Pathmark? I told you not to let them bag the groceries in those awful plastic things that are bad for the environment."

"I need to define myself," I went on. "I refuse to go on being de-fined by women—Grandma, Mom, you, the women at the office."

Mrs. Polonia said, "What about the paper bags?"

"Uh, I checked all the checkout counters. I even looked under-neath. None had paper bags," I replied apologetically.

"You have to demand paper bags. Did you ask the manager?"

"I would have, but he wasn't around," I lied.

Mrs. Polonia inspected the box of grade A large eggs to make sure none were broken. Fortunately for me, all 12 were intact.

"So can I join the men's movement?" I asked.

She said, "Is this men's movement another thing where you go off to the diner and drink coffee and tell stories with your friends all night?"

"No, this is much deeper," I explained. "Bill Moyers had a thing on TV about the men's movement, and there's a couple of best-sell-ers about it—*Iron John* by Robert Bly and *Fire in the Belly: On Being a*

Man by Sam Keen. Men go camping in the woods and beat on drums and howl at the moon to express the woundedness we've kept bottled up since childhood. All the pain comes out around the campfire."

Mrs. Polonia looked skeptical.

"Hundreds of men's-movement groups have sprung up nationwide," I said. "This will do for us guys in the '90s what feminism has already accomplished for you."

"What was that?" wondered Mrs. Polonia, rinsing the coffeepot.

"You know, liberation," I explained.

She said, "Camping in the woods? How could you sleep outdoors? You're afraid of bugs."

Mrs. Polonia has an exasperating way of focusing on something minor and missing the larger issue.

"I'll put on repellent and sleep in a tent," I promised.

"What if you have to go to the bathroom? You've been living in this house 20 years and you can't find the bathroom when you wake up in the middle of the night. You walk into walls. In the woods you'll wander off a cliff."

I ignored that and came out with the clincher. "Just as women resent being sex objects, men resent being success objects. I won't be a success object any longer." I exited grandly, marching in a manly way into the living room.

"Success object?" I heard her say. Then Mrs. Polonia laughed.

If she's in a good mood I guess that means I can join the men's movement. "Whooooeeeeeee!" Get the campfire going, guys, I wanna howl.

July 10, 1991

Living Life on the Cutting Edge of Style

Those of us who never had a lifestyle—a mere life was the best we could do—are reassured by the cover story in this week's *Time* magazine announcing the latest trend in America and dubbing it "The Simple Life."

"After all these years I'm finally in style," I told Mrs. Polonia. I read *Time* at the kitchen table while she made dinner.

By the way, I call my wife Mrs. Polonia because she is of Polish extraction. Outer-borough guys like myself often hang nicknames on our wives instead of calling them Ms.

"I knew your clothes would come back some day if you just kept wearing them," she said.

"Not my clothes, my whole life," I said. "Listen to what *Time* says:

'After a 10-year bender of gaudy dreams and godless consumerism, Americans are starting to trade down. They want to reduce their attachments to status symbols, fast-track careers and great expectations of Having It All. Upscale is out; downscale is in.'"

Mrs. Polonia looked up from the broccoli and said, "You definitely are in the forefront of the avant garde. This house had its original 1926 kitchen until last year. And we still have the original 1926 bathroom. You were way ahead of your time in rejecting gaudy status symbols."

And we have a pedestal sink in our upstairs bathroom—which is not only our upstairs bathroom but also our only bathroom. A one-bathroom family! What could be more in vogue with the simple life than that? Just call me With-It Reel.

"At least you got your high-tech kitchen before gaudiness, gadgetry and glitz went out of style," I told her.

We had a new kitchen put in last spring. I fought it all the way. My bride insisted, however. She was tired of standing over a hot stove. She wanted a microwave and a dishwasher. Also, the old linoleum floor was buckling. She finally shamed me.

"Do you know what Ursula's friends call our house?" she said. Ursula is our daughter. "They call our house 'The Little House on the Prairie.'"

So I hit up the trusty home equity account—every fashionable outer-borough homeowner who sends three kids to college has a chic home equity loan—and hired a construction crew to come in and disrupt my house for three weeks.

For a mere $20,000, a 21st century kitchen was forthcoming. The stove looks like the control panel of a jet plane. We acquired this status symbol before the rush to simplicity proclaimed by *Time*.

"More good news," I told Mrs. Polonia. "*Time* quotes theologian Martin Marty as saying that spirituality is 'in' as folks renounce the shallow materialism of the '80s."

She slumped visibly over the broccoli. "Oh, dear," she said.

"What do you mean, 'Oh, dear?'" I got a little testy. "I've been calling for spiritual renewal in my column for years. I'm a herald of what's happening, baby. An oracle of the revolution."

She sighed. "I'm afraid you'll get carried away and decide to become a deacon or something."

Not a bad idea. "Preaching the new gospel of less is more," I said, contemplating myself in the pulpit.

"I just don't want to have to listen to your sermons, or iron your vestments."

"I wouldn't wear vestments. Casual simplicity is all the rage today. I'd wear my usual flannel slacks and herringbone jacket."

Mrs. Polonia nodded. "Wouldn't it be wonderful," she said, "if just once your clothes and your ideas were in style in the same decade?"

It could happen. The '90s could be the best thing to happen to Reel since the '50s.

April 5, 1991

OH, BROTHER, CAN YOU SPARE A TUX?

I don't go to big Manhattan charity dinners, and not just because I rarely get invited. Hotel ballrooms are always too hot or too cold. Crowds conjure up my claustrophobia. Undercooked food was served at the few charity dinners I was dragged to over the years.

And formal clothes are too expensive and uncomfortable. I don't own a tuxedo and refuse to rent one. I don't look any better in black tie than in a plain suit. I don't look too smashing in a plain suit, to be honest.

I prefer to arrive home early to dine on Mrs. Polonia's tasty victuals, watch a few baskets on TV and get myself betwixt the lily whites no later than 10 P.M. Then I wake up feeling good and come into the office early to dream up something to put here.

But I was going to make an exception to my rule and attend a big charity dinner upcoming. A card arrived a month ago that said: "SAVE THIS DATE. Tuesday, June 1, 1993. Center on Addiction and Substance Abuse at Columbia University. Awards Benefit Dinner. Invitation to follow."

I put the card prominently on my desk as a reminder not to commit to a church social in Staten Island that night. The Center on Addiction and Substance Abuse was announced a year ago by Joe Califano, an admirable guy in my book. Brooklyn boy Joe rose from humble beginnings to hold important government posts beginning in the Johnson administration. Distressed by the toll addiction takes on us—abuse of alcohol, narcotics and nicotine consumes $300 billion annually in health care, disability payments, lost productivity, accidents and crime, and causes untold personal tragedy and suffering—Califano quit a lucrative law practice and founded CASA as a think tank and advocacy group to study the prevention and treatment of addiction and promote the findings.

Great idea. Long overdue. Just what America needs. Heart disease, cancer and AIDS each receive over $1 billion annually in research funds compared to only $300 million for a leading cause of them—addiction.

So I was up for the first annual CASA dinner. Sure enough, an invitation arrived yesterday. I ripped open the envelope to learn that a "leadership table" for 10 guests at the Pierre could be mine for . . . $25,000.

Or, if I wished to lead alone, I could buy a single leadership ticket for $2,500. Or I could be a piker and purchase a "benefactor" ticket for a mere $1,000, or a "patron" ticket for a paltry $500.

Alas, there was no "ex-drunk" ducat for $10 or $15, so I tossed the invite in the wastebasket. Master of ceremonies Barbara Walters and guest speaker Art Buchwald will have to go on without me in the audience.

Anyway, I already attended my one—and probably only—charity gala for 1993. This was the Recovery in Action buffet celebrating the 15th anniversary of the Employment Program for Recovered Alcoholics, a vocational counseling program that's put some 3,500 sober folks to work. The affair came off one Friday night last month in the basement of St. Francis Xavier Church on West 16th Street. Tables, chairs and decorations were set up by EPRA staffers and alumni. Pasta primavera was catered by Hot Stuff of Queens. Dress code was strictly casual.

Tickets were $15 per copy. I sprung for $30 and brought Mrs. Polonia. The only snafu came when the 400 guests, off booze but still hooked on caffeine, drank all the coffee by 8 P.M. Trying to keep up with demand, the executive director of EPRA, Richie Masterson, plugged in all the coffeepots at once and blew a fuse.

"Otherwise the evening was a huge success. After expenses, EPRA netted $1,400," Richie told me yesterday.

Best of luck to CASA, but I'll dine with EPRA, thank you.

May 7, 1993

HAVE MY HEART, BUT DON'T HOLD MY HAND

There was a story in the paper about a wife and mother who spent more than $600 on Valentine's Day presents for her family. That made an impression on this husband and father, who spent less than $4 for Valentine's Day cards, one for my daughter and one for my wife.

My card to my daughter expressed regret that I was unable to find the perfect Valentine's Day gift for her: a chocolate-covered telephone. My card to Mrs. Polonia said that my deep love for her causes me to tingle all over like my arm does when I fall asleep on it. Am I romantic or what?

Haven't heard from my daughter yet, but my wife loved the card I gave her (it cost $1.79 with tax; she would consider anything more expensive too extravagant) because of the reference to what in our mid-50s, after 30 years of marriage, has become our favorite mutual activity—sleeping. There's nothing my bride and I enjoy more than going to bed early, and we don't apologize for it, either. Just reading about people who sip and sup into the wee hours at charity balls or stay up to watch David Letterman makes our eyes droop.

On the card to Mrs. Polonia I drew a heart and wrote "I Love You!" in the middle of it. I tell her I love her all the time. She tells me she loves me. We feel a little silly saying it because it sounds corny, but we mean it.

As a certified fogy I often find myself celebrating the past, but one distinct improvement of the present is that we moderns express love more easily than our parents and grandparents did. That's my impression, anyway. We aren't too self-conscious or repressed to say "I love you." This is a healthy development.

"Love" was a word that folks used sparingly in the so-called good old days. I never heard my parents say they loved each other, although I certainly hope they did. My kids have heard their parents say it a thousand times. Maybe it rubbed off, because at the end of every phone conversation with my daughter, she tells me she loves me. When she was a kid, whenever I dropped her off to visit a friend, she leaned over and gave me a kiss before she got out of the car. I was always pleasantly surprised.

My family of four when I was a kid never displayed affection or said "I love you" to one another. I wish we had. My parents were old and dying when, for the first time since I was a little boy, I told them I loved them. I'll always regret that so many years elapsed during which we were too blocked emotionally to say how we really felt. We deprived ourselves of that consolation.

I'm still not a hugger or a hand-holder, though. Hugging has become epidemic, and I'm not sure I approve. Guys hug each other with gusto at Mass during an annual retreat I attend. I join in halfheartedly and uncomfortably. At church a few Sundays ago a married couple representing Marriage Encounter, a spiritual movement devoted to strengthening marriages, addressed the congregation, and the fellow and his wife made a show of holding hands. My wife and I could never hold hands in public. Why not? Oh, residual repression, I suppose. (And we'll be eternally grateful to all Marriage Encounter zealots who resist the temptation to try to talk us into hand-holding.)

I didn't buy my wife a Valentine's Day present. Chocolates don't agree with her and anything with alcohol in it makes her doze off, so candy isn't dandy and liquor isn't quicker (except at inducing snoring) chez Reel. And Mrs. Polonia wouldn't be pleased if I showed up with a little something from Victoria's Secret. Ours must be the only house in America that doesn't get the catalog. She thought it was tacky and canceled it. Mrs. Polonia has a mind of her own, and that's one of the reasons I love her.

February 15, 1995

THE GRADUATE SCHOOL OF FAMILY FINANCE

Seems like yesterday I was wondering how I would ever be able to afford college educations for my three kids. "My goodness, a year at a private university or liberal arts college costs $15,000!" I fretted.

Couldn't have been yesterday, though, because the figure for a year of higher learning at Prestige U. is more like $25,000 nowadays. Must have been a decade ago, when my oldest was about to enter his senior year in high school, and he and my wife and I spent weekends driving around to various groves of academe to find one that suited him.

He went off to college in 1984, and his brother in 1985, and their sister in 1989. You readers may find this hard to believe because I'm the father, but all three graduated!

Yeah, I know, they take after their mother.

Sending the kids to college was expensive, but it was the way we preferred to spend our money. When I say "our money," I mean the bank's money, of course. Middle-class families go into debt to pay for college. Even wealthy families must borrow when the bill for four years tops $100,000, as it does at many Ivy League and similar schools.

I never thought it would come in handy that I had flunked out of college, but it did when my older boy called one night during his sophomore year and said, "Dad, come and get me." Seems he was failing all his courses. A chip off the old block.

I understood and sympathized because the same thing had happened to me. "Don't worry about it," I consoled him, "you're only following in the great family tradition." I drove to New England the next morning and picked him up, and he came home and worked for the next two-and-a-half years, acquiring a certain maturity plus $20,000 in savings to take the load off the old man. Then he went back and earned a diploma. Changed his major from aeronautical engineering to math, a humble and wise retreat, and everything worked out well in the end.

Had an interesting phone call from the other guy during his sophomore year in college, too. At the time he was in a fraternity, which he later had the good sense to quit. In the course of the conversation he mentioned that he and his fraternity brothers had spent the day lugging bags of sand into the fraternity house. "What the hell for?" I inquired. I was a tad testy, having just borrowed thousands from the bank to cover his room, board and tuition for the semester. "Uh, for our dance this weekend," the heir explained. "The theme is a beach party. Only there's no beaches around here, so we're making one in the house."

I wasn't happy, but I didn't say anything. I'm glad I kept my mouth shut. No use haranguing sophomores. Let them live and learn.

Our daughter graduated from college in May, and liked academic life so much she took a job as an intern in the college administration. She began work this week. My wife and I drove to North Carolina to help her get settled. We were in a furniture store Saturday afternoon. My wife liked a certain bureau. "No, that's too expensive," our 21-year-old told us.

"Notice how frugal she is now that she's paying the bills," I remarked to my wife. Our daughter's prudence was a revelation to me, but it shouldn't have been. It's known as growing up.

Kids grow up before you know it. In my mind's eye I see my three in diapers, in Little League, in college. Now they're adults.

This is the first August since 1983 we don't have to borrow money to pay a college bill. And guess what? The Reel house needs a new roof.

The cost? About $8,000. No problem, we'll just think of shingles as tuition.

August 4, 1993

HOLD THE BOOZE BUT PASS THE BUTTER

Obsessed with diet and health, I devoured the latest confirmation of the perils of overweight: Thin men are far more likely to live long lives than fat men, and are much less likely to die of heart disease, according to major new research reported in yesterday's paper.

Age has a lot to do with preoccupation with health. In my mid-50s, seems like everybody I know has some ailment or other. Stopped the other evening at Hinsch's, the landmark ice cream parlor on Fifth Avenue in Bay Ridge, and was all ears as proprietor

Johnny Logue related details of his recent visit to Long Island College Hospital. Seems Johnny had a plumbing problem, as so many guys our age do. He was up on a table having something unspeakable done to him by the good doctor, and when he got down after it was mercifully over he felt a need to go directly to the bathroom. Where he passed out.

"I came to lying on the floor with four nurses bending over me," Johnny related. "I was stark naked. I looked up at them and said, 'I think I've died and gone to Heaven. But how come I'm the only one with no clothes on?' The nurses busted out laughing. So did I. Even the doctor had to laugh. Everything turned out fine."

Johnny, fully recovered, never looked better. We had a wonderful gab. But in the course of the conversation it came up that many of our friends have got one thing or another wrong with them. One guy is going to Maimonides for heart bypass surgery after the holidays, another is getting radiation for prostate cancer, another had an operation for an acute sinus condition but it provided little relief—his head is still clogged half the time.

Meanwhile, middle-aged moderns solemnly watch what we eat and hope to eke out a few more years than we would if we ate what we wanted. It requires an iron will—especially this time of year—to practice self-discipline at the table. I must have Italian whole wheat bread, for example. When I confessed this during my last checkup, Dr. Imperio said, "No problem. Italian whole wheat bread is good for you." Honesty compelled me to add that I put butter on it. Dr. Imperio's face fell. "No butter! You must watch your cholesterol!" he scolded.

I'm still eating half-a-dozen chunks at dinner—with butter. Can't stop. I'm powerless when it comes to Italian whole wheat bread with butter.

I tell myself it's ridiculous to feel guilty. My grandfather Billy Reel had a huge potbelly. A widower, he cooked his own meals and ate mainly pork chops and pound cake. He made his own beer and drank copious amounts of it. He never exercised. In his 70s he developed numbness in his toes. My father took him to a specialist, who diagnosed hardening of the arteries and told him to quit Camel cigarettes. Leaving the doctor's office, he lit up a Camel. "Pop, you know the doctor said you shouldn't smoke," my father reminded him. My grandfather replied, "What's the use of living if you can't enjoy yourself?" He died in his favorite chair at home at age 76. I doubt he ever thought about his health, much less worried about it.

My father, Joe Reel, who likewise ate, drank and smoked to excess without giving it much thought, suffered a severe stroke and massive internal bleeding in his early 70s. Miracles of modern medicine kept him alive, and he spent the final three years of his life in a wheelchair, unable to speak. He was happiest when I showed up at the nursing home with chocolate candy.

Billy and Joe, may they rest in peace, would wonder about me—off booze and cigarettes for years, a conscientious fruit and vegetable eater, strictly a pasta and chicken guy—no beef!—yet always anxious and concerned about what I might be eating that could kill me. Go ahead and butter your bread, they'd probably advise, and for God's sake stop worrying yourself to death.

December 17, 1993

I'LL TAKE RUNYON OVER RUDOLPH ANY DAY

The Christmas music coming from the stereo in the lobby gave me a hollow feeling in the pit of my stomach. Happens every year. Christmas music is supposed to cheer us up, but it makes me sad.

My father, may he rest in peace, hated Christmas music. Maybe hate is too strong a word, but he sure disliked it. This left an impression on me as a kid that won't go away, apparently.

"Can't they play anything but this G-damned Christmas music?" Pop would complain when "Jingle Bells" and "The First Noel" and "Rudolph" came over the radio incessantly.

G-damned Christmas music. Kind of a paradox, that. In later years my mother and sister and I got a good laugh whenever we recalled Pop's way of expressing his criticism of the genre.

When you're a kid, you're upset when your parents are upset. You adopt their emotions. Christmas music made my old man melancholy, and therefore it had that effect on me. It still does after all these years.

As I've gotten older, though, I've learned that there's value to the discomfort—it enables me to identify and sympathize with folks whose emotional hangovers from youth are much more severe than mine.

Looking back on it, I think my father probably suffered bouts of depression, although no one would have diagnosed it as that at the time.

"Pop's in a bad mood," I'd say to my mother. She'd nod, looking pretty grim herself. When I was growing up in the '40s and '50s, the word "depression" referred exclusively to the '30s—economic hard times, not mental or emotional illness. An unhappy person was merely "in a bad mood." It was his or her fault. Why didn't they cheer up?

Maybe my father inherited his aversion to Christmas music from his father, or maybe he just thought it was lousy on its merits. Pop was a pretty hip guy whose idea of a good sound was the Dorsey band doing "Marie," or Hoagy Carmichael rendering "Stardust," or Eddie Condon's Dixieland band, with Wild Bill Davison on cornet, swinging into "There'll Be Some Changes Made."

I owe my column to my father, come to think of it. When I was about 10 years old, he gave me a paperback book of Damon Runyon short stories. I devoured them. I'd read choice paragraphs aloud to him, and we'd laugh. My mother never could understand what we thought was so funny. She was highly intelligent, and much better read than my father, but the Runyon characters who so amused us left her cold.

My father was a mailman in our hometown in rural Connecticut. As a young man just out of high school, he had gone to New York to make his fortune. He worked in a bank for a couple of years. But for some reason—he never said why, and I never asked—he went home and took a job with the post office.

Pop retained a keen appreciation of New York. He wanted to be sure to pass that along to me. Several times during my teenaged years he brought me to the city for a couple of days after Christmas. We walked around midtown and marveled at the tall buildings like a couple of country boys, watched basketball at the old Madison Square Garden on 50th Street and Eighth Avenue, and took a cab to Greenwich Village to tap our feet to Dixieland jazz at smoky, boozy Eddie Condon's. Unforgettable.

At a Knicks game at the old Garden one night, a fan whose view of the court was partially obstructed by a pillar piped up, "This game is only a rumor from here." My father and I laughed at that real-life Runyonism. It was around then—almost 40 years ago—that the thought of some day writing for a New York newspaper occurred to me.

I like to think that where Pop is, St. Peter does him a favor this time of year and cans the Christmas carols in favor of some good Eddie Condon.

November 26, 1993

DAD'S DOUBLE STANDARD ON THE DIAMOND

My sons and I used to spend Easter week playing ball. Happiest days of my life. The boys enjoyed themselves, too, although probably not as much as their old man.

School was out, I took off from work, and our family visited Grandma in Hamden, Connecticut. The boys and I would hit and pitch and field grounders and shag flies for a couple of hours in the morning and a couple more in the afternoon on a field near Grandma's house.

It was bliss. We must have been rained out a time or two, but memory recalls nothing but bracing air, blue skies and sunshine.

"Just like Felix Millan!" I'd exult after one of the boys made a good backhand stab. Or, "Lookin' like Del Unser!" after a running catch of a fly ball.

This was in the late '70s, when they were in Little League. Life revolved around baseball. Seems kind of ridiculous now, but that's the way it was then. A lot of families go through a Little League phase and live to laugh about it. No regrets.

My wife and daughter and mother-in-law did whatever they did while my sons and I enjoyed our version of spring training. I don't think my daughter resented being left behind when her father and older brothers ran out the door with bats and balls and gloves right after breakfast and again after lunch—although she was perceptive enough to sense that I felt guilty about spending so much more time with them than with her.

"Dad, when are you going to play ball with me?" Ursula would say occasionally. Her tone hinted that equal time was in order.

"Uh, you want me to pitch to you?" I'd reply.

"Yes!" she'd exclaim, thrilled and delighted.

I'd pitch underhand. She could barely wield the bat. She grew bored quickly. When pitching to my sons I never let them quit on a swing and a miss—they had to finish with a line drive for confidence—but whenever Ursula was ready to pack in batting practice, so was I. A sexist double standard, I have to admit.

Her self-esteem was unaffected. One chilly spring afternoon I took the kids to a Yale baseball game and the Yale coach, a gracious guy whose name I've forgotten, appointed them bat boys and bat girl for the game. Ursula, 6 or 7 at the time, was beside herself with excitement. She threw herself into gathering bats in front of the Yale dugout. When the coach gave her instructions on how to arrange them, she assured him, "That's what I intended to do."

Later, Ursula played Little League softball. Before her first game she asked me, "Dad, when I go up to the plate to bat, should I smile?" For once in my life I was speechless. I laughed, and so did she.

Ironically, she was the best natural hitter in the Reel family, but she lost interest and quit softball after a year or two. I didn't care, although I certainly would have pushed a son with equal talent to keep playing. She played soccer in high school. Many an afternoon I ducked out of the office to get to her games. Rooting for a daughter was as much fun as rooting for a son—and much less of a strain on an aging male's ego.

Oh, I know, I'm rambling here. I would have taken this week off, but there was no one to play ball with. We drove to Grandma's on Easter Sunday and stayed only the day. The Reel boys are adults. They had to get back for work.

Their sister, a senior in college down South, called to wish us a happy Easter. She mentioned an event she was looking forward to attending this week. I wondered if she was going with anyone. Yes, with a friend who plays on the college baseball team, she said.

I got a kick out of that. Made me think that some day I'd sure love to have a couple of boys to play ball with. Boys or girls. Wouldn't matter as long as they let me play.

April 14, 1993

HEALTHY LIFE—BETTER LATE THAN NEVER

Went cross-country skiing for the first time last Saturday. Took a few flops. Looked ridiculous. Got all wet. Improved as the day went on, however, and enjoyed myself immensely.

As a beginner, I avoided anything resembling a hill, venturing down only the slightest of inclines. The intrepid Mrs. Polonia, truly my better half, stepped onto skis and went right down the first modest slope she saw. I was petrified for her. And for me.

"Don't kill yourself! Who'll make my dinner?" I yelled as she began the descent. To my great relief, she arrived at the bottom upright.

We were guests for the day of Lou and Mary Ann, our friends since the 1950s. They took up cross-country skiing a dozen years ago, right around the time they quit smoking. We drove to their house in Cheshire, Connecticut, and Lou drove the four of us to nearby Farmington, where scenic ski trails slither through pristine woods.

I found skiing arduous but invigorating. Muscles that hadn't been used in decades, if ever, flourished in the fresh air and sunshine. I should have felt tired but didn't after so much long striding (and several ungainly falls in the snow that made Mrs. Polonia laugh heartily).

A great day. Lou and Mary Ann and Mrs. Polonia and I, all in our early 50s, agreed that we never felt better in our lives than following three hours of cross-country skiing.

We ate a big turkey dinner, allowable since we'd worked off quite a few ounces during the day, and then Mrs. Polonia and I drove home. Very sound sleep for eight hours followed.

"If somebody had told me 25 years ago that in middle age I'd be on skis, I'd have laughed at the absurdity of it," I remarked on Sunday as we took our regular brisk walk of a couple of miles through the park in our neighborhood. "I never dreamed I'd be exercising."

And that's a fact. Exercise? Exertion? Perspiration? Don't be ridiculous! That stuff's for kids. I'm an adult, so gimme a drink and a smoke, and for dinner I'll have roast beef, rare.

That was the way I, and everyone I knew, looked at it in the slothful '60s. I'll bet plenty of you middle-agers (and baby-boomers and oldtimers, for that matter) can identify with my old attitude. Now many of us are regular joggers or walkers or gym-goers or cross-country skiers or whatever. I'll bet most of you, a decade or two or three ago, never dreamed you'd be putting your old bones through a vigorous regimen in the '90s. You probably figured, as I did, that you'd be slouched by the fire with a cold beer or a hot toddy and a fat cigar, looking forward to lobster thermidor for dinner.

But as it's turned out, you cut drinking drastically, you no longer smoke and, for dinner, you now prefer poultry or pasta (you can remember when it was called spaghetti).

We have no choice, of course. We exercise and watch our diet and shun nicotine out of necessity. We have to do everything we can to improve the odds of staying healthy. We can't afford, say, a heart attack. Too expensive. With health-care costs out of control, we wouldn't be able to pay the doctor or the hospital. Those of us fortunate enough to have health insurance know it won't cover everything, and we worry that what it doesn't cover will break us.

Moreover, we know it's only a matter of time before insurance companies refuse to cover sick people. They'll only accept customers in perfect health who sign an agreement to stay well permanently and die suddenly. No costly lingering.

That's for me. At 95, I hope to be hurtling down a steep slope and hit a big oak tree head-on.

March 10, 1993

THIS YEAR, JUST PLAIN "MERRY" MOOD

It's only two weeks until Christmas and I'm not depressed yet. Maybe I'll make it through the holidays in a good mood for once. Mrs. Polonia would appreciate that. When I get blue, she does, too. (Don't you love that last sentence? I should write rap lyrics.) And when I'm in good spirits, so is she. (Obviously I couldn't sustain the rhyme. No rap writing career awaits Reel, on second thought.) After

30 years of marriage, Mrs. Polonia and I tend to mirror each other's moods, so she's grateful that I'm coming up copacetic for Christmas.

For decades I always got depressed beginning a few weeks before Christmas. My annual mope generally extended through January 1. I never welcomed Thanksgiving because I knew a major downer was imminent. It was as though all the turkey with trimmings I ate that day settled somewhere between my ears and weighed me down emotionally for weeks to come.

A big part of my Christmas depression, I think, was resentment against society's expectation that people should be happy during the holidays. It was the season to be jolly, yet joy perversely eluded me. Other folks brimmed with good cheer, and they assumed I should rejoice with them. Their presumption rubbed me the wrong way. They were happy and I wasn't, and they thought I ought to be, making me grimmer still.

By the way, when I say I was depressed, I don't mean in the way a therapist might use the term. I never was afflicted with what could be diagnosed as clinical depression, a serious condition that may require medication or even hospitalization. I wasn't that bad, thank God. I was merely down in the dumps for a few weeks before and during the holidays. I wanted to stay in bed and eat cannoli all day, then fall asleep facedown in the crumbs on the pillow, but never succumbed to the temptation.

All the hustle and bustle and busyness of Christmas seemed too much. I hated to go shopping for presents. Not because I'm cheap. I am cheap, but that wasn't the reason. Aversion to the crush of humanity in the aisles made me want to flee the department stores. (Truth be told, shopping is an ordeal for me at any time of year. I contrive to leave the buying to Mrs. Polonia.)

One morning a decade or so ago I was at a mall near my home around this time of year. Somehow I had managed to put dread at arm's length and plunge into the madding crowd of Christmas shoppers. No one was smiling, I remember. Everyone looked harried and frantic. In the eddying mob around me in mid-mall I heard a middle-aged woman say, "Where's mother?" She and her husband and their kids stood together, looking around. Her elderly mother had wandered off, apparently. The woman repeated, in an alarmed voice, "Where's mother? Have we lost mother?" And her husband blurted out, "I hope so!"

His wife shot him a look that could kill. Just then, her mother reappeared and the tension lifted, but I've often thought that this was all too typical of how the Christmas rush can strain if not sunder family relations. The fellow was glad his mother-in-law was a missing person, and didn't mind admitting it. He was past Christmas depression and into the next stage, Xmas exasperation.

I always hated to go for a Christmas tree. There were years when I stayed home and Mrs. Polonia drove to the lot and picked out and purchased the tree. Then I felt guilty for not going with her. Guilt made my depression worse. I recall a year—it was in the mid-1970s, if memory serves—when she bought the tree and drove it home and I hauled it down off the top of the car and put it in the garage. I neglected to close the garage door. A neighborhood cat wandered in and wee-weed all over the tree. This escaped our notice until days later when we brought the tree in the house, put it up, decorated it, arranged the presents under it—and then were struck by a nose-wrinkling aroma. "What's that smell?" Mrs. Polonia wondered. One of the kids got close to the tree and took a whiff and announced, "Cat wee-wee!" This incident deepened Daddy's Christmas depression.

I never enjoyed decorating the tree. I steadfastly refused to decorate my house (and still do). I dreaded all Christmas preparations. I'd rather lie on the couch and watch a basketball game. Wrapping presents was a tedious and boresome chore that I rushed through. The piece of wrapping paper I cut always turned out to be too big or too small for the box, causing me to utter words unfit for a season of spiritual uplift.

Christmas parties didn't bother me, but that's only because I refused all invitations to attend them. They'd have bothered me plenty if I'd shown up. Nothing depresses me more than standing in a room for two or three hours and watching other people drink. I'm uncomfortable around the cup that cheers since I can't partake without, sooner or later, falling into the Christmas tree. (Talk about depressing!) Seltzer, my drink of choice, is a thirst-quencher but not a mood-changer. If I arrive at a social occasion feeling anxious and insecure and self-conscious and fresh out of wry repartee, which is my normal condition, and I drink two or three tall glasses of seltzer with plenty of ice and a twist of lemon, the effect is that I'm still anxious and insecure and self-conscious and fresh out of wry repartee. Meanwhile, normal social drinkers have gotten tipsy. They're laughing at each other's jokes. They're listening to each other's opinions. They're ogling each other's significant others.

What's the opposite of Christmas depression? Cool Yule? Nativity Tranquillity? Or just plain old Merry Christmas? This year I think I'll have the latter. You too, I hope.

December 11, 1994

Why Isn't Anybody All Ears Anymore?

Lately I've noticed that nobody wants to listen to what I have to say. I'll meet someone and start talking, and right away the other party interrupts with what's on his or her mind.

This isn't because I'm boring. I am boring, but that's not the reason people cut me off the second I slow down for a comma. I was always boring, but they used to hear me out anyway.

I'll bet you've had the experience of trying to tell someone something and before you finish your thought or even your sentence, he or she barges in with a monologue. You stand there like a dummy, frustrated and demoralized while they ramble on.

Good listeners are a vanishing breed. Most people nowadays have lost the capacity to listen. They must talk! It's a compulsion. Maybe there should be a Babblers Anonymous where they could meet and learn to thank each other for not sharing.

People used to have the courtesy to hear each other out before weighing in with their own anecdote or opinion. I'm damned unhappy about the trend to silence me. It galls me that I can't get a word in edgewise anymore.

The other Sunday my wife and I were out for our walk when we met a couple we know. They were coming home from church. We paused to chat. They said their pastor had warned that their church was going broke for the usual reasons—declining attendance, rising expenses, parsimonious parishioners. Mrs. Polonia and I politely listened.

It so happened I had something to say on this subject, so I put in (or, rather, I began to say), "The other day I was talking to the pastor of a church in Florida. The previous Sunday he had two collections at his six masses. The first brought in almost $40,000 for the parish, as it does every Sunday. The second, for Catholic Relief Services, the international aid agency, brought in $31,000."

I expected—foolishly, it turned out—that this would fascinate folks concerned about their failing church, and that they would want to know more about how Monsignor Mort Danaher inspires such generosity in the 2,200 families who attend Christ the King Church in Jacksonville. (He does it by asking them to sacrifice for their faith.)

But the ordeal of listening was too much for the couple, and he loudly interrupted, "Oh yeah, no kiddin'. Hey, did I tell ya our son belongs to the biggest church in Jersey blah blah blah . . ." I got so disgusted I turned on my heel and went home, proving that I can be a lousy listener, too.

Mrs. Polonia politely stood there, nodding her head and feigning interest until her ears lapped over. When she got home she reprimanded me for being rude. I shut up and listened. I knew better than to interrupt Mrs. Polonia, lest she let her rolling pin do the talking.

Listening has fallen to such a low state that people won't even listen to sex talk. "Every time I try to tell my best friend about sexual problems I'm having with my boyfriend, she talks about her own similar experiences. I never finish and end up frustrated and disinterested in what she's saying," a reader wrote to newspaper sex guru Dr. Judy Kuriansky.

"Too many people like your friend selfishly turn all the attention back on themselves," Dr. Judy sympathized in her reply in yesterday's paper. The good doctor counseled that all of us should dedicate ourselves to what she called "active empathetic listening." Sounds good. ("I love it when you talk dirty and I listen empathetically!")

Dr. Judy advised the writer to discuss the sexual problems that she and her boyfriend are having not only with her girlfriend but with . . . her boyfriend! That's easy to say, but the guy probably won't hear of it. She can't find anybody to listen to her talk about sex except Dr. Judy and her readers.

Thank God for readers! You can't interrupt. I love it when you read empathetically.

June 8, 1994